THE COMPLETE GUITAR PLAYER

Konecky & Konecky
72 Ayers Pt. Road
Old Saybrook, CT 06475

Further information relating to this book and other music information
can be found at www.musicfirebox.com

First published in 2004

Created and produced by **FLAME TREE PUBLISHING**,
Crabtree Hall, Crabtree Lane, Fulham, London SW6 6TY

ISBN 1-56852-513-3

A copy of the CIP data for this book is available from the British Library

Printed in China

Special thanks to:
Lucy Bradbury, Sara Robson, Julia Rolf, Colin Rudderham, Nick Wells, Polly Willis, Tom Worsley

THE COMPLETE GUITAR PLAYER

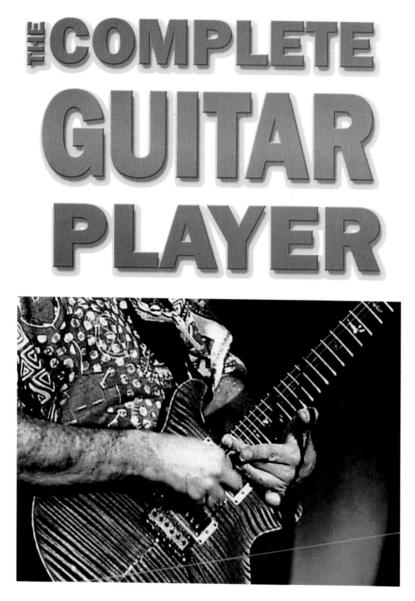

**Joe Bennett, Trevor Curwen, Cliff Douse,
Douglas J Noble, Richard Riley,
Tony Skinner, Harry Wylie**

KONECKY&KONECKY

CONTENTS

SPECIAL FEATURE SPREADS

INTRODUCTION

Have you ever been to a gig and wished you could play like the guy (or the girl) with the great looking guitar and fingers that seemed to spin a web of solid sound around the room? For some people it's the band in a seedy bar that inspires them, for others it might be the virtuoso in a classical concert hall, or the singer in a dingy cafe. Sometimes, it's just the sound that hits - a lead break of sublime super-humanity from Jeff Beck; the sheer poetic precision of Segovia; the frenetic ingenuity of Jimi Hendrix or the passion and pain of Paco de Lucia.

A Rickenbacker 360 can look so good it forces you to go out, buy it and hold it for as long as possible before even trying to play it. Some love the magic of Joe Satriani, with his multiple effects pedals stoking up his sound through massive valve stack amplifiers. For others, it's the glorious mini-orchestra found within the six strings and simple wooden sound hole that dignifies Classical, Spanish and Folk music.

Whatever your reasons for wanting to know more about the guitar, this book is a great place to start. It's written, edited, photographed and designed by real enthusiasts, with a very wide range of musical experience.

The themed approach has allowed us to pack in an enormous amount of information while keeping the format very straightforward. Here you can find entries on great guitarists of every kind, and learn how to play in a variety of different styles. We've tried to keep things as clear and unfussy as possible so that sections on reading music and repairing your guitar show you what's possible and give you just enough to whet your appetite without boring you with too much information. If you're starting out, the book will give you plenty of choices, encouraging you to sample as many different techniques and guitars as possible. For the more experienced player, *Complete Guitar Facts* will quickly show you other ways of playing and hearing so that you can decide which direction to take next.

We have deliberately used real, and in some cases absurdly old, gear in the shoots because that's often the experience of a guitarist: the most polished guitars and pedals, like bright new strings, don't always give the best to the music, or represent the true spirit of the passion. With old gear, there is history and character, a sense of authenticity and a feel for music rather than the show of it. Brian May still uses the hand-made guitar he put together thirty years ago; the late 1950s Strats play much better than their 1980s counterparts.

The best accompaniment to this book is, of course, music, so we've set aside a series of web pages on the Internet so that you can hear and download mp3s of the music examples, chords and scales (www.musicfirebox.com). This can be really useful if the notation is just a step ahead of what you want to do or if you're simply impatient to get on with playing. Of course the more friends (and strangers!) you actually play with, the more gigs you go to, the more CDs, mp3s or old scratchy LPs you listen to the better and more interested you will get. Experiment too with a variety of sounds and instruments – playing a large bodied Martin acoustic guitar is physically a very different experience to holding and strumming a medium-sized Yamaha and can really affect how comfortable you feel and ultimately, how you play.

John Lee Hooker died at the age of 83 and although he had given up gigging in his last few years he was well known for grabbing the mike and taking over the stage while out drinking at a club. Like so many budding guitarists, the brilliant Carlos Santana regarded Hooker as his inspiration: 'When I was a child he was the first circus I wanted to run away with.' We hope you'll enjoy this book and the places it can lead you.

HOW TO PLAY

'ANJI' ('ANGIE')

The finger-style instrumental 'Anji' was originally written by Davy Graham, one of the most influential British folk guitarists of all time. In 1964, 'Anji' was recorded by Scottish-born folk guitarist Bert Jansch on his first, eponymous album and achieved wide-spread fame. The song's inclusion on Simon and Garfunkel's *Sounds of Silence* album ensured further popularity and the piece rapidly became, and has remained, a mainstay of any folk guitarist's repertoire. With its descending bass pattern and fluid picking style, the piece is a lasting tribute to Graham's writing style and influence on British folk music.

➤ *Folk, Picking, Paul Simon*

BELOW: Eric Clapton, who penned 'Layla', jams with some friends.
RIGHT: Jimi Hendrix, composer of 'Purple Haze' and for some, the greatest guitarist ever.
ABOVE: The classic instrumental 'Angie' appeared on Bert Jansch's debut album.

CAVATINA

Cavatina is the title given in classical music to a short, slow and sentimental piece. A single-section aria is often known by this name. In the guitar world,

the most famous Cavatina was written by Stanley Myers for the film *The Deerhunter*. The soundtrack features Australian-born classical guitarist John Williams playing a beautifully melodic part over a sublime orchestral accompaniment. Williams went on to make an arrangement of the piece for solo classical guitar. The beauty of this arrangement and Williams' delicate playing brought the sound of the classical guitar to the ears of many non-classical listeners for the first time.
➤— *Classical, John Williams*

'JOHNNY B GOODE'

This classic Chuck Berry 12-bar is one of the most inspirational in electric-guitar music. The song has been covered by numerous acts since it was first released in 1958, and even today it remains a stalwart encore piece for bands in the pub-rock scene. The rhythm guitar part comprises a fast blues rhythm over a 12-bar blues sequence. The much-copied lead guitar part is based on double-stopped fourths played in a driving triplet rhythm, mixed with slides and string bends. The solos and licks on this track rank as some of the most influential in the entire history of electric guitar playing.
➤— *Blues, Chuck Berry, Twelve-Bar Blues*

'LAYLA'

This very popular Eric Clapton song first appeared on the Derek and the Dominoes 1970 album *Layla And Other Assorted Love Songs*. The fine guitar playing on the track is particularly notable for the fast slurred introduction (which features a fluid combination of hammer-ons and pull-offs), a riff which countless guitarists ever since have copied. The track also featured fine interplay between Eric Clapton's guitar playing and that of the other guitarist on the album, Duane Allman from the Allman Brothers. In 1992, Clapton released an acoustic 'unplugged' version of the song which emphasized its melodic and romantic nature.
➤— *Eric Clapton, Hammer-On, Pull-Off*

'PURPLE HAZE'

'Purple Haze', released in 1967, was the second single from the Jimi Hendrix Experience. Hendrix's unique use of wah-wah and distortion on this track, and

his wild stage pyrotechnics when performing it live, brought the electric guitar to the forefront of popular music culture. His performance on this track was one that could only be reproduced on the electric instrument, and it brought the electric guitar into a new era – one where it was no longer played just as an amplified version of the acoustic guitar, but as a unique and individual instrument. Hendrix's playing and guitar style has had an influence on many rock guitarists who have followed him.
➤— *Jimi Hendrix*

ROMANCE/ROMANZA

This traditional and very popular Spanish melody is often played as a classical guitar solo piece. It typifies the character of Spanish guitar, and demonstrates how the instrument can combine harmonic and melodic playing. The melody, which is almost entirely on the first string, is often played with rest strokes to create a full and sonorous tone, often enhanced with the use of vibrato. Meanwhile, the triplet accompaniment on the lower strings is played with light free strokes so as not to distract attention from the melody. The piece is in two distinct sections: the first in E minor, the second in E major. The second section is far more difficult to play, involving some wide fingerboard stretches.

➤— *Classical*

'SMOKE ON THE WATER'

This classic Deep Purple track from the 1972 album *Machine Head* is most memorable for its opening guitar introduction. This stark and powerful four-bar phrase has become one of the most often-played guitar parts in rock music. Deep Purple's guitarist, Ritchie Blackmore, created this timeless riff using only the first four notes of the blues scale. He made the sound stronger by harmonizing the riff: using double-stopping to add an interval a fourth below each note of the riff.

➤— *Blues Scale, Riff*

'STAIRWAY TO HEAVEN'

'Stairway To Heaven', from Led Zeppelin's 1971 album *Led Zeppelin IV*, has become the best-known rock anthem of all time. The fingerstyle guitar introduction played by Jimmy Page has been emulated by guitarists worldwide ever since the record's release. The introduction is a good example of simple minor-key contrapuntal movement, with a descending bass-line played over a minor chord, whilst melody notes are played in an ascending direction. After the wistful introductory verses, the song turns to a more heavy-rock style with Page, who often used a double-neck guitar for live

LEFT: Jimmy Page plays the rock classic 'Stairway To Heaven'.
BELOW: Symbols, known as Led Zeppelin 4, *included 'Stairway To Heaven'.*

performances, using power chords, distortion and taking an extended guitar solo.

➤— *Jimmy Page*

BLUES, TWELVE-BAR

This is the most common chord progression in the history of popular music. Tens of thousands of songs, particularly from the fields of blues, rhythm & blues and rock 'n' roll are based around this 12-bar sequence of chords.

There are a few common variations on the basic 12-bar pattern:

$$\| \ C7 \ | \ C7 \ | \ C7 \ | \ C7 \ |$$

$$| \ F7 \ | \ F7 \ | \ C7 \ | \ C7 \ |$$

$$| \ G7 \ | \ F7 \ | \ C7 \ | \ G7 :\|$$

🎸 The chord in the second bar is often played as IV7 (e.g. F7, in the key of C)

🎸 The chord in bar 10 is sometimes kept as V7 (e.g. G7, in the key of C)

🎸 the chord in the last bar is sometimes kept as I7 (e.g. C7, in the key of C).

➤— *Blues, Rhythm & Blues, Rock 'n' Roll*

PRACTISING/WARM-UP TIPS

Warming up

In order to avoid straining muscles or tendons in the hands or arms it is essential to do a few warm-up exercises before launching into a difficult guitar piece. A few simple stretching exercises should precede any serious practice session, and should also be incorporated into any lengthy practice regime; these will help dispel the toxins that may have built up in the muscles. Rotating the wrists, elbows and shoulders will help to keep the joints and muscles loose. Any stretches should never be forced or held for too long.

Hand position

Many novice players have limited finger-span and experience tightness in the fretting hand. This can be alleviated by opening the hand wide and allowing the fingers to stretch apart, and then very gently flexing all the fingers against a wall or table whilst keeping the wrist clear of the surface. This exercise can be followed up by tightly closing the hand, and then allowing the fingers to rapidly and forcefully flick outwards as the hand opens. Guitar playing is made much easier if players observe the minimum-movement principle, i.e. cutting out any unnecessary finger movement. In most playing situations, each finger should ideally be assigned to a separate fret. Using this technique, scales, melodies and riffs can be played with ease.

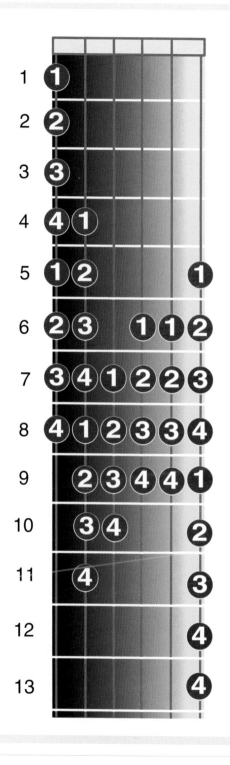

The chromatic scale (left), being the only scale that uses all four fretting fingers on every string, can serve as an ideal warm-up exercise. If this scale is played across three octaves, most of the fingerboard is covered, and the fingers will have experienced a good workout.

Practice

It is important to differentiate between playing guitar and practising guitar. The boundaries often get blurred, and it is all too easy during a practice session to slip into playing things which do not really help improve your playing or your technique. Whilst it is important to enjoy your playing and to play through things you've done before, practice sessions should be set aside for learning new things and consolidating and improving your technical ability. As most people's spare time is limited, it is important to make the best use of these practice sessions. A practice session should last no more than 40 minutes, as the concentration will diminish after this time. If you have more time to spare, it is best to leave the guitar, take a 20-minute break, and come back to it feeling fresh. In any case, try not to play for more than 20 minutes at a time without taking a short break to rest the hand and forearm muscles.

A well-structured practice session for an electric guitarist will consist of some of the following:

♩ A few warm-up and stretching exercises
♩ Scale practice – playing some scales you already know, learning some new ones, or trying existing ones in new fingerboard positions
♩ Chord practice using both old and new chords, which you can incorporate with some rhythm playing into a song
♩ Practising new techniques, such as string bends or harmonics
♩ Playing through songs you already know
♩ Working out a solo from a recording
♩ Improvizing your own solo over a backing track.
➤— *Lead Guitar Tips*

TOP LEFT: Practising scales is essential for any guitarist.
FAR LEFT: Practice sessions need not be dull – playing with others can improve your playing in many ways.

RHYTHM GUITAR TIPS

In a band situation guitarists spend the vast majority of their time playing chords, so honing your rhythm guitar skills is essential to increasing your chances of joining a band.

Changing chords

Leaving gaps between chords when strumming through a song or chord progression is a recipe for musical disaster: the performance will sound fragmented and, if you're playing with a singer or other musicians, it will prove impossible to keep in time. It is essential that chord changes are crisp and prompt. Changing between chords can be made much easier if you follow the minimum-

movement principle. This involves making only the smallest finger movements necessary between chords, and avoiding taking fingers off the strings or frets only to put them back on again for the next chord.

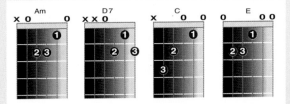

Notice the common fingering between each chord and, in particular, how the first finger stays on the first fret and how the second finger stays on the second fret throughout.

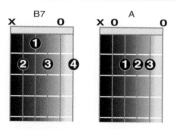

Changing between the B7 and A major chords, the first finger can be slid along the fourth string, between frets one and two.

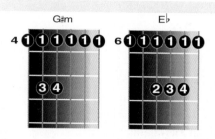

G♯m barre chord using an E minor shape moved to the fourth fret; E♭ barre chord using an A major shape moved to the sixth fret.

If you look carefully at the fingering for various chords, you will notice that some have one or more notes in common. For example, the open-position Am and D7 chords both include the note C (first fret on the B string).

Even if different chords do not contain too many common notes, changing between them can still be made easier if you look out for any relationships and visual links between them.

No matter how seemingly remote a chord change is, there will always be some kind of link between the chords that, once spotted, will make changing between them easier. When confronted with a chord change you're not used to, ask yourself the following questions:

❦ Can I slide one finger along a string?
❦ Can I keep some fingers where they are?
❦ Can I maintain the same shape but just change string?

If you keep these questions in mind, you'll effectively be implementing the minimum movement principle, which is the secret to fluent rhythm playing. However, if all else fails, you can mask any gap between chord changes by using an open vamp. This simply involves strumming the open strings whilst your fingers move to the new chord, thereby maintaining the overall fluency and momentum of the performance. Some players actually make a feature of this technique to bring out accents within their rhythm playing. Whatever technique you use, the golden rule in rhythm playing is 'never stop – always keep strumming'.

Using barre chords

The advantage of using barre chords is that the same shape can be moved up or down the fretboard to create new chords; thus avoiding the need to memorize a myriad of different fingerings for each chord. By using barre chords, you can also access more unusual chords (like G♯m, or E♭) that are simply unobtainable in open position.

Furthermore, as barre chords do not involve open strings they can sound great with distortion, and punchy rhythmic techniques (like staccato) are much more easy to use.

Playing barre chords involves moving an open-position chord higher up the fretboard, with the original chord shape re-fingered so as to leave the first finger spare for making the barre. Here are the essentials of good barre-chord technique:

❦ Keep the first finger straight and in line with the fret rather than at an angle to it.
❦ The barre finger need not be completely flat – it can be slightly tilted away from the fret towards its outer edge.
❦ Position the barre finger so that the creases between its joints do not coincide with the strings. Adjust your finger position until all the notes ring clearly.
❦ Position all the fretting fingers as close to the fret wire as possible.
❦ Press down firmly, but avoid using excessive pressure with either the first finger or the thumb.

When you move barre chords around the fretboard, make sure that the thumb at the back of the fingerboard also shifts at the same time, – so that your whole hand position (not just the fretting fingers) is moving with each chord change.

➤— *Barre Chords*

LEFT: Two of the finest rhythm guitar players in rock – Bo Diddley and Keith Richards.

PLAYING A SOLO

Creating an effective guitar solo requires more than just using scale patterns; attention must also be given to phrasing, tone, dynamic range, structure, style and harmonic awareness.

Getting in key

Before you play a lead solo you need to identify the key of the song. It does not matter how fast and flashy your lead playing is; if you use the wrong scale for the key of the song, then you're certain to hit notes that will clash with the backing chords and your solo will be ruined. Fortunately, in most pop and rock songs the key can be easily identified by noting the starting chord, which will normally be the key chord. Don't be misled by any introductory chords; look to the chord that starts the main section of the song.

Once you're sure which scale to use, practise playing the scale up and down until you are totally familiar with the sound of it; this will help you get a feel for the overall tonality of the key.

Relating to chords

Whilst knowing the correct scale will enable you to play in tune, if you have a good knowledge of arpeggios, you will be able to make your solo relate more to the chord structure – because an arpeggio contains exactly the same notes as its related chord. Practising arpeggios is very useful in helping you identify the notes contained within each chord. You can then use this knowledge to target certain chord tones whilst improvizing. This technique can help you reflect and enhance the harmonic content and movement of the accompaniment. Alternatively, you can use your knowledge of arpeggios deliberately to avoid chord tones (particularly at the start of a bar), to create a sense of musical tension that can then be released by reverting to a chord tone.

Solo style

When creating a guitar solo, always pay attention to the overall musical style and listen carefully to what is being played on other instruments. Try to make your solo relate in some way to the mood of the song and the melody of the vocal line. The ability to reflect the melodic lines and rhythms of other instrumentalists and vocalists is a core skill of any good lead soloist. This approach will help you bring a more natural feel to your solo than the mechanical approach of just allowing your fingers to lead the way.

At the same time it is important to remain musically open-minded. Although most genres of music have stylistic traditions, which broadly define the borders between one style of music and another, there are no definitive rules about what sort of thing you can or cannot play in a particular style of music. Careful experimentation, with a monitoring of musical appropriateness, is recommended. Above all, trust your own musical taste to guide you.

Structure and phrasing

When constructing a solo, experiment with playing phrases of different lengths, and listen carefully to your playing to hear which ones best suit the musical style of the song. You can avoid making your phrasing sound too predictable by not always starting phrases on the first beat of the bar. Instead, try playing a few lead-in notes before the start of the bar. Ensure that you use a wide variety of note lengths, playing some notes quickly and allowing others to ring on. Listen carefully to the overall sound of the song, and relate your solo to the song's main musical features and style – allowing your ears, rather than your fingers, to guide you as to what works best.

Tone

No matter how many techniques you master or how elaborate your playing is, what people listen to most of all is the overall sound and tone that you produce. Take time to set up the volume and tone settings on your amp and guitar so that you achieve a sound that is suitable for the song you're soloing in. Whether this is a warm mellow tone or a rasping distorted tone should depend entirely upon what you think is appropriate for the song. Spend some time working on tone production when you're practising: try picking near to the bridge and then close to the fingerboard to create different tonal textures; create some light and shade by using different amounts of attack when you pick the strings; try selecting a different pick-up for different sections of a solo.

Muting notes by damping the strings is a useful way to control the sustain of each note and to introduce staccato and accent effects. This can be done by using the side of the picking hand pressed against the strings near the bridge, or by flexing the pressure of the fretting finger.

Alternating between damped and normal notes is a good way of establishing rhythmic accents within your phrasing.

In order to sound really effective, guitar solos often need a few finishing touches. Using string bends, slides, vibrato, slurs and other techniques can help make your solo sound more distinctive and personal. You should practise these techniques until they become second nature, then you'll be able to incorporate them into your soloing with ease.

➤ *Lead Guitar Tips*

LEFT: George Benson in flight.
ABOVE: Gary Moore lets rip during a solo.

LEAD GUITAR TIPS

To turn your improvization into a real guitar solo you'll need to use some specialist guitar techniques to add character and style to the solo.

Slurs

Using slurs will make your playing both faster and smoother. Slurring consists of two main techniques: hammering on and pulling off. Both techniques allow you to sound two or more notes for each pick of a string.

To hammer on a note, instead of picking the string again, quickly and firmly hammer the tip of your fretting finger on to the note – making sure to hammer on right next to the fret wire in order to ensure clarity.

To pull-off a note, first fret a note and pick the string, then pull your fretting finger lightly downwards until it plucks the string and the lower note is sounded. If the lower note is fretted (rather than an open string) then you need to have another finger in position fretting this note before executing the pull-off, and you should also ensure that it is held with firm pressure so that the pulling finger does not cause it to move and alter the pitch.

Once you've mastered basic slurring you can combine hammer-ons and pull-offs to create very fast and effortless-sounding lines.

Slides (glissando)

Sliding between notes is a highly effective musical technique that is ideally suited to the guitar. You can slide quickly to a note from a few frets below or above; it does not matter which note you start from providing you don't linger on the initial note. Alternatively, you can play and hold a lower note in a scale before sliding slowly to a higher note in that scale, allowing any intervening passing notes to sound.

Vibrato

Vibrato involves repeatedly varying the pitch of a note very slightly by moving the fretting-hand finger. Vibrato is widely used by most guitarists to add sustain and

RIGHT AND FAR RIGHT: Two great lead guitarists – Carlos Santana and Jimi Hendrix. Follow the tips given here, and who knows what may happen … CENTRE: Bending a note.

character to their playing. You can get a vibrato effect by repeatedly waggling the tip of your fretting finger vertically up and down very slightly whilst holding a note. If you are fretting the note with your first finger then you can use wrist vibrato, where the pitch of the note is altered by the rotation of the wrist, whilst the first finger holds down the note.

String bends

You can change the pitch of a note without altering string or fingerboard position by fretting a note and pushing the string upwards whilst you pick it – this is known as string bending. String bends are a great way of adding expression to your playing. Nearly all rock and blues

guitarists use string bending as an integral part of their technique, and as a way of expressing emotion through their playing.

When string bending with the third finger always keep your first and second fingers on the string to give support and control to the bending finger. Pivot from the elbow, to use the strength of the whole forearm when string bending. This way you'll avoid any risk of injuring your finger. Don't be scared to position your thumb over the top of the fingerboard if you find that this gives you extra leverage.

Be careful to pitch the note exactly in tune when bending. Generally, you should bend a note until it reaches the pitch of the next note in the scale. One way to practise this is to fret a note and sing the pitch produced; then using this as a target note, play a note two frets lower and slowly bend it upwards until it becomes in tune with your singing. Practise string bending in different keys, as the amount of pressure that will be needed to bend a note into tune will vary depending upon the fingerboard position: bending notes higher up the fingerboard requires less pressure than when bending in fingerboard positions closer to the nut.

There are numerous types of bends that you can try:

❦ Hold bend: bend the note slowly until it is in tune, then just hold it there.

❦ Rising bend: pick the string repeatedly whilst bending it up very slowly.

❦ Choke bend: bend the note, then quickly choke the sound by letting the picking hand touch the strings.

❦ Teasing bend: use several very small bends before fully bending the note into tune.

❦ Pre-bend and release: bend the note up without picking

it, then pick it and slowly release it.

❦ Double bend: bend the note up, let it down, then bend it up again.

➤— *Bend, Glissando, Hammer-On, Pre-Bend, Pull-Off, Slide, Vibrato*

IMPROVIZING

 Guitar improvization is often thought of as 'making up a lead solo freely on the spot'. In some senses this is true, but for improvization to take place there needs to be some structure and foundation behind it. To solo over any chord sequence a scale is required, as this is what defines the choice of notes that will fit with the backing chords. However, not all the notes of the scale need to be played, nor in any particular order (and certainly not in the set order). Once the scale has been learned, the aim is to use it in a melodically inventive and creative way, which ensures that the resulting playing does not sound too scale-like. Short phrases should be used, rather than a continuous flurry of notes and it does not matter if there are gaps. All the notes of the correct scale will fit over all of the backing chords, although some will sound better than others. However, playing the wrong scale over a chord sequence will sound pretty dire: the song's key should be indentified before any improvization begins. Since nearly all songs begin with the tonic (i.e. home key) chord, the easiest method is to check the first chord of the song. For example, if the first chord is A minor, it is pretty certain that the song is in the key of A minor.

Phrasing and rhythm

The rhythmic aspects of improvization should be given as much thought as the melodic content: rather than playing the scale in straight time, a far more musical and inventive sound can be acheived by playing some notes quickly whilst allowing others to ring on. Originality is not the main aim of improvization: it is more often an amalgam of things that have been played before.

A good way to start improvizing is to use a well-known melody as a template for rhythm and phrasing. The notes of the melody don't need to be played, instead some of its rhythmic aspects can be borrowed to give the improvization structure and direction.

By repeating certain series of notes, well-defined phrases will begin to be established, which will give the improvization structure. Once an acceptable phrase has been identified, it can be varied slightly when it is played again – that way it will sound fresh, whilst still giving the listener something recognizable to latch on to. Leaving some gaps between phrases is a good idea as it gives the music space to breathe.

Simply playing scales up and down is not enough to make a good solo. Scales only set the range of notes that will be in tune in any key. It is up to the player to create melodically and rhythmically interesting phrases from the scale.

Style

The improvization should fit with the style of the backing: the accompaniment and the vocal line should be listened to to ensure that the improvization sounds right in the context of the song. Improvization can be practised with other musicians, or over backing tracks or records, all of which help listening and playing skills, skills which are key to good improvization. Lengthy periods of improvization practice without any harmonic backing should be avoided, as it is very difficult to develop a good sense of phrasing and style this way, and playing can often be become overbusy as it is hard to leave gaps when there is no accompaniment.

LEFT AND BELOW: Whether you play in the style of Eddie Van Halen or BB King, being able to improvize is crucial to lead guitar playing.

It is important to listen not only to other guitar players but also to the improvizations of other instrumentalists. Their ideas and approaches to phrasing can be adopted, and variations of their musical ideas can be incorporated into future improvizations.

➤— *Lead Guitar Tips*

GIGGING

Getting a gig

The first step towards getting a gig is to discover which venues have live music. Although it is possible to approach venues that do not normally have live music, this could prove fruitless as it is unlikely they will have a valid music licence. Without such a licence from the local authority no more than two people can perform; which is OK if you're in a duo, but not so good if you're part of a band. Check your local paper, listings magazines and the music press for venues that host live bands.

The next step is to telephone the venue to discover if they book bands direct or through an agent, noting the name of the person responsible for booking acts. You should then send a tape or CD of your music to the booker. There is no need to put more than three tracks on this demo-tape; three will be sufficient to give the booker a good idea of your style and standard. Do not save the best till last – put your best track first; whoever it is may never get as far as listening to the last track. Make sure

that you include a contact telephone number with the tape. Include a photo of the band, and some basic publicity information. A full, 10-page biography of every member will probably remain unread, but a concise flyer summarizing your style and gigging experience, with excerpts from any reviews you've had, would be ideal.

Allow a week for your demo to be listened to and then make a follow-up telephone call; many venues are regularly inundated with demos, and you can't rely on them to take the time to call you. You may prefer to appoint a friend or family member to act as your agent or manager and liaise with venues on your behalf.

Most venues will insist on a cut of the door takings (often about 50 per cent) if tickets are sold, whilst others will offer a straight fee. Some venues operate a pay-to-play policy: they provide the PA (public address) system and expect you to contribute to the costs, which are then reimbursed to you if you manage to sell enough tickets. In general, you should try to avoid such schemes.

Trying to get onto the books of a legitimate agent or manager would take away some of the burden of gig-hunting. Although you will have to pay them a percentage of your fees (normally 10 to 20 per cent) it is usually worth it to take advantage of the contacts they have, resulting in more and better-paid gigs.

An alternative to trying to get gigs at established venues is to put on your own gig. This will involve hiring a hall and having a budget for publicity and promotion. Whilst this will mean that you have to find some money in advance, at least all the ticket receipts will come straight to you. However, you should be certain that you can attract a large enough audience to make the venture worthwhile.

Supporting a well-known band with a similar musical style is often a great way to get started. You will benefit from exposure to the right type of audience, who will then hopefully return to see you perform when you headline your own gigs. This is such an effective way of gaining an audience that some record companies pay considerable sums to buy their new bands support slots on tours with major bands.

Playing a gig

It is essential that you bring the right equipment to the gig. If the venue is supplying a large house PA system, a small guitar amp will suffice, as this can be miked up or DI-ed (direct-inputted, or plugged into the PA system). If only a vocal PA is supplied, then bring the biggest amp you have or hire one: a small amp that sounds loud in a small room may not project or have sufficient tonal range in a large venue. If you're playing with a drummer, then 50 to 100 watts is the minimum output you'll require. Make a checklist of all the things you need to bring in your gig bag:

- leads
- effects units (inc. spare batteries or mains adaptors)
- mains extension lead and multi-socket
- tuner
- strap
- spare strings
- plectrums
- towel and change of clothes
- gaffa tape to keep all the leads
  in place on-stage
- guitar stand
- flight case – useful for protecting your treasured guitar
  when it is in the gig van.

LEFT: Who knows where jamming with your friends at gigs will lead? Keith Richards, Neil Young and Chuck Berry (leaning back) had to start somewhere!
BELOW: Ensure that your gig bag contains the correct equipment and accessories.
BOTTOM: Whether the venue is big or small, gigging can be a great experience.

Once you're on-stage the essential thing is to enjoy yourself – hopefully this feeling will spread to the audience. All the preparation should have been done in rehearsals beforehand, and the show should be tight and flowing: avoid talking to other band members between songs, or working out what song to play next – decide a set list in advance. Although you do not necessarily need to run around the stage playing the guitar behind your head, show some commitment to putting on a show to create an energy that will let the audience know this is a performance and not a rehearsal.

➤ *Lead Guitar Tips, PA System, Playing A Solo*

TUNING

The musical pitch of each guitar string can be altered manually by turning the pegs located on the headstock. These pegs rotate the guitar's machine heads. While some musicians use unconventional tunings,

most guitarists tune to a pattern known as standard or Spanish tuning. Typically, the modern guitarist will use an electronic tuning device to ensure that the notes are at the correct pitch; these devices can indicate either the specific notes that each string should be tuned to, or can be chromatic and therefore able to show every note. As you play each string, the tuner will show the note you are playing and the direction you need to turn the peg to achieve the correct pitch. Electronic tuners allow the guitar to be tuned without interference from surrounding noises in the room or on stage.

Standard tuning

Standard tuning (see top right) requires the six strings of the guitar to be tuned, starting from the thickest and lowest string, to the notes E, A, D, G, B and E. For the sake of convenience, the strings are usually numbered from one to six, the sixth string being the lowest and thickest. The highest-sounding string (also called the first string) is tuned exactly two octaves above this lowest (or sixth) string. For correct concert tuning the A string (fifth) will be at a musical frequency of 110 Hz, and the first string will be tuned to E above middle C on a piano. However, you do not need a piano or an oscilloscope to tune your guitar.

The most frequently used method is to tune each string relative to a fretted note on the string above it. To start

with, if you have a tuning fork or pitch pipe, you will be able to generate a reference note (usually E above middle C on a piano). The open E string (the sixth) will be tuned to a note exactly two octaves below this. Alternatively you can tune the sixth string relative to the other instruments you might be performing with, using an electronic tuner as outlined previously. Once you have generated this reference note, you will be able to tune all the other strings relative to it using the few easy steps outlined below. If you are unable to provide a reference note, you can still use these steps and tune your guitar relative to itself, but it could well be out of tune with other instruments.

Relative tuning

To tune a guitar this way (see left), play the note on the fifth fret on the sixth (lowest) string. Then turn the peg that adjusts the tuning of the fifth string, while also plucking the open, unfretted fifth string. Keep turning the peg up or down until both notes are identical (also known as in unison). Be careful not to tune any string too high or you may break it, or even damage the neck of the guitar.

Now repeat this process, but this time pluck the fifth fret of the fifth string while plucking the open fourth string. Make sure these notes are identical.

Next, play fret five of the fourth string and tune the third string until the notes are identical. Now play the fourth fret (this is the exception) of the third

FAR LEFT: Tuning a Spanish guitar.
LEFT: Standard tuning.
BELOW LEFT: Relative tuning.
BELOW: If you play a left-handed guitar, as Albert King, you will still use the same tuning techniques as for a conventional right-handed guitar.

string, and tune the second string to this note. Finally, use the fifth fret of string two to tune the first string once again.

Now try playing a commonly used open chord, such as G major or E major, to see if each string sounds correct. You may need to repeat the tuning process until the guitar sounds perfectly in tune.

LICK

A lick is a small musical motif such as a phrase or riff that can be incorporated into a lead guitar solo. All good solo players have a vocabulary of licks which they use in their lead lines.

➤ *Lead Guitar Tips*

STRUMMING

To achieve a fluid and easy strumming action it is essential that the strumming hand pivots from the wrist. Therefore, it is important that the wrist is loose and relaxed when strumming. If the wrist is stiff and not allowed to move freely, excessive arm movement will occur, as the strumming action will be forced to come from the elbow instead. As this can never move as fluently as the wrist action, a loss of smoothness and rhythmic potential is almost inevitable.

Good strumming does not always have to be fast and furious. Steve Cropper, one of most respected rhythm guitar players, says that the secret of his rhythm guitar style is based on his adage: 'It is not so much what you play, as what you do not play'. Rather than filling all the beats of a bar with relentless strumming, if only certain beats are accented, a groove is set up. It is important that the strummed rhythm interacts well with what the drums and bass are playing. There's no need to keep the rhythm exactly the same throughout; adding subtle variations is the key to good rhythm playing.

Resting the side of the strumming-hand lightly on the strings, just by the saddle, a choked or muted sound can be achieved by deadening the sustain of the chords. This

HYBRID PICKING

Most guitar players have a right-hand technique which falls into one of two categories: plectrum style or finger-style. Some players, however, use a combination of plectrum and fingers to play their instrument. This is known as hybrid picking.

> *Finger-Style, Picking, Plectra*

RASGUEADO

Rasgueado (or *rascuedo*) is an instantly recognizable flamenco technique where the fingers of the picking hand strum individually across the strings in rapid succession. A *rasgueado* can be performed as a downward or upward strum, or both. To hear *rasgueados* played by some of the finest flamenco players, look out for recordings by any of the following: Paco Peña, Paco de Lucía, Ramon Montoya, Carlos Montoya, Tomatito, Vicente Amigo, Gerardo Nuñez and Juan Mañuel Canizares.

technique can be used to achieve a staccato effect after a chord has been strummed. The technique can also be used to bring out accents in a rhythm by maintaining the muting effect throughout and releasing intermittently on the beats to be accented.

Experiment by strumming just the top three or four strings on chords; this gives a thin, crisp sound, highly suited to soul and funk styles.

> *Palm-Muting, Rhythm Guitar Tips, Soul*

COMPING

Comping is a jazz term for accompanying. It usually means playing rhythm chords over which a singer can sing or a lead performer can play a solo. When you're comping it is important to remember to keep things as simple as possible so that your playing complements and brings the best out of the soloist – if you try to do anything too clever, you'll end up clashing with other members in the band. The other thing to remember is to stick to the rhythm of a piece and play a part that highlights the groove that the bassist and drummer are laying down.

> *Improvizing, Jazz*

ABOVE LEFT: James Taylor strumming his guitar.
LEFT: Strumming is an essential technique for the rhythm guitarist to master.
FAR LEFT AND ABOVE: Pete Townshend and Albert King, who both have their fair share of great licks.

SWEEP-PICKING

Sweep-picking is an advanced technique where a guitarist plays notes across the neck with economical pick movements. This technique can be used to facilitate execution of ultra-fast arpeggios. Electric

guitar virtuosos like Frank Gambale (Chick Corea Electric Band) and Paul Gilbert (Mr Big) have used it to incredible effect.

➤ *Picking*

RAKE

A rake is an interesting effect a guitarist can produce by rubbing one of their fingers or hands along one or more of the guitar's strings. A harsher effect can be achieved by using a hard object, such as a plectrum. Raking is particularly pronounced on round-wound strings which have a more uneven surface than plain metal or gut strings.

➤ *Harmonics, Round-Wound Strings*

FINGER-STYLE

Whilst electric guitarists generally regard use of the plectrum as the best method for picking the strings, acoustic guitarists often prefer to use the fingers. Classical and flamenco styles are completely based on finger-style playing.

The picking-hand fingers are identified by letters: 'p' for the thumb, 'i' for the index finger, 'm' for the middle finger, 'a' for the ring finger, 'c' for the little finger; although, because of its shorter length, the little finger is rarely used except in some flamenco techniques.

In finger-style playing the thumb normally picks the bass strings, whilst the fingers pick the treble strings. This approach means that the picking hand can stay relatively stable.

Memorizing the letters that identify each of the picking-hand fingers is particularly useful in folk-based music, because it is often based on repeated picking patterns. If each finger is assigned a treble string to pick whilst the thumb picks the bass strings, then most picking patterns can be quick to learn. For example, **p i m i a m** would mean: '**p**' picks the bass strings, '**i**' picks the third string, '**m**' picks the second string and '**a**' picks the top string. The thumb normally will alternate between two bass notes within the chord, rather than remain on the root note.

Typical folk-picking pattern

In more advanced finger-style the treble strings may be picked simultaneously with the bass notes, or at cross-rhythm to them, to form their own melodic line.

Finger style with treble string melody

In blues and some traditional folk-based music sometimes only two fingers are used to pick the treble strings, with the third finger resting on the soundboard of the guitar to give the hand stability. This is often called the claw-hammer technique because of the shape made by the hand in this position. The thumb will normally pick bass notes comprising the root and fifth of the chord, whilst the 'i' and 'm' fingers pick the treble strings.

Clawhammer-style finger picking

Because of the angle of the hand when using this technique, the palm can easily be tilted slightly onto its side to rest on and dampen the strings, giving a typical acoustic blues sound.

Classical and flamenco finger-style

Classical and flamenco players generally use their nails to pluck the strings. This gives a stronger sound to the guitar than if using the flesh, and because classical and flamenco guitars use nylon strings the nails do not break as easily as they would if used on steel-strung acoustic guitars. Even so, amongst professional and serious guitarists, great care

needs to be taken to maintain the nails in good condition. Careful filing with a range of graded emery papers is required in order to achieve and maintain the correct nail profile that will result in a smooth sound. Extra nutrients, such as gelatin and B vitamins, are often added to the diet to ensure nail growth and strength, and sometimes (particularly amongst flamenco players) hardening fluids are applied to the nails. If all else fails, artificial nails that can be glued on are available from specialist guitar shops.

Classical and flamenco guitarists employ two main picking techniques:

Apoyando (often called rest strokes): this is when the picking fingers are kept fairly straight, and once a string has been struck the finger comes to rest on the adjacent string below. This creates a very strong sound, and most single-line melodies are played in this way in order to achieve a good level of volume and tone. Downward rest strokes played with the thumb can be used if the bass notes need to be accented.

Tirando (often called free strokes): this is when the fingers are slightly curled, and strings are plucked freely towards the palm (without touching the lower strings). This technique is used for chordal and arpeggio-based music.

The two techniques are often combined together in solo pieces, with the melody being highlighted by the use of apoyando strokes whilst the accompaniment is executed using tirando techniques.

➤ *Classical, Flamenco, Folk*

FAR LEFT: Sweep-picking.
TOP LEFT: Raking the strings will add colour to your solos.
ABOVE: John Martyn demonstrates the art of finger-style playing.

FLAT-PICKING

 Flat-picking is a playing style where all notes, scalic and chordal, are articulated with a plectrum or thumb pick. In a flat-picking style the bass note from a chord (and sometimes a short bass-line fill) is picked first, followed by the treble notes which are struck either with the plectrum or, if using a thumb pick for the bass strings, with the some of the fingers. Rhythm players who use this technique tend to alternate between single-string bass notes and strummed chords, while some country lead flat-pickers are capable of playing incredibly fast scalic solos while alternating between upstrokes and downstrokes with their picking hand. This style of playing has the advantage that, providing the bass-note finger is placed first, more time can be taken to place all the fingers needed for the chord on the fretboard.

➤— *Country, Folk, Plectra, Thumb Pick*

ARPEGGIO

An arpeggio is the sounding of the notes of a chord in succession rather than all simultaneously. Arpeggios can be played individually while holding a chord down or by picking out the notes separately on the fingerboard, just as you would when playing a scale. A major arpeggio consists of the first, third and fifth notes of a major scale (e.g. C, E and G in the key of C), while a minor arpeggio is the first, flattened third and fifth notes of the scale (C, E♭ and G in the key of C). Arpeggio notes produced with a held-down chord are not always in their exact order according to music theory.

PICKING

If you hold the plectrum (also known as a pick) the wrong way it could slow down your playing for years to come. The best method is to grip the plectrum between the thumb and index finger – this leaves the other fingers free for possible simultaneous finger-picking (called hybrid picking). Position the plectrum so that its point is about half a centimetre beyond the fingertip. If you let it poke through too much, it may snag on the string; too little and you may miss the string totally. Be careful how you grip the plectrum: if you use too much pressure, your hand muscles will tighten and so reduce your fluency, but don't hold it so loosely that you keep dropping it.

Hold the plectrum so that it is in line with your index fingernail. At all costs, avoid holding it at right angles to your index finger as this will cause your wrist to lock. To gain speed and fluency, it is essential that the picking movement stems from the wrist, not from the elbow.

To get a clear tone and good attack the plectrum tip should be at a right angle, parallel to the string it is striking. Although interesting tones can be achieved by varying this angle, these should be used for special effect, not as a general rule.

Unless you're trying to produce a particular effect, you should always alternate down and up plectrum strokes. This approach will allow you to achieve much greater speed and fluency than using either only up- or only down-strokes.

Sweep picking is an effective method, often used in rock, of playing fast, arpeggio-based runs, – where notes

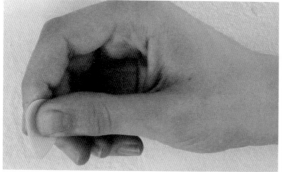

that comprise the lick are each on an adjacent string. Sweep picking is one technique in which the plectrum direction stays constant: all down-strokes for ascending runs and all up-strokes for descending runs. The plectrum is literally just swept across the strings, with each fretting finger being released after its note has been picked.

Plectra come in a variety of shapes and sizes. They are normally made of plastic, although some players prefer metal ones. The most common gauges are known as 'thin', 'medium' and 'heavy'. The latter two are best for lead playing, whilst thinner, more flexible plectra suit strumming styles.

➤— *Finger-Style, Plectra, Strumming, Sweep-Picking*

PALM-MUTING

A guitar's strings can be muted by placing the picking hand lightly across them. This technique is very useful when playing at high volume to stop the strings ringing out. It can also be used to add more colour and texture to a rhythm. Al Di Meola, a highly respected fusion guitarist, pioneered a palm-muting technique called the mutola effect, for playing extremely fast muted scales in his solos. Guitar strings can also be muted by placing the fingerboard hand lightly over them on the neck so as to exert minimal pressure.

➤— *Al Di Meola*

FAR LEFT AND ABOVE: Carlos Santana and Angus Young picking their guitars in their own distinctive ways.
ABOVE LEFT: This is the correct way to hold a plectrum.
LEFT: Palm-muting is achieved by placing the picking hand across the strings.

BEND

One of the most common lead guitar techniques is string bending, where the player plays a note on one string and pushes it up towards the next string, while still holding the note down. The most common note bends are a semitone (a bend to a note that sounds like the one in the next fret) and a tone (a bend to a note that sounds like the one two frets up). Note bending is normally carried out on the top three strings and, unless you have incredibly strong fingers, can only be played comfortably with light to medium-gauge strings. You can bend one, two or even three strings at the same time.

➤— *Lead Guitar Tips*

HAMMER-ON

A hammer-on is a technique where you play a note behind a fret on the fingerboard, then hammer down one of your other fingers behind another fret higher up on the same string. It is one of the most common lead-guitar techniques used by blues, rock, jazz and even classical players. You can use hammer-ons to play several notes on the same string. Some players, like Allan Holdsworth, use a lead technique whereby they pluck one note of a scale for each string and hammer down the rest of the notes on the string to produce a smooth, legato sound.

➤— *Lead Guitar Tips, Pull-Off*

ABOVE: Bending strings is one of the oldest techniques of lead guitar playing.
ABOVE RIGHT: It may take time to master the pre-bend, but it is worth the effort.

PULL-OFF

A pull-off can be seen as the reverse of a hammer-on. A note is played, then the finger playing that note is pulled off the string to sound a lower note that is either an open string or one fretted by another finger. When performing this technique, care must be taken not to create extraneous noises by bumping the fingers into adjacent strings.

➤— *Hammer-On*

PRE-BEND

A pre-bend is when you bend a note before you play it. In this situation you play the string from the top of the bend and then pull it back into its original

position. This technique requires a little bit of patience to perfect, as it will only work if the top of the bend is perfectly in tune.

➤— *Bend*

SLIDE

This effect is produced when you play one note on the guitar and, while still holding the note down, slide up or down the guitar neck to another note.

In a true slide, the only two notes you can hear clearly are the first and last notes, at the beginning and end of the slide, whereas a glissando is a sliding effect that is played in such a way that every note under the finger is articulated. Slide is also another name for a bottleneck guitar slide and the techniques used in bottleneck slide-guitar playing.

➤ *Bottleneck, Glissando*

BOTTLENECK

In some styles of blues, country and rock music a bottleneck (also known as a slide), rather than the fingers, is sometimes used for fretting notes. Using a bottleneck is a way of sliding between notes and achieving smooth glissandos (in the style of a pedal-steel

or Hawaiian guitar). Elmore James and Duane Allman are some of the best-known bottleneck players; also listen out for Ry Cooder and his soundtrack to the 1980s film *Paris, Texas*.

Originally, the term bottleneck literally meant just that: the neck of a bottle. Whilst some bottlenecks are still made this way (Ry Cooder uses the sawn-off end of a bourbon bottle), or from materials such as porcelain and bone, the majority are specially manufactured tubes made from glass or, more often, metal. The metal versions are technically known as slides, although in practice the terms slide and bottleneck are interchangeable. Glass bottlenecks tend to give a smoother, more rounded tone than their metal equivalents. Bottlenecks can be full-size (i.e. roughly the width of the fretboard) or half-size (these tend to be used mainly for lead playing). If you're serious about learning bottleneck techniques you should try both glass and metal slides as they each produce different sounds.

Bottlenecks are normally slipped onto either the third

or fourth fingers; using the fourth finger enables the third finger to remain free for normal fretting, but this is dependent upon the fourth finger being large enough and strong enough to support the bottleneck.

ABOVE: Elmore James was one of the finest exponents of slide-guitar playing and influenced countless guitarists, including Chuck Berry and Brian Jones. ABOVE LEFT: Playing using a bottleneck, or slide.

Bottleneck playing is often combined with special tunings that enable chords to be played across one fret with the bottleneck alone. There are a wide range of tunings in common usage, but the most popular bottleneck blues tuning is, from the lowest to the highest string: DADF♯AD. With this tuning a D major chord can be played with the bottleneck across the twelfth fret.

When playing bottleneck it is important to rest the centre of the tube directly over the fret, rather than just behind it as with normal fretting. The tube should not be pressed down to fret the note in the normal way; instead it should lightly touch the strings. Pressing the strings too hard with the bottleneck will cause fret buzz and result in the notes being out of tune.

A very high-action setting is ideal for achieving clear bottleneck playing, and for this reason many players tend to use a different guitar, especially set up for this purpose.
➤— *Blues, Country, Glissando, Rock, Slide, Tuning*

DOUBLE-STOP

A double-stop refers to two adjacent strings of the guitar played simultaneously. Most guitar solos are single-note melodies punctuated with ornaments such as bends, hammer-ons and pull-offs. A player can colour a solo even further by introducing two-note licks known as double-stops. These can be picked straight, slid up or down the neck or even played as hammer-ons or pull-offs. The double pull-off is perhaps the easiest, with the player holding down two strings at the same fret with the third finger and pulling it off to two notes held down with the first finger two frets further down the neck.
➤— *Bend, Hammer-On, Pull-Off*

TREMOLANDO

Tremolando is a classical and flamenco guitar technique in which the first, second and third fingers of the picking hand play a continuous, repeating pattern on one note. If brought up to speed, this technique produces a smooth, flowing effect. You will hear it on many recordings by classical guitar virtuosos such as Andrés Segovia, John Williams, Julian Bream, Christopher Parkening and Manuel Barrueco.
➤— *Classical, Flamenco*

VIBRATO (TECHNIQUE)

Vibrato is a fingerboard-hand technique where a played note is moved rapidly to produce a fluctuation in pitch that gives more richness to the tone. Vibrato can be applied vertically (across the neck) or horizontally (along the neck). Vibrato is used extensively in classical guitar music, and in blues, jazz and rock guitar solos. Some blues and blues-rock players such as BB King and Eric Clapton are renowned, among other things, for their heavy vibrato techniques.
➤— *BB King, Eric Clapton*

STACCATO

Staccato notes are short and abrupt. Such notes are used to add accents and colour to guitar solos. The most extreme example of staccato is Al Di Meola's mutola effect, with which he plays lines of fast staccato notes by muting the strings with his picking hand while he is playing phrases. When written on a staff, staccato notes have dots underneath. The opposite of staccato is legato, where notes are played smoothly and connectedly.

➤— *Reading Music*

HARMONICS

Harmonics enable notes to be played that are much higher than the pitch that can be reached by normal fretted notes. Harmonics give a high-pitched, bell-like sound. If using an electric guitar, harmonics will be easier to execute if you select the treble pick-up and add extra gain and treble on the amp; picking near the bridge also helps.

Various forms of harmonics can be played on the guitar.

🎸 Natural harmonics: these are easiest to learn at first. Play the high E string and then touch the string directly above the 12th fret; do not press the string on to the fretboard, just touch gently, directly above (rather than behind) the fretwire.

🎸 Natural harmonics occur on all strings on frets 12, 7 and 5 (and 12 frets up from these). Natural harmonics also occur on frets 9 and 4, although making these ring clearly is a bit harder. The harmonics on the 5th and 9th frets produce a different note to the one normally produced on that fret.

🎸 Touch harmonics: these are most easily played by fretting and picking a note as normal and then touching (rather than pressing) the same string directly over the fret that is 12 or seven frets higher. A variation of this technique is known as tapped harmonics, in which the harmonic note is achieved by rapidly tapping the higher fret. This effect can be used for incorporating one or two high notes into a phrase of normally fretted notes.

🎸 Fretted harmonics (or artificial harmonics): these are similar to tapped harmonics, in that the string is touched 12 frets higher than the fretted note. However, in this technique, instead of picking the fretted note first, the string is picked with the third finger of the picking hand only after the first finger has been positioned over the harmonic notes.

🎸 Pinched harmonics: these are mainly used in rock music. This technique can make screeching high notes appear out of nowhere in the middle of a phrase. The effect is achieved by fretting a note as normal and picking the string with the side edge of the plectrum, then immediately allowing the side of the thumb to touch the string, thus creating a harmonic. The quality and pitch of the sound achieved depends upon where the string is picked – the easiest place being the nodal point, which is the equivalent of 24 frets (i.e. two octaves) higher than the note being fretted.

➤— *Harping*

FAR LEFT: Duane Allman, one of rock music's greatest slide players.
CENTRE: Two adjacent strings being played simultaneously: a double-stop.
ABOVE: Through harmonics, notes higher than the pitch reached by normal fretted notes can be reached.

HARPING

This comprises combining natural harmonics with open strings, thereby creating a harp-like sound in which notes over-ring against each other. A very similar effect can be achieved by sustaining fretted notes on some strings whilst playing other strings open. This is known as *campanellas* (bell-ringing).

➤— *Harmonics*

GARGLING

A number of clever tremolo arm (whammy bar) techniques have evolved over the years. Some rock and avant-garde players make their guitar 'gargle' by smacking or yanking the bar hard so that it vibrates.

Ritchie Blackmore used to do it with Deep Purple during the 1970s, and the likes of Steve Vai, Joe Satriani and Yngwie Malmsteen have since developed the technique into a fine art.

➤— *Tremolo Arm*

GLISSANDO

When a guitarist plays a glissando, he or she is sliding up or down the guitar neck in such a way that every note under the fingerboard hand finger is articulated. This is different from a basic slide where the only notes that can be clearly heard are the first

and last notes played by the fingerboard hand finger. Pianists can also produce a glissando effect by sliding rapidly over their instrument's keys, whereas singers, violinists and trombone players can only produce a smooth, 'portamento' slide effect from one note to another.

➤— *Bottleneck, Slide*

TAPPING

During the late 1970s, rock guitarist Eddie Van Halen popularized the two-handed playing technique known as tapping (or finger-tapping) – influencing a whole generation of rock guitar players such as Steve Vai, Randy Rhoads and Joe Satriani. Eddie

explained the philosophy behind finger-tapping as 'since you've got fingers on both hands, why not use both of them to fret notes'. As the name suggests, tapping involves a finger from the picking hand tapping a string onto the fretboard in order to sound a note.

Tapping enables guitarists to intermix high and low notes on the same string to stunning effect, greatly expanding the interval range that can be achieved when compared with normal fretting.

Whilst some players tap with the first finger, most players use either the second, or third, finger of the picking hand. This means that the plectrum can still be held between the thumb and first finger. Whichever finger is used, it is essential to tap with the bony tip, rather than the fleshy pad, of the finger; this will ensure that the sound is clear. Be careful to tap exactly at a right angle to the fretboard; this way you will avoid hitting other strings, and also avoid bending notes out of tune. To get a good

tone, tap the fingerboard with a fast, strong action just behind the fret. Although you can tap with a clean sound, it is easier at first to use some distortion; the extra compression and sustain means not having to tap so hard to fret each note.

Tapping is also often combined with fret-hand slurs to create fast and expressive licks with a wide interval range. Some advanced players, such as Joe Satriani, use two-finger tapping, i.e. simultaneously tapping with two fingers of the picking hand. This approach greatly opens up the harmonic possibilities of the technique.

➤— **Hammer-On, Pull-Off**

ABOVE: Tapping, or finger-tapping: this enables guitarists to mix high and low notes and to expand the intervals achieved through conventional fretting.
FAR LEFT: Ritchie Blackmore of Deep Purple used the gargling technique on many of the band's 1970s releases, such as 1972's Machine Head.
LEFT: Eddie Van Halen, who popularized the tapping technique.

MUSICAL STYLES

BLUES

Blues guitar playing can be divided into two distinct styles: country-acoustic blues and urban-electric blues.

Acoustic blues

Leadbelly, Son House, Big Bill Broonzy, Mississippi John Hurt, Blind Lemon Jefferson, Robert Johnson, Brownie McGhee, John Lee Hooker and Sam Lightnin' Hopkins are some of the best-known early blues players. Although some of them, particularly in the later periods of their careers, used electric guitars, their style of playing remained barely unchanged from its acoustic roots, and all of these legendary bluesmen were finger-style players who could play a bass part and melody simultaneously. In this style of playing the thumb plays the bass strings as an accompaniment to the melody, which is picked normally using just the index and middle fingers – the third and fourth fingers can be anchored on the guitar scratchplate to give the picking hand stability. The thumb has to play independently, regardless of what the fingers are doing. It is important that the thumb holds a steady beat and sets a regular 'groove'. Whilst you play the bass part with your thumb, the fingers can pick some blues licks or a melody.

To get an authentic blues sound, rest the side of the picking hand across the strings near the bridge. This will mute the bass notes and stop them overpowering the melody.

Much of the music in this style was mostly improvised, and designed to accompany a blues vocal line; therefore, to get the right feel it is important that your playing does not become too rigid – include variations for each verse you play.

Most traditional acoustic blues pieces are written in guitar-friendly keys, such as E and A, so that greatest

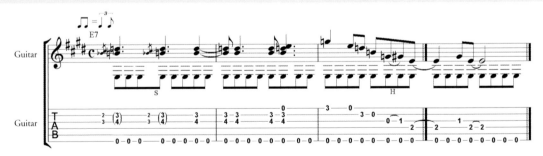

Example of acoustic blues finger-style playing: The low E string is played repeatedly with the thumb establishing a traditional blues rhythm in the bass. The opening chord is a D7 shape slid up to become E7; acoustic blues songs often feature slide-guitar playing and, even when they do not, the player often imitates a slide-playing style. Notice the contrast between the G and G♯ notes (minor and major thirds) which creates a typical blues sound.

advantage can be taken of the open bass strings; other keys occur mainly when a capo or an altered tuning is used.

Electric blues

Once blues players migrated from the country areas of the Mississippi Delta to the urban environments of cities like Chicago, they began increasingly to use electric guitar and perform with backing bands. Guitarists like BB King, Buddy Guy, Muddy Waters, Freddie King and Albert King were the pioneers of electric blues playing. More recent blues players like Eric Clapton, Stevie Ray Vaughan and Robert Cray all drew their style from these players. Because electric blues players played within the context of a band, the emphasis shifted to lead and rhythm playing rather than finger-style playing. A wider range of keys was used – such as B♭, F and C – which suited the saxophone-and-trumpet horn sections that were often included in the band line-up.

The core of electric blues lead playing comes from the blues scale. This is enhanced by the use of a wide variety of string bends and vibrato – blues soloing does not sound authentic unless these techniques are employed.

Blues music has an unusual harmonic structure in that the chords used tend to be dominant sevenths (or their extensions) – which are extensions of major chords – whilst the lead playing is based on the blues scale – which is a variation of a minor scale. It is this harmonic 'clash' which gives blues soloing its unique tonality and character. However, many of the best blues players (most

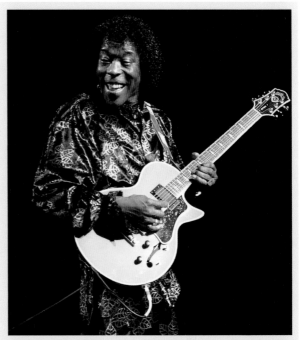

notably, BB King) go beyond the basic blues scale and include chord tones (often major third notes) in their lead playing. This gives their soloing a more lyrical and melodic sound than could be achieved using the blues scale alone.

➤— *Blues Scale, Finger-Style, Twelve-Bar Blues*

LEFT: Lightnin' Hopkins – one of the blues pioneers.
ABOVE: Buddy Guy – one of the original electric blues lead guitarists.

Example of electric blues solo: a 'lead-in' before the bar, and the use of string bends, makes this a typical Chicago-style solo. Notice how the major thirds of each chord are added to the basic blues-scale notes to create a more melodic sound. The basic dominant seventh chords have been extended to become dominant ninth chords in order to give a more mellow and sophisticated sound.

CLASSICAL

The classical guitar repertoire can be divided up into clearly defined sections:

- Transcriptions of music originally written for earlier instruments, most commonly the lute. Early music (e.g. that of John Dowland) and baroque music (e.g. that of JS Bach) is often arranged for the classical guitar.
- Guitar music from the classical and romantic periods forms the bulk of the classical guitar repertoire, with many pieces being by guitarist-composers, for example Fernando Sor, Mauro Giuliani and Francisco Tárrega.
- Spanish music is well-suited to the guitar, and whilst some pieces have been specifically written for the instrument by Rodrigo and similar composers, some of the most popular music consists of arrangements of piano or orchestral works by composers such as Albéniz and Falla.

- Andrés Segovia and Julian Bream did much to extend the classical guitar repertoire in the twentieth century by commissioning new pieces from contemporary composers, including William Walton and Villa-Lobos. The classical guitar has also been used by some players, for instance Charlie Byrd and Earl Klugh, to perform other styles of music, such as jazz.
- Compared to rock music the audience for classical guitar is rather limited, making it difficult for more than a relatively small number of top professionals to earn a living solely by performing. Some of the most respected masters of the instrument today are John Williams, Julian Bream, Carlos Bonell, David Russell, John Mills and Ray Burley.

Classical guitar technique

Classical guitar pieces are normally written in standard music notation – so a good ability to sight-read music will prove useful, particularly if you wish to play in classical ensembles rather than solo.

Picking-hand technique combines the use of *apoyando* (often called rest strokes) – in which the picking fingers are kept fairly straight, and once a string has been struck the finger comes to rest on the adjacent string below; and *tirando* (often called free strokes) – in which the fingers are slightly curled and strings are plucked freely towards the palm (without touching the lower strings).

Fret-hand technique can include chordal-based playing, or melodic single-line playing – for which a strict one-finger-per-fret technique is normally employed.

A footstool, or some kind of apoyo device, is normally used to ensure that the guitar neck is held at an angle which will facilitate the optimum hand position.

To capture the spirit of certain pieces classical guitarists use a range of musical effects:

Rubato: this literally means 'robbed'. It involves using subtle tempo changes, especially at the end or beginning of phrases; the performance slowing down in places and then speeding up again to make up lost time. The ability to use rubato effectively and appropriately is one of the distinguishing characteristics of a good classical guitarist.

LEFT: John Williams – one of the most highly respected classical guitarists performing and recording today.

Dynamics: this involves varying the volume to create a dramatic effect. For example, playing some phrases very softly can draw the listener into the music. Volume changes can help to emphasize melodic shaping and phrasing.

Rallentando: this means 'slowing down', normally at the end of a phrase, allowing the performer to shape the melody in an individual way.

Vibrato: wavering the pitch of the note on the classical guitar is achieved by gently, but repeatedly, rocking the fretting finger horizontally; this technique can be used to add sustain and to help embellish the melody.

Glissando: this involves sliding smoothly from one note to another.

Legato: this is the technical classical term for slurs (hammer-ons and pull-offs), which are used to lend fluency and smoothness to a musical phrase.

➤— *Classical Guitar, Glissando, Vibrato, John Williams*

Excerpt from Francisco Tárrega's *Étude in E minor*

Like very many classical guitar pieces, this study consists of a melody with an arpeggiated chordal accompaniment. If you look closely at the music you'll notice that some notes (normally the first of every triplet) have a tenuto line above them: these lines indicate the melody notes which should be emphasized, so that they sound clearly above the accompaniment. When played together, the two parts should give the listener almost the impression of hearing two guitars. There are many ways of interpreting a piece of this nature, and of getting the contrast in volume and tone between the two voices. The most obvious method is to use a rest stroke for the melody notes; another method is to use free strokes throughout, but to angle the third finger anticlockwise so as to extract extra volume from the melody notes without making them sound too forced. Either system will suffice – the important thing is to ensure that the accompaniment is not too loud. Like many pieces from this period, the study is chordal-based, so it is important to hold down the chord shapes within each bar to achieve a smooth legato (over-ringing) sound.

COUNTRY

Country music has always been popular in the southern USA, but new country acts like Garth Brooks, Travis Tritt and Dwight Yoakam are now selling

more albums globally than pop stars like Michael Jackson. Despite its traditional homespun image, country music has always had its fair share of quality musicians, and country guitarists like Albert Lee, the late Danny Gatton

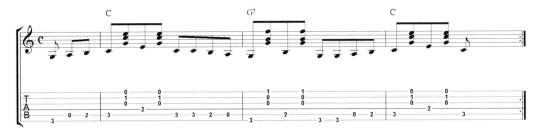

Traditional country-style rhythm playing. Separating the chord into treble strings and bass notes is a popular technique in country music. Having two bass notes per chord creates a sense of movement and emphasizes the rhythm. This type of piece can either be played finger-style, or with a thumb pick and fingers.

and Jerry Donahue are world-class players whose musicianship and dexterity can more than match that of the best rock players. Albert Lee's *Country Boy* shows his virtuoso country lead playing at its best.

Country rhythm

The easiest way to add a country feel to rhythm playing is to separate the bass notes from the treble notes during chord playing. Instead of strumming all the strings simultaneously, pick the bass note of the chord first, followed by the top three strings. The next stage is to alternate between two bass notes for each chord; these are normally the lowest note of the chord, plus the adjacent higher string. Open position D chords are an exception: because the lowest note is the fourth string, the next string up (i.e. the third) would already be part of a treble-string strum; so in open D chords use the fifth string instead for the alternate bass note.

Adding some bass runs leading up to each chord is a particularly effective technique, which works especially well when playing alone without the benefit of a band (and bass player).

Country lead

One important aspect of country lead playing is knowing the way around the pentatonic major scale – this has traditionally been the mainstay of country playing. The term pentatonic means 'five note', so the pentatonic major scale is just a normal (do-re-mi) major scale, but with the fourth and seventh notes omitted. Leaving these notes out makes the scale much easier to improvize with,

as there's less chance of scale notes clashing against certain chords. The pentatonic major scale's simplicity and clarity of sound are ideally suited to the straightforward chord sequences that tend to be used in country music.

String bends are often used in country playing, particularly the harmony bend, in which some notes are held whilst another is bent; this emulates the sound of a pedal-steel guitar. Hammer-ons, pull-offs and slides are also widely used to aid speed and fluency.

Some country players, particularly in the styles of country-swing and new country, find the basic pentatonic scale a little bland, and so they add in the minor third as a passing note. When this is combined with the pentatonic major scale it gives a slight bluesy edge to the sound, and is known as the country scale.

Country sound

The Fender Telecaster has always been the favoured instrument of country guitarists, as it has a clean and bright sound, with a cutting edge to the tone. If you haven't got a Telecaster you can emulate its sound by selecting the treble (bridge) pickup on your guitar, and cutting back on the bass and mid frequencies on your amp. To get an authentic country sound use a clean amp setting with little or no distortion. Clean country electric guitar sounds frequently use a compressor effect.

➤— *Compressor/Limiter, Country Scale, Fender Telecaster, Pentatonic Major Scale*

LEFT: Albert Lee – one of country music's finest guitar pickers.

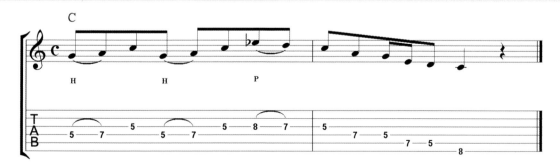

Country-style lead playing. This example uses the country scale, and includes some typical new-country use of slurs.

features of any flamenco show. It is only relatively recently that flamenco guitar has come to be performed and recorded as a solo instrument, pioneered by Ramón Montoya in the first half of the twentieth century. Montoya is widely regarded as the father of solo flamenco guitar playing, and was a big influence on later generations of virtuoso flamenco players including his nephew, Carlos Montoya, Paco Peña and Tomatito. To hear flamenco playing at its best today, listen out for:

FLAMENCO

The invasion of southern Spain in the fifteenth century by the Moors from North Africa resulted in a very distinctive and exotic influence on the music of Spain. Consequently, southern Spanish music developed a unique character – compared with the classical music of its northern European neighbours. The typical flamenco guitar style that we know today has been developed largely from this tradition, and has remained particularly pure to its roots amongst the gypsy populations based in the Andalucia region of Spain.

Traditionally, the guitar plays a supporting role to the singers and dancers, who are considered to be the main

ABOVE: Flamenco came from a musical tradition begun in southern Spain.
RIGHT: Juan Martín's recordings, books and videos have helped widen flamenco's appeal.
FAR RIGHT: A flamenco guitar.

- Paco de Lucía – responsible for bringing jazz harmonies into flamenco guitar playing. He also happens to have one of the fastest, most intricate finger-picking techniques in the world.
- Paco Peña – one of the greatest living exponents of the pure flamenco style.
- Juan Martín – a renowned flamenco educator, who has broadened its popular appeal and introduced fusions of other cultures with flamenco.

Whether played solo or in an accompaniment role, all flamenco guitar is based on a range of traditional dance rhythms such as *alegría*, *bulería*, *sevillana*, *malagueña* and *soleá*. Each has its own unique *compás* (underlying rhythm) that sets the mood and feel of the music.

Flamenco techniques

- **Tremolo**: this involves using the picking-hand fingers in a quick and flowing pattern to repeatedly play one note. This technique is often used to bring out a melody on the top string and is a method of emulating the very long sustain of a note that can be more easily achieved on bowed or wind instruments. There are various finger patterns that can be used for a tremolo, but the most common is a repetition of **a m i**.

- **Rasgueado** (or *rascuedo*): this is an essential flamenco strumming technique. The hand is held tightly closed, then the strings are strummed by releasing the fingers in quick succession; the fingers roll rapidly across the strings, striking them one after another with the front of the nails. The resulting sound is powerful and piquant.

- **Golpe**: this is a percussive effect achieved by striking the body of the guitar with the ring finger. *Golpes* are used to emphasize accents within the rhythm of the piece. Flamenco guitars are fitted with perspex *golpe* plates to avoid damaging the instrument.

Flamenco pieces often require a strong attack with the thumb to bring out a bass melody. The approach is often far more aggressive than that used in classical guitar playing; quite often, rest strokes are used with the thumb in order to achieve a forceful tone.

Fast and lyrical scale runs are a characteristic feature of flamenco playing. Sometimes slurs can be used to facilitate playing runs at speed, but the ability to alternate the index and middle fingers rapidly when picking is a prerequisite of an accomplished flamenco guitarist.

➤— *Finger-Style*

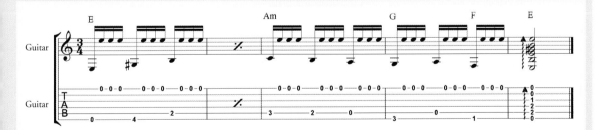

Malagueña: a well-known and traditional flamenco piece.

Like much flamenco guitar music, although it is based in the key of A minor, the dominant chord of E major plays an important harmonic role – this is reflected in the use of the Gn note which gives a Phrygian-scale tonality to many flamenco pieces. In this arrangement a tremolo technique is used on the top E note, whilst the melodic movement lies in the bass. A rasgueado strum finishes the excerpt. In flamenco, whilst the rhythms of the various dances are strictly defined, the use of tremolo or rasgueado effects is left to the performer's discretion, and the exact guitar lines played are normally improvised around a standard theme.

FOLK

Although guitar-based folk music by the likes of Woody Guthrie had been around for many years, it was the widespread success in the 1960s of folk singer-songwriters like Bob Dylan, Joan Baez and Paul Simon that brought folk music to a far wider audience. Folk music's influence served to introduce political ideas into pop music and its lyrics. Folk pioneer Bob Dylan has had his songs covered by many rock acts, such as Jimi Hendrix and Guns N' Roses.

Folk music comes from an unwritten tradition and is rarely notated – instead tunes and picking styles are usually passed on from player to player by demonstration, or learnt by ear from recordings. The essence of much British folk music can be traced back directly to the days of the Renaissance lutenists – this style of folk is exemplified by guitarists such as John Renbourn, Bert Jansch and Martin Carthy. Celtic influences are also very evident in the styles of some modern folk players, such as Gordon Giltrap and Dick Gaughan.

Ragtime, blues and jazz music influenced the playing style of many folk guitarists, such as Davy Graham and Stefan Grossman, in the 1960s and 1970s. In recent years, world music influences, from African rhythms to eastern European scales, are becoming quite prevalent in folk music, and the boundaries of what constitutes folk music are becoming increasingly blurred. Although folk music is traditionally played on an unamplified acoustic guitar some players, such as John

Martyn, amplify the instrument and use effects. Today, having an electric guitarist in a folk band is not at all unusual – an indication that folk music is alive and continuing to grow and develop as it has always done.

Folk guitar technique

Although plectrums and strumming are used in folk music, typically most traditional folk guitar playing is based on finger-picking. Whilst the folk guitar can be used as a solo instrument, it is far more commonly used to accompany the voice. The bass strings are usually picked by the thumb, whilst the index, middle and ring fingers are used to pick the treble strings. With some notable exceptions, such as Gordon Giltrap, it is very rare for the little finger to be used. In the most straightforward forms of folk music, once a basic finger-picking pattern is established it is used throughout the song, or at least for a whole verse or chorus. Playing this style of accompaniment is easiest if each finger is assigned a treble string to pick. The thumb can then play either just the root note of the chord, or alternate between bass notes within the chord. Some folk guitarists prefer to rely on just the index and middle fingers to pick the treble strings, with the other fingers resting on the table of the guitar, thereby giving the hand a sense of stability.

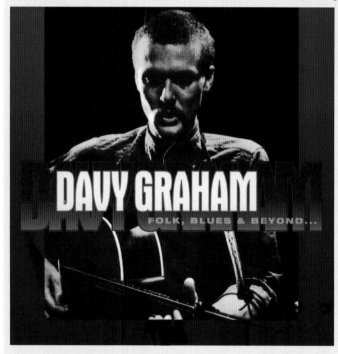

DAVY GRAHAM
FOLK, BLUES & BEYOND...

Typical folk finger-picking accompaniment pattern

Solo folk-guitar style

Folk flat-picking style

In more advanced folk finger-picking, particularly in instrumental solo pieces, the picking may be far more elaborate, with the treble and bass strings written as separate voices forming their own melodic lines (as in the style of a classical guitar piece). The palm is often tilted slightly on to its side so as to rest on and dampen the bass strings, thereby preventing them from overpowering the thinner treble strings. Flat-picking technique is also used by some players.

➤— *Flat-Picking, Plectra, Strumming*

TOP AND LEFT: Roy Harper and Gordon Giltrap picking folk songs.
FAR LEFT: Davy Graham's Folk, Blues & Beyond… *fused traditional folk songs with jazz, blues and world music inflluences.*

JAZZ

Jazz music first emerged as a distinct musical style in the early part of the twentieth century. It developed in the New Orleans region of the USA as a fusion of brass-band music, blues and ragtime, with strong African rhythmic influences.

The guitar was first used in the Dixieland and New Orleans styles of jazz (often referred to as 'trad jazz'), its main role being to act as part of the rhythm section, conventionally playing chords in a solid four-to-the-bar rhythm. It was only in the 1930s that guitarists such as Eddie Lang and Lonnie Johnson began to play single-line lead solos.

During the late 1930s and 1940s swing music came to the fore. Whilst the guitar still largely played a steady rhythmic role, guitarists such as Django Reinhardt and Charlie Christian made full use of the newly invented electric guitar to play guitar solos more in line with a piano or saxophone style of improvizing.

Swing was later superseded by bop, which involved

small groups when compared with the larger swing bands, but far more complex music. Bop compositions by saxophonist Charlie Parker, and trumpet player Dizzy Gillespie remain challenges for jazz musicians today. Bop guitarists of the time include Jimmy Raney, Tal Farlow and Barney Kessel.

Cool jazz developed as a mellower and less frenetic variation of bop, typified by the relaxed smooth style of guitarists such as Jim Hall and Howard Roberts.

A reaction to the placid nature of cool jazz in the 1950s was the development of the more unrelenting and sometimes funky rhythms contained in hard bop, as played by Wes Montgomery and Kenny Burrell.

During the 1960s and 1970s, fusion developed as a mix of jazz and rock music. This style continues to be developed today, with guitarists such as John McLaughlin, Larry Coryell, Larry Carlton and Pat Metheny being some of the best exponents.

Jazz improvization

Good jazz players are generally considered to be some of the most skilled improvizers. What makes this type of improvization challenging is that most jazz tunes involve

A Dorian Modal scale   G# Dorian Modal scale   F# Whole Tone scale

|| Am7 | D9 | G#m9 | C#13 | F#7#5 | F#7#5 |

B Lydian Modal scale   B Lydian Modal scale   E Myxolydian scale

|| Bmaj9 | A#m7#5 | Dmaj7 | C#13 | E7 ||

Example of the scales used for jazz improvization

some modulation (i.e. changes of key) which means that the improvizer has to have a good knowledge of scales and harmony in order to play over the changes. To cope with the key changes and complex harmony, modal scales and altered arpeggios are often used.

Another challenge of jazz playing is to incorporate notes outside the main scales and arpeggios – this is called chromaticism. Adding these outside notes can create a real sense of musical tension and add colour to improvization, making solos less predictable and more individual. The best way to begin using chromaticism is to play auxiliary notes, i.e. moving to chord tones from a note above or below. For example, over a D minor chord, a C# could be played before playing the root note D. The C# note is outside both the key scale and the chord. The longer this is held, the greater the sense of dissonance and tension created, and the more dramatic the release will be when it is resolved. Another technique is to begin on a chord tone or scale tone and create tension by passing through non-chord/scale tones before releasing the tension with the final note.

Jazz chords

Jazz players often use extended chords rather than basic triads or sevenths in order to produce a more sophisticated sound.

|| C | Am | Dm | G ||

can become:

|| Cmaj9 | Am11 | Dm9 | G13 ||

Example of jazz chord extensions

|| Cmaj9 | Am7♯5 | Dm7♭5 | G 7♯5♯9 ||

Example of jazz chord substitution

|| Cmaj9 | E♭7 | A♭9 | D♭13 ||

Example of altered jazz chords

Often the fifth or ninth interval within a chord is altered (raised or lowered by a semitone) by jazz guitarists in order to create a sense of musical tension.

Chord substitution is a technique used by jazz players to enhance the harmonic interest of a simple chord progression. One common type of substitution is the tritone (or flattened fifth); this involves replacing a chord with a dominant seventh (or its extension) with a root note a flattened fifth higher than the original chord. For example, E♭7 could be substituted for Am.

Jazz sound

To get a typical jazz sound use a clean, mellow sound with lots of low mid-range tone and with the treble control rolled back a bit. Try using slides rather than string bends. Listen to some of the great jazz saxophone and trumpet players to get ideas for phrasing.

➤— *Arpeggio, Improvization, Jazz Melodic Minor Scale, Modes, Slide*

LEFT: Barney Kessel – a pioneer of bebop guitar playing.
ABOVE: A fine exponent of jazz-fusion genre, John McLaughlin.

Example of chromatic playing in jazz improvisation

METAL

Heavy metal music emerged as a distinct form in the late 1970s. It was pioneered by bands such as Van Halen and Iron Maiden. Metal took its influences from the heavy rock of the early 1970s, but incorporated much of the style and attitude of punk rock, which in many respects was its main precursor.

Sub-genres of metal soon emerged during the 1980s, the most successful of which were:

- Thrash metal: performed by bands such as Metallica, Slayer and Megadeth, was played at high speed and emphasized raw energy and aggression.
- Death metal: performed by bands such as Napalm Death and Death, explored a deeper, darker side of metal, often using discords and augmented or diminished intervals to create an unsettling musical effect.

Metal sound

An authentic metal sound relies on plenty of distortion. A distortion pedal will probably be necessary, as metal distortion tends to be more extreme than that which can be achieved through a standard amplifier.

Most metal players use guitars with low actions and very light-gauge strings as this facilitates the fast playing and slurring that is typical of the style. Metal guitarists often use instruments with a tremolo arm (also known as a whammy bar) and a locking nut so that extreme 'dive-bombing' and other tremolo effects can be achieved without the strings going out of tune. The guitars will also normally have humbucker or other powerful pickups to aid volume and distortion levels.

Metal chord techniques

When using an overdriven sound you can achieve a much tighter and more easily controlled sound by just using the root, fifth and octave from a chord. These chords are known as 'power chords' and form the backbone of metal rhythm playing.

To play a power chord, fret a note on any bass string using your first finger and then add a note two frets up on the adjacent higher string with your third finger; this will give you the fifth. Now add the octave with the fourth finger; this will be on the same fret as the fifth interval, but on the adjacent higher string.

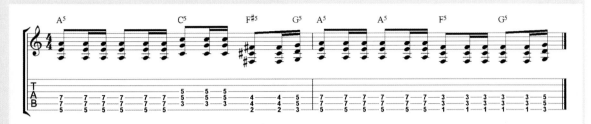

Example of metal rhythm playing using sixteenth notes and power chords

The rhythmic style of metal chord playing is often quite relentless, such as using sixteenth beats in an insistent and repetitive rhythm. Down-strokes are mainly used when playing power chords in order to emphasize the strength of the bass strings. The side of the strumming hand is often rested against the strings, near the bridge, to mute the sound; this can then be released to create powerful accents.

In order to play power chords clearly, check that you are doing the following:

- Adapting your hand stretch to the size of the fret you're playing at (frets get narrower as you progress up the fingerboard).
- Moving your whole hand (not just reaching with the fingers) when you change fret position.
- Only strumming the strings that you are fretting – beware of hitting unwanted open strings.

Metal lead techniques

One of the main features of metal lead playing is speed. This requires a very secure plectrum technique with a fast alternate picking action (See 'picking'). However, other ways of picking are sometimes used, such as sweep-picking, in which the plectrum direction stays constant – ascending lines all being played with down-strokes, and descending lines all being played with up-strokes. This technique is often used in metal, but it only really works when the notes that comprise the phrase are on adjacent strings; the plectrum can then just be swept across the strings, with each fretting finger being released after its note has been picked.

Another method that is used in metal to achieve fast playing is multi-slurring. This is the combining of hammer-ons with pull-offs (and sometimes with tapped notes). By using short repetitive slurred phrases, often including open-string notes, fast playing becomes much easier than if all the notes were picked. Although a light touch is required in order to enable the speed that is required, it is important that notes are hammered firmly enough so that their pitch can be clearly heard – If they are not, the notes can become just a blur of sound, whereas with the best metal players all the notes can still be heard clearly despite the speed of their execution.

➤ *Action, Distortion, Hammer-On, Lead Guitar Tips, Power Chords, Pull-Off, Tremolo Arm*

LEFT: Steve Harris from Iron Maiden – the most successful band to emerge from the new wave of British metal.

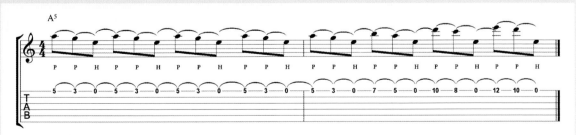

Example of metal lead playing using multi-slurring

REGGAE

The rhythm style known as reggae is used in a wide range of musical styles, far beyond its traditional Jamaican roots.

Aswad, Toots and the Maytals, and Bob Marley and the Wailers are some of the most successful reggae bands. British artists such as the Police, the Clash, Eric Clapton and UB40 have achieved wide commercial success by making use of the reggae sound.

The whole rhythmic emphasis of reggae revolves around the bass-line, which is often far more prominent than in other musical styles. The guitar part consists of very sparse chord chops (known to reggae musicians as skanks, or drops), which are played on the back beats (beats two and four) rather than the main beats of the bar. The overall aim is to create a very steady, even rhythm, with the bass and guitar parts complementing each other.

The chord drops are normally played using down-strokes. To get a crisp sound, chords should be played

Single-skank reggae rhythm: play a single short down-stroke on beats two and four; you do not need to strum all of the strings in each chord – playing just the top four treble strings will give a crisper sound.

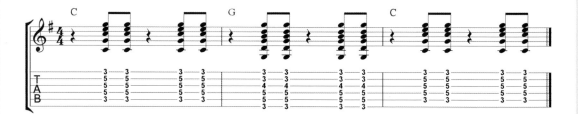

Double-skank reggae rhythm: after each down-stroke immediately 'bounce back' with an up-stroke across the first two or three strings.

Example of ska-style rhythm playing

staccato. This means that as soon as the chord is sounded it is damped, by allowing the strumming hand to rest against the strings in between strums.

Long guitar solos are not normally a feature of reggae; most guitar lines in reggae music consist either of short licks or improvization based on the melody line. Nevertheless, this can be very effective – particularly if, like the best reggae players, you use interesting rhythms and a variety of string damping using the fretting hand.

Ska

Ska is sometimes thought of as a speeded-up version of reggae, although it has its own unique style and mood, and is in fact the precursor of reggae. The development of ska can be split into three main waves: original ska (pioneered by artists including Derrick Morgan and Prince Buster); two-tone (popularized by bands like The Specials and Madness) and ska-core (a fusion of metal, punk and ska pioneered by bands such as No Doubt and the Mighty Mighty Bosstones).

All types of ska adhere to the same basic rhythmic style known as skanking, as described on page 130.

In order to get the crisp guitar sound that is used in ska, all chords should be played using only upward strums across the top three or four strings, and you should mute the strings after each strum. You can do this by allowing the strumming hand to rest against the strings in between strums and by slightly releasing the finger pressure with the fretting hand.

Lead guitar solos are few and far between in traditional ska and two-tone, as the guitar normally plays a mainly rhythmic role, using a clean, undistorted sound, in order

not to overpower the vocals and horn section. However, modern bands such as the Mighty Mighty Bosstones tend not to feature the distinctive ska rhythm throughout their songs, alternating instead between this and some metal or punk-inspired riffs.

➤— *Eric Clapton, Bob Marley, Strumming*

LEFT: *Peter Tosh – whose influential reggae guitar style was central to Bob Marley and the Wailers' sound.*
ABOVE: *The late, great Bob Marley, reggae superstar.*

RHYTHM & BLUES

The most influential rhythm & blues guitarist of all time was Chuck Berry. Berry played his blues-based music with a fast rocking rhythm and a unique guitar style that influenced a generation of guitar players. His hits, such as 'Johnny B Goode', 'Roll Over Beethoven' and 'Reelin' And Rockin'', are some of the most covered songs in the history of rock music.

Chuck Berry used the commonplace blues scale as the mainstay of his playing. He achieved a strikingly strong and individual sound by using only down-strokes and often playing two notes at once, a technique known as double-stopping. Berry didn't fly around the fingerboard too much, and he wasn't particularly worried about following the chord changes; he was quite content to stay on a one-position riff whilst his band members did the work of changing chords. This thrifty technique meant that although his melodic riff might remain static, its harmonic effect would change with each chord.

Rhythm playing

The rhythmic basis of much early rhythm & blues music is the shuffle rhythm, normally played just using two notes of each chord on the bass strings: the root and fifth, alternating to the root and sixth. This is often also called the dotted rhythm, because it comprises the alternation of long dotted notes (dotted quavers) and short notes (semiquavers). Most rhythm & blues songs will use this rhythm riff throughout the song, changing the pitch for each chord and normally following a standard 12-bar blues progression.

Berry and many other rhythm & blues performers modernised the blues shuffle rhythm by speeding it up and playing it in straight eights, i.e. with a more even rhythm. Many rock bands, such as Status Quo, later used this rhythm to great effect.

Another common variation is to include the dominant seventh in this rhythm riff. This gives a more bluesy tonality.

Muting the strings by resting the side of the fretting hand lightly against the strings near the bridge will help you get an authentic rhythm & blues sound.

Lead playing

The main factor that distinguishes rhythm & blues lead playing from other styles is the emphasis on double-stopping: although the blues scale is the core of rhythm & blues soloing, the notes often tend to be fretted two at a time. This can be achieved by laying your fretting fingers flat across two strings on the same fret, and pressing with the pads rather than the tips of your fingers. The powerful sound achieved by this technique makes single-note runs sound weak in comparison, so these are used mainly as lead-ins to double-stopped licks. Slides and unison string bends are also a common feature of the style.

Riff playing

Arpeggio runs, normally from dominant seventh chords, are frequently used in rhythm & blues to create repetitive riffs that move with the chords. These are normally played on the bass strings in order to give a strong sound and provide a solid foundation to the song. Some advanced players, such as Mick Green and Wilko Johnson, are able to combine lead licks with arpeggio or rhythm riffs.

➤— *Arpeggio, Chuck Berry, Dominant Seventh Chords, Lead Guitar Tips, Riff, Rock, Twelve-Bar Blues*

ABOVE: Chuck Berry — a man who knows a thing or two about rhythm & blues.

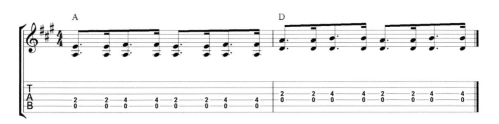

Rhythm & blues shuffle rhythm

Rhythm & blues straight-eights rhythm

Rhythm & blues straight-eights rhythm using sixths and dominant sevenths

Rhythm & blues lead licks

Rhythm & blues arpeggio riff

ROCK

The early 1960s saw the emergence of groups, such as the Beatles and the Rolling Stones, who began to write their own songs and found phenomenal commercial success. In the late-1960s popular music took two different paths: pop singers specialising in catchy hit singles, and rock bands performing more musically complex and improvized material, aiming more for album sales. Since then, rock music has diversified into numerous subgenres, ranging from the complex and lengthy soloing of guitarists such as Ritchie Blackmore of Deep Purple to the shorter, more song-based soloing of Noel Gallagher from Oasis.

Classic rock

Guitarists in the 1960s such as Jimi Hendrix and Eric Clapton laid the foundations of rock guitar playing. Their playing relied upon the blues scale and pentatonic minor scale. There was much use of string bends, and the influence of blues music was quite evident (the main difference between rock and blues being the more distorted rock sound achieved by overdriving the amps, and the far wider range of chords that were used in many rock songs). Improvizations tended to be quite free and sometimes lengthy, becoming as important a feature of

the song as the vocal line, an approach that before then had only occurred in jazz. Previously, guitar solos had been relatively short and were often viewed as just a fill between vocal choruses. In classic rock, repetitive guitar riffs often opened and then formed the basis of the songs.

Progressive rock

During the 1970s, guitarists such as Ritchie Blackmore of Deep Purple and Jimmy Page of Led Zeppelin expanded the possibilities of rock guitar playing even further. They introduced quasi-classical influences into a musical style that became increasingly complex: the harmonic structure of songs became more developed and, although

pentatonic playing still remained the backbone of soloing, other scales such as the harmonic minor became more widely used. Soloing became increasingly lengthy, and the speed of guitar playing came to be seen as an important musical feature, laying the foundations for metal music.

A classic rock riff

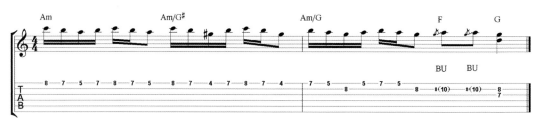

Progressive-rock lead licks

Punk

In the late-1970s, punk-rock groups such as the Sex Pistols and the Clash rejected the technical excesses of progressive rock, and concentrated on raw energy and an aggressive attitude to get the message of their songs across. There was normally a fairly minimalist harmonic structure: major barre chords were often used exclusively throughout a song, with lots of distortion. This combination created a powerful, slightly dissonant sound.

Any featured solos tended to be fairly short, normally limited to eight or 12 bars, and these were more about feel and rhythm than melody. Double stops were often used in order to maintain the powerful sound.

Grunge

It was from this punk background that grunge-rock bands emerged in the early 1990s, such as Seattle's Nirvana and Pearl Jam. Grunge playing tended to have a little more

FAR LEFT: Ritchie Blackmore has expanded the horizons of rock guitar playing.
LEFT: The Sex Pistols' raw energy negated the need for any technical finesse.
BELOW: Despite his short-lived career, Kurt Cobain of Nirvana wrote the rulebook of grunge guitar playing.

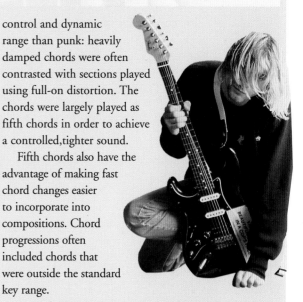

control and dynamic range than punk: heavily damped chords were often contrasted with sections played using full-on distortion. The chords were largely played as fifth chords in order to achieve a controlled, tighter sound.

Fifth chords also have the advantage of making fast chord changes easier to incorporate into compositions. Chord progressions often included chords that were outside the standard key range.

➤— *Bend, Blues Scale, Distortion, Fifth Chords, Harmonic Minor Scale, Improvizing, Pentatonic Minor Scale*

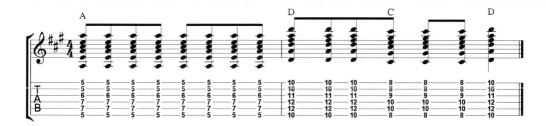

Punk rhythm playing – it is essential to use some distortion to get the right sound

Grunge rhythm playing

ROCK 'N' ROLL

Taking the blues as inspiration and mixing in influences from country and jazz music, rock 'n' roll came to popularity in the late 1950s. Early rock 'n' roll guitarists developed their style from either country music (as in the case of Chet Atkins) or jazz and jump jive (as in the case of Scotty Moore). Certainly in rockabilly styles of rock 'n' roll, the strong country music influence can be clearly heard. Many rock 'n' roll riffs also bear a strong resemblance to the bass lines of boogie-woogie piano playing.

Most rock 'n' roll songs are based on the standard 12-bar blues format, apart from the doo-wop subgenre, which was based on the I-Vim-IV-V chord progression.

Rock 'n' roll guitarists tended to use a clean, undistorted sound, but often added echo and reverb.

Rock 'n' roll riffs

Guitarists in some rock 'n' roll groups, such as that of Little Richard (which at one stage had Jimi Hendrix as a member), often played the main instrumental riff of the songs in unison with either the bass, piano or horn section. This would often be based around a major-sixth arpeggio, which became the trademark of some styles of rock 'n' roll. The arpeggio-based riff would be transposed

Example of rock 'n' roll guitar riff

Example of rock 'n' roll rhythm playing

to match each chord change, normally following a standard 12-bar blues progression.

Rock 'n' roll chords

In rock 'n' roll rhythm playing, major chords are often extended to become major sixth chords, and sometimes dominant seventh chords. Chords tend to be played as stabs, or accents, rather than being strummed all the way through each bar. This style of playing emulates the stabs that were often played by the horn section in the swing and jump-jive music which preceded rock 'n' roll. Sometimes chords are slid into pitch from a fret below the destination fret. Such passing chords are not normally written in the chord chart; it is left to the performer's discretion as to when they are included. Quite often only partial chords are played, omitting the bass strings. This creates the clear tonal contrast between the bassist and the guitarist that is often a feature of rock 'n' roll recordings.

Rock 'n' roll lead

Despite the seemingly straightforward nature of rock 'n' roll chord progressions, the lead soloing of the best rock 'n' roll guitarists, such as Scotty Moore, Cliff Gallup and Brian Setzer, is actually quite complex. This style of lead playing uses a combination of the pentatonic major scale (to reflect the brighter, major sixth elements of rock 'n' roll) with the blues scale (to reflect the blues influence of the music). It also takes influences from jazz: the use of chromaticism and targeting of chord tones,

LEFT: Eddie Cochran was a great rock 'n' roll guitarist and had hits with classic songs such as 'C'mon Everybody', 'Somethin' Else' and 'Summertime Blues'. BELOW: Cliff Gallup played lead guitar in Gene Vincent's Blue Caps.

and the emphasis more on slides than string bends. Fast repetition of short licks or single notes is also a feature of this style of lead playing.

➤— ***Dominant Seventh Chords, Lick, Major Sixth Chords, Twelve-Bar Blues***

Example of rock 'n' roll lead playing

SOUL (AND MOTOWN)

Playing guitar in a soul music context is all about timing and the interaction between instruments; the guitar style is often quite sparse, establishing a groove but allowing the music space. The rhythm guitar normally consists of short, repetitive chops, with any lead playing largely consisting of short, repetitive licks. Rather than filling all the beats of the bar with relentless chordal strumming, the trick is to accent only certain beats. This is exemplified by guitarists such as Steve Cropper, who performed with Otis Redding and featured on many of the most influential soul recordings of the 1960s.

Soul-style rhythm guitar playing

Funk-style lead licks – X indicates fret-hand muting

Funk

Although the overall sound of a funk track may seem quite busy, the rhythm guitar playing is often quite sparse, consisting of short, rhythmic licks. These rarely start on the first beat of the bar, instead fitting around the vocals, drums and bass-line of the tune. There are three main ingredients that you need in order to play in a truly authentic funk rhythm guitar style:

🎸 Partial chords: instead of playing full six-string chords, just play the treble strings. As the bass guitar plays an important role in funk music, you do not even need to play the root notes of the chords, as the bass will be doing this.

🎸 Slideable chords: as funk guitar chords normally consist of only three or four fretted treble strings, they are very easy to move from one fret to another. Sliding chord shapes up or down a fret or two will create a sense of movement in the music.

🎸 Extended chords: often in funk music, rather than just playing normal majors and minors, the chords are extended to become ninths.

Rather than playing long, elaborate solos, funk players tend to play short, rhythmic riffs (often with string muting) that are repeated with slight variations throughout the song.

Soul and funk sound

Go for a crisp, clean sound. If you have a compression unit, this will help achieve the well-defined tight sound used in these styles of music. Wah-wah pedals are quite often used in funk and disco.

➤── *Lick, Palm-Muting, Rhythm Guitar Tips, Riff, Wah-Wah*

LEFT: Nile Rodgers – a great exponent of funk-guitar playing.
ABOVE: Nile Rodgers and Bernard Edwards of the funk band, Chic.

PEOPLE

ATKINS, CHET

American, 1924–2001. Country-based finger-picking acoustic and electric guitarist. With a career spanning six decades, Atkins worked as a session guitarist, solo artist, songwriter, producer and record-label executive. He played with the Carter Sisters, Hank Williams and Elvis Presley. As an A&R director with RCA he helped shape the careers of Elvis Presley and the Everly Brothers, and as a producer he is generally credited with shaping traditional country into a more mainstream musical form. His playing style, based on finger-picking with thumb and three fingers, includes solo finger-picking tunes with cleanly plucked melodies above alternating bass lines and accompaniment, and lightning-fast, cascading arpeggios. 'I've said that Merle Travis and I pretty much taught America how to finger-pick.'

He recorded many solo albums including *A Session With Chet Atkins* (1958) and *The Early Years Of Chet Atkins And His Guitar* (1964). He collaborated with Mark Knopfler on *Neck And Neck* (1990) and with Knopfler, George Benson and Eric Johnson on *Read My Licks* (1995). He has influenced many guitarists, including George Harrison, Mark Knopfler, George Benson and Eric Johnson. Honouring his stature as a guitarist, both Gretsch and Gibson made Chet Atkins signature-model guitars, the semi-acoustic Super Chet and the solid-body nylon-string Chet Atkins Standard CE respectively.

➤ *Arpeggio, Country, Finger-Style, Gibson, Gretsch*

BARRUECO, MANUEL

Cuban, born 1952. Classical guitarist. Barrueco's family relocated to the USA in 1967, where he has been based since. He studied at the Peabody Conservatory in Baltimore, where he was a full-scholarship student under Aaron Shearer, a soloist with the Peabody Orchestra and a winner of the Peabody competition (Barrueco was the first guitarist to achieve any of these honours). He was also co-founder of the guitar department at the Manhattan School of Music. Barrueco has a unique way of memorizing pieces one hand at a time – he will memorize the plucking-hand movements alone before fretting any notes. His recordings include the traditional guitar repertoire such as *Falla, Ponce & Rodrigo* (1987), *JS Bach: Sonatas for solo violin nos 1, 2, 3 (BWV 1001, 1003, 1005)* (1997), *Rodrigo: Concierto de Aranjuez & Fantasia para un gentilhombre & Songs for tenor & guitar* (1997), recorded with the London Philharmonic Orchestra and Placido Domingo. He has also released genre-breaking collections such as *Sometime Ago* (1994), which includes music by Chick Corea, Keith Jarrett, Paul Simon and Lou Harrison, and *Lennon & McCartney Songs* (1995), with Leo Brower arrangements recorded with fellow classical guitarist David Tanenbaum and the London Symphony Orchestra.

➤ *Classical, Paul Simon*

BATTEN, JENNIFER

American, born 1962. Rock guitarist. Her influences include Jeff Beck, jazz performer and instructor Joe Diorio, and fusion electric bassist Jaco Pastorius. Batten was the first woman to graduate from Hollywood's Guitar Institute of Technology in 1979, later returning to teach there. She has written several guitar instructional books, including *Two-Handed Rock* (1984). She reached a wider audience touring with Michael Jackson in 1987/8 and 1992/3. Batten has released two solo albums as Jennifer Batten's Tribal Rage: *Above Below And Beyond* (1992) and *Momentum* (1997), the latter heavily influenced by world music. Invited to join Jeff Beck's band, she subsequently played on Beck's *Who Else!* (1999) and *You Had It Coming* (2001), then appeared with Beck on the supporting tours. A highly schooled and highly skilled guitarist, Batten wrote a 'Wire Tapping' instructional column for the esteemed US magazine *Guitar Player* from April 1990 to June 1992, sharing all aspects of her two-handed tapping technique. Besides being well versed in post-Van Halen techniques, Batten has also embraced technological advances, using MIDI set-ups with Beck. Batten plays Washburn Maverick guitars with Roland GK-2A guitar-synth pickups. For guitar sounds she uses a DigiTech GSP2101, Digitech Whammy and Boss Acoustic Simulator, amongst other effects; for keyboard sounds she uses a Roland GI-10 MIDI converter, Akai samplers and a Roland JV-1080 sound module.

➤— *Jeff Beck, Electro-Acoustic, MIDI, Rock, Tapping*

BECK, JEFF

British, born 1944. Rock guitarist. Beck played in the Deltones and the Tridents before replacing Eric Clapton in the Yardbirds in 1965. He embarked on a solo career in 1966, guided by producer Micky Most, and had a hit single as vocalist with the uncharacteristically poppy 'Hi Ho Silver Lining' (1967). He formed the Jeff Beck Group which, with an ever-changing personnel, recorded albums including the blues/rock *Truth* (1968) and the funky *Rough And Ready* (1972). He formed the short-lived Beck Bogert & Appice, releasing one eponymously-titled album in 1973. He returned to a solo career, this time favouring instrumentals. The 3-CD set *Beckology*

BELOW: *The incredible Jeff Beck.*
BELOW LEFT: *Chet Atkins – country music musician and producer and the guitarist who 'taught America how to finger-pick'.*

(1992) chronicles Beck's career from 1965–89. His career highlights include a Grammy for *Guitar Shop* (1989) and a BAFTA for the *Frankie's House* soundtrack (1993). With the Big Town Playboys he released *Crazy Legs* (1993), a tribute to Gene Vincent's guitarist, Cliff Gallup, one of Beck's biggest influences. Highly regarded by his peers, in 1990, British Sunday newspaper the *Observer* conducted a 'Guitarists' Guitarist' poll with assorted top guitarists, and Beck won. Long gaps in his recording career are filled with Beck's other passion, restoring hot-rod cars. He was more active towards the end of the 1990s, releasing *Who Else!* (1999) and *You Had It Coming* (2001). He plays a Fender Stratocaster and has a signature Strat built according to his specifications with a particularly thick neck. He uses minimal effects and plucks the strings with his fingers. Beck was one of the first guitarists to explore the full sonic potential of the tremolo arm to add astonishing depth, colour and range of sound to his electric, bombastic style.

➤— *Eric Clapton, Fender Stratocaster, Finger-Style, Rock*

BENSON, GEORGE

American, born 1943. Electric jazz guitarist and rhythm & blues vocalist. Benson recorded his first tracks as a singer aged 11, and became a professional musician at 15, singing and playing rhythm & blues. He joined the Jack McDuff Quartet in 1963, gaining a solid foundation in swing, blues and jazz before embarking on a solo career in the mid-1960s. Early solo albums *It's Uptown* (1965) and *Benson Burner* (1966) demonstrate Benson's bluesy bebop style, influenced by Kenny Burrell and Wes Montgomery, with *Beyond The Blue Horizon* (1971) seeing Benson stretching out as an accomplished and exciting soloist. After signing with Warner Brothers, *Breezin'* (1976) broke into the mainstream with a smoother, more laid-back sound concentrating on his soulful vocals rather than on his guitar playing. His stature as a pop artist was consolidated with *In Flight* (1977). Since then, Benson has concentrated on his singing and mainstream career, although he still occasionally cuts loose with his distinctive jazz sound. *Absolute Benson* (2000)

sees a balance in favour of his jazz side, which involves scat-singing along to his own guitar lines. He plays Gibson Johnny Smith and Ibanez semi-acoustics – Ibanez make a George Benson signature model.

➤ *Blues, Gibson, Jazz, Rhythm & Blues*

BERRY, CHUCK

American, born 1926.

Rock 'n' roll guitarist, singer and songwriter. Influenced by Carl Hogan, the guitarist in Louis Jordan's jump-jive Tympany Five, blues guitarists T-Bone Walker and Elmore James, and saxophonist Illinois Jaquet, Berry combined these influences with country and western to form his unique brand of rock 'n' roll. A gifted lyricist who wrote lyrics teenagers could relate to, Berry was one of the first pop performers to write his own material. Several of Berry's songs, such as 'Johnny B Goode', 'Roll Over Beethoven' and 'Carol' start with variations on Berry's trademark lick – a three-note pickup into repeated double stops (i.e. licks involving playing two notes at once) on the top two strings. *The Great Twenty Eight* (1984) and *The Collection* (1988) include Berry's greatest hits; *The Chess Box* (1989) looks in depth at his early career on the Chess label. *Chuck Berry: The Autobiography* (1987) offers many revealing insights into his musical career, personal life and dealings in the music business. His influence extends beyond rock 'n' roll – Berry was an effect on the music of many rock and pop guitarists, including the Rolling Stones' Keith Richards and the Beatles' George Harrison. He plays Gibson ES-350T and 355 semi-acoustics.

➤ *Gibson, Rock 'n' Roll*

BELOW: Chuck Berry, one of the most influential songwriters and guitarists of all time, was renowned for his fast-moving, double-stopped licks.
FAR LEFT: George Benson cuts loose.

BREAM, JULIAN

British, born 1933. Classical guitarist and lutenist. At the age of 13 he received lessons from Segovia and later won a full scholarship to the Royal College of Music where he also studied piano, cello, harmony and composition. He recorded for RCA, winning many awards, including two Grammys and an Edison award. He has played and recorded guitar music in almost every style: Renaissance, Baroque, Classical, Romantic and Modern. He has persuaded many contemporary composers to write for the guitar, thus enriching the repertoire; works instigated by Bream include Sir Michael Tippett's *The Blue Guitar* and Sir William Walton's *Bagatelles*. He recorded the duet albums *Together* (1971) and *Together Again* (1974) with John Williams, uniting arguably the two foremost classical guitarists in the post-Segovia generation. *Guitarra: The Guitar In Spain* (1985), which accompanied a BBC TV series about the history of the guitar, includes Bream playing music on the appropriate period instruments, including the Renaissance guitar, *vihuela* and the Baroque guitar. Known as a very expressive player, Bream varies the position of the picking hand to take full advantage of the classical guitar's different tones and is not afraid to take risks in the pursuit of musical expression. He has recorded using Hauser and Romanillos classical guitars.

➤ *Classical, Lute, John Williams*

CARTHY, MARTIN

British, born 1940. Folk singer-songwriter. After leaving school, he worked as an assistant stage manager for a number of theatrical companies. He joined a skiffle band, the Thameside Four, in 1959 and played the London folk-club scene as a solo artist during the early 1960s. His first album, *Martin Carthy* (1965), featured adaptations of traditional songs 'Scarborough Fair' and 'Lord Franklin', which were later taken up by

Paul Simon and Bob Dylan respectively. He was also a music scholar who frequently studied the notes of well-known folk collectors such as Percy Grainger, and had an interest in Indian classical music. Carthy's formidable guitar and mandolin playing can be heard on his many recordings, which include *Byker Hill* (1967), *But Two Came By* (1968), *Prince Heathen* (1969), *Shearwater* (1972), *Crown Of The Horn* (1971), *Landfall* (1977), *Because It's There* (1979), *Right Of Passage* (1988), *Life & Limb – Live* (1991), *Skin & Bone* (1992), *Signs Of Life* (1999) and *Both Ears & The Tail* (2001). He is also considered to be the father of the English folk revival that spawned the likes of Steeleye Span, Brass Monkey, the Albion Band, Swarbrick and Fairport Convention.

➤— ***Bob Dylan, Folk, Mandolin, Paul Simon***

CHRISTIAN, CHARLIE

American, 1916–42. Pioneering jazz guitarist. The son of a trumpeter, Christian gained a wide musical education courtesy of his school music director, a Mrs Zelia Braux, and played double bass, piano and acoustic guitar. Influenced by saxophonist Lester Young, he got his break when joining the Benny Goodman Sextet. He started as a swing player, but developed a more sophisticated style that laid the foundations for bebop, hence the naming of the track 'Swing To Bop'. Harmonically, his style included the use of diminished and augmented chords; melodically, his solos included long, swinging phrases of unusual lengths. One of the first electric guitarists, he demonstrated that freed from the volume limitations of the acoustic guitar, the electric guitar could play a prominent part in any band's line-up. Recordings include *Solo Flight* (1941), *Live At Minton's Playhouse* (1941) including 'Swing To Bop', and *Live 1939–41* (1941) with Benny Goodman. He influenced Django Reinhardt – who in turn influenced Christian – and the whole generation of post-swing players including Wes Montgomery, Barney Kessell and Jim Hall. He played a semi-acoustic Gibson ES150, Gibson's first electric guitar. Christian died prematurely from pneumonia in 1942.

➤— ***Gibson, Jazz***

FAR LEFT: Julian Bream, classical guitarist and lutenist.
BELOW LEFT: Martin Carthy, a leader of the 1960s London folk scene.
BELOW: Eric Clapton, one of England's finest players.

CLAPTON, ERIC

British, born 1945. Rock and blues guitarist. Clapton started his career with the Yardbirds, left them to join John Mayall's Bluesbreakers and then recorded the highly influential *Blues Breakers* (1965). On this album he redefined electric blues in his use of an overdriven amp to achieve sustain and in his fiery playing, inspiring 'Clapton is God' graffiti in London.

He left to form Cream, who legitimized lengthy on-stage jamming for rock musicians, recording *Fresh Cream* (1966) *Disraeli Gears* (1967), *Wheels Of Fire* (1968) and *Goodbye* (1969). He formed Derek And The Dominoes, with whom he recorded *Layla And Assorted Love Songs* (1970), which includes the rock classic 'Layla'. He battled heroin and

alcohol addiction. Since 1970, Clapton has pursued a solo career, generally with a more mainstream sound than his earlier work, with highlights including the acoustic *Unplugged* (1992), a return to the blues on *From The Cradle* (1994) and a collaboration with blues guitarist and singer BB King on *Riding With The King* (2000). He was influenced by Robert Johnson, BB King, Freddie King and Albert King, and in turn has been an influence on many blues and rock guitarists, including Free's Paul Kossoff, Queen's Brian May and Edward Van Halen. With the Bluesbreakers he played a Gibson Les Paul through a Marshall 60-watt combo; after Cream, he changed to a Fender Stratocaster and has a signature-model Strat.

➤— ***Blues, Fender Stratocaster, Gibson Les Paul***

CLARKE, STANLEY

 American, born 1951. Fusion bassist. Clarke started playing the violin aged 12, and later switched to double bass, cello and bass guitar. Influenced by JS Bach, Jimi Hendrix, James Brown and the Beatles, he studied double bass at the Philadelphia Musical Academy. In 1970 he worked with jazz musicians Joe Henderson and Stan Getz, joining Chick Corea's fusion outfit Return To Forever in 1972 with whom he recorded *Where Have I Known You Before?* (1974) and *Romantic Warrior* (1976). He also recorded solo albums *Stanley Clarke* (1974), *Journey To Love* (1975), which features Jeff Beck and *Schooldays* (1976), on which he demonstrates his mastery of double stops (two-note chords). Musically, Clarke seamlessly mixes rock and jazz, gaining a new audience for both. Technically, Clarke is a highly accomplished player in funk slap and popping, chords and fast, single-note work, produced with a distinctive and individual tone from his Alembic bass. Influenced by Larry Graham and Scott LaFaro, Clarke was himself a major influence on Level 42's Mark King, Marcus Miller, Stu Hamm and others. Such is his stature that Alembic have a Stanley Clarke signature model. Clarke has continued to release solo albums including *Rocks, Pebbles and Sand* (1980), *Find Out* (1985) and *East River Drive* (1993) as well as recording with various musicians including Al Di Meola, Paul McCartney and John McLaughlin.

➤ *Bass, Jazz, John McLaughlin, Al Di Meola, Rock*

DE LUCÍA, PACO

 Spanish, born 1947. Flamenco guitarist. De Lucía's father is the flamenco guitarist Antonio Sanchez Pecino. According to de Lucía's biographer DE Pohren, Sanchez Pecino had a 'master plan' to mould de Lucía into the greatest flamenco guitarist. He began playing the guitar aged five and practised up to 12 hours a day. He accompanied the Jose Greco ballet in America when he was 12, and further built his reputation by accompanying Spain's greatest dancers and singers until he was 18. *Los chiquitos de Algeciras* (1961) with brother Pepe de Lucía drew attention to this new talent; with his other brother, Ramon de Algeciras, he collaborated on *Musica clasica transcrita para guitarras* (1966) and *Dos guitarras flamencas en America Latina* (1967). Early albums *El duende flamenco de Paco de Lucía* (1972), *Fuente y caudal* (1975) and *En vivo desde el teatro real* (1975) were based on traditional flamenco, although 'Entre dos aguas' from *Fuente y caudal* topped the Spanish pop charts in 1975. In New York, de Lucía met flamenco guitarist Sabicas who told him guitarists have to play their own music; he started to compose. De Lucía's music pushed back the boundaries of flamenco with new techniques and harmonies, and was criticized in his early years by flamenco traditionalists, despite de Lucía's efforts not to stray from the basic flamenco

rhythms. *Almoraima* (1976) saw a break from tradition with jazz-influenced chord progressions.

In 1981, he recorded the million-selling *Friday Night In San Francisco* with fusion guitarist Al Di Meola and jazz guitarist John McLaughlin, further pushing back the boundaries of flamenco guitar and reaching new audiences. The trio followed this up with *Passion, Grace and Fire* (1983).

He successfully ventured into the classical guitar repertoire with a recording of Rodrigo's *Concierto de Aranjuez* (1991); composer Rodrigo described de Lucia's live performance of the slow movement as the best he had heard. He is fiercely committed to improvization in music, to the extent of not practising between tours and albums to avoid developing mechanical habits and to force him to come up with something new. He also plays with non-flamenco musicians.

He has written and performed film soundtracks for *La Sabina*, *The Hit* and *Carmen*, and played on pop artist Bryan Adams' UK number one single 'Have You Ever Really Loved A Woman?' (1995) from the film *Don Juan de Marcos*. He reunited with Di Meola and McLaughlin for *The Guitar Trio* (1996). *De Lucia's Luzia* (1999) mixes old and new flamenco. His main performing guitar is a Hermanos Conde that he has owned for over 25 years.

➤— *Classical, Al Di Meola, Flamenco, Finger-Style, John McLaughlin*

DI MEOLA, AL

American, born 1954. Fusion guitarist. Di Meola started learning the guitar when he was nine; his early influences included Tal Farlow, Kenny Burrell and George Benson. He studied at Boston's Berklee College of Music and joined Return To Forever when he was 19, playing on *Where Have I Known You Before?* (1974), *No Mystery* (1975) and *Romantic Warrior* (1976). He left to pursue a solo career, recording *Land Of The Midnight Sun* (1976), *Elegant Gypsy* (1977), *Casino* (1978) and *Splendido Hotel* (1980), his main instrument being a Gibson Les Paul. His formidable picking technique is explained in his tuition book *Al Di Meola's Picking Technique* (1983) – he often plays lightning-fast passages whilst damping the strings with the palm of the picking hand to help the notes 'pop' out (the 'mutola' effect).

On acoustic guitar he recorded *Friday Night In San Francisco* (1981) with jazz guitarist John McLaughlin and flamenco guitarist Paco de Lucía, followed up by *Passion, Grace and Fire* (1983). Acoustic-based solo album *Cielo e Terra* (1985) marked a change from previous solo albums as did *Soaring Through a Dream* (1985), *Tirami Su* (1987) and *Kiss My Axe* (1991), which feature guitar, synthesizer and vocals. With the acoustic World Sinfonia he recorded *World Sinfonia* (1990) and *Heart Of The Immigrants* (1993).

➤— *Paco de Lucía, John McLaughlin, Picking*

ABOVE: *Al Di Meola, a respected fusion guitarist.*
ABOVE LEFT: *Stanley Clarke, still one of the world's premier bassists.*
LEFT: *Paco de Lucía, who began playing the guitar at the age of five.*

DYLAN, BOB

American, born 1941. Folk-rock singer-songwriter. Born Robert Allen Zimmerman on 24 May 1941, Dylan started playing the guitar at the age of 12 and, as a teenager, became influenced by the legendary folk singer Woody Guthrie. Determined to become a famous folk singer himself, he dropped out of the University of Minnesota in 1960, adopted the name Bob Dylan and travelled to New York to perform in Greenwich Village. His earthy acoustic renditions of traditional songs and idiosyncratic harmonica playing caused a stir, and CBS signed him up in 1962. His debut album, *Bob Dylan* (1962), was well received, but the following two albums, *The Freewheelin' Bob Dylan* (1963) and *The Times They Are A-Changin'* (1964), made him famous. Featuring protest songs such as 'Blowin' in the Wind' and 'The Times They Are A-Changin", they established him as a

talented and original singer-songwriter. Critical opinion on many of Dylan's later albums has often been divided, but without doubt he has been one of the most influential figures in the development of folk and rock music. His songs have been covered by countless other artists and his lyrics have inspired generations of aspiring singer-songwriters.

➤━ *Folk*

FRIPP, ROBERT

British, born 1946. Progressive rock guitarist. Fripp is a founder member of King Crimson. The band started as grandiose progressive rockers with *In The Court Of The Crimson King* (1969) and *Lark's Tongue In Aspic* (1973); *Discipline* (1981) and *Three Of A Perfect Pair* (1983) reveal a more streamlined approach but are no less intense. After a lay-off Fripp reconvened the band for *Thrak* (1994) and *The ConstruKction Of Light* (2000), the new six-piece line-up being capable of dense textures. He also formed a three-piece off-shoot of King Crimson called ProjeKct II, based on free-form improvizations, which released *Space Groove* (1998).

LEFT AND ABOVE: Bob Dylan started as a folk singer but went on to conquer the rock world with albums such as 1965's Highway 61 Revisited.
FAR RIGHT: Robert Fripp's playing is highly technical, yet quite aggressive.

Despite his highly technical and cerebral approach to playing, Fripp can be an extremely aggressive player. He developed a solo style of playing christened 'Frippertonics', involving recording himself with two reel-to-reel tape recorders then playing over what he has recorded, with which he creates elaborate sound textures. He is a respected teacher and gives 'Guitar Craft' seminars. He has worked with many other musicians including Brian Eno, David Bowie, Andy Summers, Peter Gabriel and David Sylvian.

In early days of King Crimson he played a Les Paul; with ProjeKct II he plays a Custom Fernandes with Les Paul-style body in his custom tuning of C G D A E D from bottom string to top.

➤ *Gibson Les Paul, Rock, Tuning*

GUITAR TECHNICIAN

Most top players employ a guitar technician to make sure that their guitars and amps are well looked after. Guitar technicians are highly skilled individuals who can fix guitars and amps when they are broken, restring and adjust the intonation of instruments for live performances and studio work, and carry out general maintenance on the guitars and equipment.

➤ *Luthier*

HARPER, NICK

British, born 1965. Acoustic guitarist and singer-songwriter. His recording debut came on his father Roy's album, *Whatever Happened To Jugula* (1983), a duo collaboration with Led Zeppelin guitarist Jimmy Page. Harper's first solo release was an EP entitled *Light At The End Of The Kennel* (1994), which was followed up by an album, *Seed* (1995), a year later. He was heard by former Squeeze frontman Glenn Tilbrook, who promptly signed him to his Quixotic label. Tilbrook produced Harper's second album, *Smithereens* (1998), which confirmed the guitarist's position as an inspired artist at the forefront of the current generation of acoustic performers. An original virtuoso, a soulful singer and an accomplished performer who has a warm rapport with audiences from New York to Glastonbury, he has also written lyrics and melodies of great beauty and depth. His third album, *Harperspace* (2000), established his reputation as a folk hero and his releases since – including the live album *Double Life* (2002) and *Blood Songs* (2003) – continue to suggest that his best work is probably still in the future. 'As long as the songs keep coming and I do not get arthritis,' he says, 'I'll be around for a while yet.'

➤ *Roy Harper*

HARPER, ROY

British, born 1941. Folk-rock guitarist and singer-songwriter. Roy Harper was introduced to music by his older brother. After a spell in the Royal Air Force, Harper spent the mid 1960s busking around Europe. He eventually settled in London and recorded *The Sophisticated Beggar* (1966) and *Come Out Fighting, Ghengis Smith* (1968), two quirky chronicles of his life in London at the time. By 1968 he was a cult figure with London's rapidly growing underground audience. He signed to the Harvest label in 1970 and recorded *Flat Baroque & Berserk* (1970), an uncompromising album covering a wide range of subjects and musical styles, and *Stormcock* (1971), a critically acclaimed album of extended songs with arranger David Bedford and Led Zeppelin guitarist Jimmy Page ('Hats Off To Harper' from *Led Zeppelin III* (1970) was a homage to Harper). Other significant albums include *Bullinamingvase* (1977), featuring 'One Of Those Days In England', with Paul and Linda McCartney on backing vocals, *Born In Captivity* (1984), *Once* (1990) and *Death Or Glory?* (1992). He also made a guest appearance on Pink Floyd's *Wish You Were Here* (1975). Harper's poetic lyrics and original guitar playing have inspired many folk and rock musicians since the 1960s.

➤— *Folk, Nick Harper*

HENDRIX, JIMI

American, 1942–70. Rock guitarist and electric guitar pioneer. Hendrix was influenced initially by Muddy Waters, BB King, Jimmy Reed, Elmore James and John Lee Hooker, then by Curtis Mayfield. He backed Lonnie Youngblood, the Isley Brothers, Little Richard and others, before being spotted by ex-Animals bass player Chas Chandler who brought him to London, where Hendrix formed the Jimi Hendrix Experience.

He released only five albums during his lifetime: *Are You Experienced?* (1967), *Axis: Bold As Love* (1967), *Electric Ladyland* (1968), *Smash Hits* (1969) and *Band Of Gypsies* (1970). His innovations included the harnessing of feedback, as heard at the beginning of 'Foxy Lady' from *Are You Experienced?*, the chord/melody style of playing with the so-called 'out-of-phase' pickup position for 'Little Wing' from *Axis: Bold As Love*, and the expressive qualities of the wah-wah pedal in 'Still Raining, Still Dreaming' from *Electric Ladyland*. Hendrix showed how the harmonic palette of rock could be expanded with the ear-catching diminished fifths between bass and guitar at the beginning of 'Purple Haze' from *Smash Hits*, and enriched the chord repertoire of the rock guitarist with the so-called 'Hendrix chord' of 'E7♯9', also used in 'Purple Haze'.

In 'The Star Spangled Banner' from *Woodstock* (1994) and 'Machine Gun' from *Band Of Gypsies* (1970) he incorporated the sound of warfare into the music, painting sound pictures with an unsurpassed control of the guitar and minimal effects. A left-hander, Hendrix played a right-handed Fender Stratocaster restrung for a left-hander, through a Marshall stack, generally set with

everything on the 'Hendrix setting' of '10'. He died aged 27 from suffocating after vomiting in his sleep. Most of the posthumous releases serve his legacy badly, notable exceptions being *Radio One* (1988), *Jimi Hendrix Concerts* (1989), *Woodstock* (1994) and *Blues* (1994); the Hendrix family did not regain control of the music until 1977. Hendrix influenced many electric guitarists, including Joe Satriani, Steve Vai, and Stevie Ray Vaughan. The tribute album *Stone Free* (1993) contained Hendrix songs covered by a huge range of artists affected in one way or another by Hendrix, including Eric Clapton, Jeff Beck, the Pretenders, the Cure, Pat Metheny and Nigel Kennedy, a testament to his huge influence. Fender has two signature Hendrix guitars, one which is a 'left-handed guitar strung right-handed'.

➤ *Fender, Rock, Wah-Wah*

HOOKER, JOHN LEE

American, 1917–2001. Blues guitarist and singer. Hooker learned blues licks and tunings on acoustic guitar from his stepfather William Moore. Also influenced by James Smith and Coot Harris, he was inspired by T-Bone Walker to play electric guitar. He settled in Detroit in 1943 and released his first single 'Boogie Chillen' in 1949. Like many of his early recordings, this sees Hooker accompanying his own singing with electric guitar and his tapping foot. It is thought to have sold over a million copies. In the 1960s he was championed by British bands such as the Rolling Stones and Cream; the Animals had a hit with Hooker's 'Boom Boom'. Despite blues falling out of favour in the 1970s and early 1980s, Hooker

continued to tour and record companies repackaged his early work. The blues resurgence in the late 1980s saw Hooker united with many younger musicians whom he had influenced, including Carlos Santana, Bonnie Raitt, Los Lobos and Robert Cray for *The Healer* (1989), resulting in one of the best-selling blues albums. The follow-up, *Mr Lucky* (1991), saw Hooker working with Ry Cooder, Van Morrison and Albert Collins. He played many instruments throughout his career, latterly a Gibson ES-335 and an Epiphone Sheraton.

> *Blues, Epiphone, Gibson 335*

HOWE, STEVE

British, born 1947. Progressive rock guitarist. Howe played in Tomorrow, then joined Yes in 1971, becoming one of the band's major songwriters. One of the few rock guitarists not to be significantly influenced by blues players, he instead was influenced by Merle Travis, Chet Atkins, Julian Bream, Carlos Montoya and Wes Montgomery. A proficient electric and acoustic player,

Howe has an extensive guitar collection. Howe's first release with Yes, *The Yes Album* (1971), includes his signature acoustic guitar instrumental 'Clap' (mistakenly known as 'The Clap', to Howe's disgust), influenced by Chet Atkins, and was followed by *Fragile* (1971), which includes the Montoya-influenced 'Mood For A Day', *Close To The Edge* (1972), the live *Yessongs* (1973), the triple-LP concept album *Tales From Topographic Oceans* (1973) and *Relayer* (1974). The band split up, then reformed with *Going For The One* (1977), *Tormato* (1978) and *Drama* (1980). Howe then joined 'adult-oriented-rock' (AOR) supergroup Asia, releasing *Asia* (1982) and *Alpha* (1983) before rejoining a version of Yes called Anderson Bruford Wakeman Howe, which released *Anderson Bruford Wakeman Howe* (1989). After renaming themselves Yes once again, the band released *Union* (1991), *Keys To Ascension* (1996), *Open Your Eyes* (1997) and *The Ladder* (1999). Howe has also released solo albums including *Beginnings* (1975), *The Steve Howe Album* (1979), *Turbulence* (1992), *The Grand Scheme Of Things* (1993), *Quantum Guitars* (1999) and *Portraits Of Bob Dylan* (1999). His main instrument is a semi-acoustic Gibson ES-175.

➤— *Gibson, Rock*

BELOW: Heavy rocker Tony Iommi cuts loose.
CENTRE: Prog rock wizard Steve Howe.
FAR LEFT: The late, great John Lee Hooker.

IOMMI, TONY

British, born 1948. Heavy-rock guitarist. A left-handed guitarist, Iommi lost the tips of two fretting-hand fingers in a factory accident early in his career; the tips of his fingers were replaced with plastic covers and he uses very light strings. He was a founder member of heavy-rock band Black Sabbath. The band's debut album *Black Sabbath* (1970) included the Sabbath anthems 'Black Sabbath' and 'NIB', both based on gloomy, doom-laden riffs, an Iommi and Sabbath trademark. The follow-up, *Paranoid* (1970), spawned the top-five single 'Paranoid' based on one of Iommi's best riffs. The band consolidated their success and style with *Master Of Reality* (1971), *Vol 4* (1972), *Sabbath Bloody Sabbath* (1973), *Sabotage* (1975), *Technical Ecstasy* (1976) and *Never Say Die* (1978). Original singer Ozzy Osbourne left to be replaced, with mixed success, by various singers for *Heaven & Hell* (1980), *Mob Rules* (1981) and *Live Evil* (1983), *Born Again* (1983), *Seventh Star* (1986), *The Eternal Idol* (1987), *Headless Cross*, *Tyr* (1990), *Dehumanizer* (1992), *Cross Purposes* (1994) and *Forbidden* (1995). The original line-up reconvened for the live *Reunion* (1998). Iommi's solo album *Iommi* (2000) features collaborations with various musicians influenced by Iommi and Sabbath, including Henry Rollins, Foo Fighters' Dave Grohl, Pantera's Phil Anselmo and Queen's Brian May. Iommi plays a custom John Diggins-style SG and various Gibson Custom Shop SGs.

➤— *Gibson, Rock*

JOHNSON, ROBERT

American, 1911–38. Acoustic blues singer-songwriter. According to blues legend, Johnson was initially taunted for his novice guitar playing, 'disappeared' for around a year and returned a proficient player having sold his soul to the devil at a Mississippi Delta crossroads at midnight, in return for his guitar-playing skills. Influenced by Charley Patton, Willie Brown and Son House, Johnson himself influenced generations of blues players and other musicians, including Muddy Waters, Elmore James, Taj Mahal, John Hammond, Johnny Winter, Rory Block, Ry Cooder, Keith Richards, Jimmy Page, Robert Plant and Eric Clapton. Clapton reworked Johnson's 'Cross Road Blues' as 'Crossroads' on Cream's *Wheels Of Fire* (1968). Johnson recorded only 29 songs, all credited as originals but based on reinterpretations of blues forms. *The Complete Recordings* (1996) includes the original 29, plus alternate versions. All songs feature Johnson playing solo. Johnson often played with a slide, always in either open A (E A E A C♯ E from bottom string to top) or open E (E B E G♯ B E). His non-slide playing was in standard tuning. He often used a capo. Johnson's death is shrouded in mystery

– he may have died after being poisoned by a jealous husband or from congenital syphilis; even the location of his body is unsure – he has three grave markers. Only three known photographs of him survive. He played a wooden-body Stella with a metal resonator, a Kalamazoo archtop and a Gibson L-0.

➤ *Blues, Gibson, Slide, Tuning*

KING, ALBERT

American, 1923–92. Electric blues guitarist and singer. King played left-handed on a guitar strung for a right-handed player, so his top string was closest to his head; he plucked the strings with his thumb. This set-up helped him to forge his distinctive lead style based on biting tone and wide bends – instead of bending upwards, he bent strings by pulling them downwards. Influenced by Blind Lemon Jefferson, Lightnin' Hopkins, Elmore James and T-Bone Walker, he was an influence on Otis Rush, Albert Collins, Jimi Hendrix, Stevie Ray Vaughan, Eric Clapton and Robert Cray. Signed to the Stax label in 1966, King established his style on *Born Under A Bad Sign* (1967) with the title track, later covered by Cream on *Wheels Of Fire* (1968), with 'Oh Pretty Woman', 'Crosscut Saw' and 'As The Years Go Passing By', accompanied by Booker T & the MGs. This was followed up by two acclaimed live albums, *Wednesday Night In San Fransisco* (1968), *Thursday Night In San Fransisco* (1968), and *King Of The Blues Guitar* (1969). He guested on Gary Moore's *Still Got The Blues* (1990) on Moore's version of King's 'Oh Pretty Woman'. King played Gibson Flying Vs he christened 'Lucille' and his favourite guitar was a Flying V built by Dan Erlewine.

➤ *Bend, Blues, Gibson*

KING, BB

American, born 1925. Electric blues guitarist and singer-songwriter. King's real name is Riley B (the 'B' is an initial only), the 'BB' standing for 'Blues Boy'. He has done much to bring blues to a mainstream audience with his exciting live performances and audience-friendly rapport, as can be heard on *Live At The Regal* (1964), and his omission of risqué lyrics. Influenced by his cousin Bukka White, Django Reinhardt, T-Bone Walker and Louis Jordan, he was an influence on Jimi Hendrix,

Eric Clapton, Peter Green and Stevie Ray Vaughan. King claims to be unable to play guitar and sing at the same time. He rarely plays chords, preferring to concentrate on his singing, guitar fills and solos; his trademark sound is his 'hummingbird' vibrato. He had hits in the 1950s with 'Three O'Clock Blues', 'Rock Me Baby' and 'Please Love Me' and his 1970 cover of Roy Hawkins 'The Thrill Is Gone', with strings accompaniment, helped him cross over into the mainstream. In his seventies he cut down from 300 gigs a year to around 200! His *Definitive Greatest Hits* (1999) compiles the high

FAR LEFT: BB King with his beloved 'Lucille'.
BELOW: Albert King popularized the 'biting' blues tone.

points from his long career, *Let The Good Times Roll* (1999) sees King paying tribute to Louis Jordan, and King guests on Eric Clapton's *Riding With The King* (2000). He plays Gibson semi-acoustic 335s and 355s and a Gibson ES signature model called 'Lucille', King's pet name for his guitars.

➤ *Blues, Gibson 335*

KNOPFLER, MARK

British, born 1949. Rock guitarist and singer-songwriter. He was a founder member of Dire Straits, whose success was based around Knopfler's songwriting, his distinctive Bob Dylan-esque voice and his tasteful guitar playing on a clean-toned Stratocaster. His songwriting is influenced by Dylan and JJ Cale. The debut album *Dire Straits* (1978) included their signature song 'Sultans Of Swing', followed up by *Communique* (1979), *Making Movies* (1980) with hits 'Romeo and Juliet' and 'Tunnel Of Love', *Love Over Gold* (1982) and the live *Alchemy* (1984). Already a highly successful touring and recording act, *Brothers In Arms* (1985) took their popularity to a new level – it's one of the best-ever selling albums – and spawned the hit single 'Money For Nothing'. The compilation album *Money For Nothing* (1988) draws their hits together, and *On Every Street* (1991) marked the last Dire Straits studio album followed by the live *On The Night* (1993). Knopfler gets his individual tone by plucking the strings with his fingers instead of a plectrum. A prolific writer, Knopfler has written soundtracks including *Local Hero* (1983) and *Cal* (1984), written songs for other artists, including 'Private Dancer' for Tina Turner, and recorded and toured with the Notting Hillbillies. Knopfler has also pursued a solo career with *Golden Heart* (1996) and *Sailing To Philadelphia* (2000). He originally played a Fender Stratocaster with Dire Straits, then a Pensa-Suhr Strat-type guitar.

➤— *Finger-Style, Fender Stratocaster, Rock*

MALMSTEEN, YNGWIE

Swedish, born 1963. Heavy-metal guitarist. Influenced by Deep Purple's Ritchie Blackmore, Jimi Hendrix, JS Bach and violinist Paganini, Malmsteen largely invented the 'neo-classical' genre – a virtuosic mixture of heavy rock and classical-style chord progressions with fast scalar runs, pivoting phrases and dramatic arpeggio sweeps. He is an influence on Vinnie Moore and Tony Macalpine. He played on Alcatrazz's *No Parole From Rock 'n' Roll* (1984) and *Live Sentence* (1984) before embarking on a solo career. His debut solo release *Rising Force* (1984) contains the signature instrumental 'Black Star'; it was followed by *Marching Out* (1985), *Trilogy* (1986), *Odyssey* (1988), *Eclipse* (1990), *Fire And Ice* (1992), *The Seventh Sign* (1994), *Magnum Opus* (1995), *Inspiration* (1996), an album of cover versions, *Facing The Animal* (1998) and *Double Live* (1998). *Concerto Suite For Electric Guitar And Orchestra In E Flat Minor* (1998) sees Malmsteen paired with the Czech Philharmonic Orchestra, followed by *Alchemy* (1999) and *War To End All Wars* (2000). Malmsteen is the most proficient and prominent player in the neo-classical genre. He plays Fender Stratocasters with scalloped fretboards and Malmsteen signature Strats through Marshall amps.

➤— *Fender Stratocaster, Improvizing, Metal, Rock*

MARLEY, BOB

Jamaican, 1945–81. The son of an English serviceman and a local woman, Bob Marley was born in St. Anne's, Jamaica. He grew up in Trench Town, a tough Kingston slum, and began playing music as a teenager on home-made instruments. Early influences included local blue-beat and ska musicians, as well as Fats Domino, Elvis Presley and the Drifters. He cut his first single, 'One More Cup Of Coffee', in 1961 with Leslie Kong, and later teamed up with fellow singers Bunny Livingston and Peter Tosh to form the Teenagers (later the Wailers). They began devoting themselves to the teachings of the Rastafari faith, which played an important role in Marley's subsequent life and music. Their album *Burnin'* (1973) featured the memorable 'I Shot The Sheriff', which was covered by Eric Clapton in 1974. Clapton's success with the song helped popularize reggae music in Britain and the US and the Wailers' groundbreaking album *Natty Dread* (1975), featuring the legendary 'No Woman No Cry', was received warmly on both sides of the Atlantic. By then, the Wailers' unique reggae sound had carved its own niche in mainstream music. Their success was cut short when, tragically, Marley died of cancer in 1981. Throughout his playing career, Marley was most closely associated with a Gibson Les Paul electric guitar.

➤— *Eric Clapton, Gibson Les Paul, Reggae*

ABOVE: *Bob Marley, reggae superstar, and his 1975* Live! *album.*
CENTRE: *Yngwie Malmsteen, who incorporates both classical and rock styles in his playing.*
FAR LEFT: *Mark Knopfler is famous for his distinctive finger-style playing.*

MARVIN, HANK

British, born 1941. Pop guitarist. Marvin started his musical career in the Five Chesternuts, releasing one single, and then joined the Drifters, Cliff Richard's backing band, who then renamed themselves the Shadows. As Cliff and the Shadows Marvin recorded and performed with Richard; as the Shadows the band played instrumentals featuring Marvin on lead guitar. The prominence of Marvin's guitar playing inspired a whole generation of guitarists including Brian May and Mark Knopfler. He enjoyed a string of instrumental hits

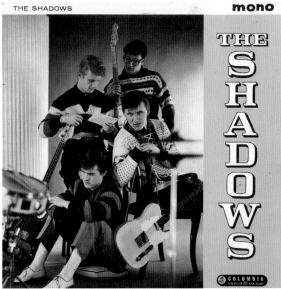

starting with 'Apache' and followed by 'F.B.I.', 'Kon Tiki', 'Wonderful Land', 'Foot Tapper' and many others. Albums included *The Shadows* (1961), *Out Of The Shadows* (1962), *Greatest Hits* (1963) and *Dance With The Shadows* (1964). Marvin's style involved catchy, straight-forward melodies played with a clean tone and frequently embellished with his use of the vibrato arm; visual trademarks were his red Fender Stratocaster and Buddy Holly-style glasses. Marvin wrote some of the material, but the Shadows relied mainly on external writers. The Shadows split up in 1968 and Marvin released a solo album, *Hank Marvin* (1969). The band reformed for *Shades Of Rock* (1970) then split, reforming again for *Rockin' With Curly Leads* (1973), and continued recording and performing until 1990, since when Marvin has toured under his own name.

➤— *Fender Stratocaster*

MAY, BRIAN

British, born 1947. Rock guitarist. May was one of four songwriters in Queen; his distinctive sweet, warm tone comes from a homemade guitar including parts from a fireplace and a knitting needle for a vibrato arm! He plucks the guitar with an old sixpence. He is influenced by Lonnie Donegan, Hank Marvin, Jimi Hendrix and Eric Clapton. Early releases *Queen* (1973),

Queen II (1974) and *Sheer Heart Attack* (1974) showed glam-rock and heavy rock influences. May's style involves harmony guitar parts as heard on 'Killer Queen' and the use of delay as heard on 'Brighton Rock', both from *Sheer Heart Attack*. The epic and operatic 'Bohemian Rhapsody' from *A Night At The Opera* (1975) took the band to a new level, musically and career-wise. They consolidated their success with *A Day At The Races* (1977), *Jazz* (1978), *The Game* (1980), *The Works* (1984), *A Kind Of Magic* (1986), *The Miracle* (1989) and *Innuendo* (1991). Queen effectively ended with the death of singer Freddie Mercury in 1991, although material Mercury was working on at the time of his death was moulded by the remaining members into *Made In Heaven* (1995). A highly successful recording and live act, Queen have released three greatest hits compilations: *Greatest Hits* (1981); *Greatest Hits II* (1991) and *Greatest Hits III* (1999). May has also released the solo albums *Back To The Light* (1992) and *Live At The Brixton Academy* (1994).

➤— *Plectra, Rock*

MCLAUGHLIN, JOHN

British, born 1942. Jazz guitarist, fluent on both electric and acoustic guitar. McLaughlin started learning classical piano aged nine. Shortly afterwards, he took up the guitar, inspired by Big Bill Broonzy, Muddy Waters, various flamenco guitarists, Django Reinhardt and Tal Farlow, later by Miles Davis and John Coltrane. He participated in the London blues boom in the early 1960s and played free jazz in the late 1960s. *Extrapolation* (1969) showcased McLaughlin's highly developed technique and a deeply expressive manner. He played on Miles Davis' *In A Silent Way* (1969) and Davis' highly influential jazz

and rock fusion *Bitches Brew* (1970). McLaughlin then formed the fusion outfit Mahavishnu Orchestra, releasing *Inner Mounting Flame* (1972), *Birds Of Fire* (1973) and the live *Between Nothingness And Eternity* (1973); their combination of cool jazz harmonies and the drive and excitement of rock reached new audiences. He collaborated with Carlos Santana on *Love, Devotion, Surrender* (1973), then re-formed Mahavishnu for *Apocalypse* (1974), *Visions Of The Emeralds Beyond* (1975) and *Inner Worlds* (1976). He joined the Indian-influenced and acoustic Shakti, playing on *Shakti With John McLaughlin* (1976) and *Natural Elements* (1977), then recorded the solo album *Electric Guitarist* (1978). He teamed up on acoustic guitar with Al Di Meola and Paco de Lucia for *Friday Night In San Francisco* (1981) and *Passion, Grace and Fire* (1983), and released solo albums *Belo Horizonte* (1981) and *Music Spoken Here* (1982).

McLaughlin again re-formed the Mahavishnu Orchestra for *Mahavishnu* (1985) and *Adventures In Radioland* (1987), which saw him expanding his sonic palette with guitar synthesizers. He returned to an acoustic setting for *Live At The Royal Festival Hall* (1990) and *Que Alegria* (1992). McLaughlin is a well-respected musician – *The Promise* (1995) contains contributions from Jeff Beck, Sting, Al Di Meola, Dennis Chambers, Paco de Lucía and many others. The acoustic *Remember Shakti: The Believer* (2000) and the electric *The Heart Of Things – Live In Paris* (2000) demonstrate McLaughlin's multifaceted musical personality and his love of improvization; both are live albums. A technically accomplished player from years of dedicated practice, McLaughlin has an insatiable desire to keep learning and pushing forward. He has played many different guitars; with Mahavishnu he played a Bogue 6 and a 12-string double-neck electric; for *The Heart Of Things – Live In Paris* he played a Gibson Johnny Smith, and for *Remember Shakti* a Gibson ES-345.

➤— *Gibson, Jazz, Twelve-String Guitar*

TOP: Brian May with his homemade guitar.
ABOVE: John McLaughlin is a diverse and inspirational player.
FAR LEFT AND ABOVE FAR LEFT: Hank Marvin of Cliff Richard's backing band the Shadows, and the band's 1961 debut album.

MITCHELL, JONI

Canadian, born 1943. Guitarist and singer-songwriter. Mitchell (originally Roberta Joan Anderson) studied art at the Alberta College of Art in Calgary, and became interested in folk music, learning how to play the guitar from a Pete Seeger instruction record. She moved to Toronto in 1964 and married another musician, Chuck Mitchell, in 1965. They performed as a duo at various Toronto coffee-houses but divorced a year later. Mitchell started developing a frank lyric style that was soon to gain her considerable critical acclaim. She moved to New York and became popular on the folk-club circuit, earning a reputation as a talented songwriter and engaging performer. Her first album, *Songs To A Seagull* (1968), demonstrated her early folk influences as well as her unique songwriting skills. She continued with *Clouds* (1969), *Ladies Of The Canyon* (1970), *Blue* (1971) and *For The Roses* (1972). During the 1970s, she displayed an increasing interest in jazz and this began to show in her music; *Court And Spark* (1974) was a sophisticated blend of folk, rock and jazz, while *The Hissing Of Summer Lawns* (1975) took these elements and fused them together with world music. *Hejira* (1976), *Don Juan's Reckless Daughter* (1978) and *Mingus* (1979) all

marched further into jazz territory and were criticized by folk and jazz purists. *Shadows And Light* (1980) was a live double album with an impressive line-up of guest musicians, including Pat Metheny and Jaco Pastorius. By then, Mitchell had forged her own unique sound that did not seem to fit into any musical category. In 1981 she was inducted into Canada's Juno Hall Of Fame by Prime Minister Pierre Trudeau. *Wild Things Run Fast* (1982), *Dog Eat Dog* (1985), *Chalk Mark In A Rain Storm* (1988) *Night Ride Home* (1991), *Turbulent Indigo* (1994), *Taming The Tiger* (1998) and *Both Sides Now* (2000) are all branded with her own unique stamp.

Fiercely independent, she has never let herself be pushed around by the forces of commerciality that so many of her contemporaries have succumbed to. No other female singer-songwriter has so bravely explored territory outside the often narrow confines of mainstream popular music. Mitchell's songs paved the way for other performers as diverse as Joan Armatrading, Patti Smith, Madonna, Suzanne Vega and Björk. Her songs have been covered by Judy Collins, Gordon Lightfoot, Fairport Convention, Big Country and many others. She is one of the most original and influential singer-songwriters of the last 30 years.

➤— *Folk, Jazz*

MOORE, GARY

Irish, born 1952. Rock guitarist. Influenced by Jeff Beck, Moore in turn influenced George Lynch and Randy Rhoads. He played in Skid Row and the Gary Moore Band, then, following a brief stint with Thin Lizzy, Moore joined jazz rockers Colloseum II for *Strange New Flesh* (1976), *Electric Savage* (1977) and *Wardance* (1978). He rejoined Thin Lizzy for *Black Rose* (1979), leaving to record a solo album, *Back On The Streets* (1979), which included the hit single 'Parisienne Walkways', a mainstay of Moore's live shows. He formed G-Force who produced one album, *G-Force* (1980), then joined Greg Lake to play on *Greg Lake* (1981). Moore embarked on a solo career playing hard rock, releasing *Corridors Of Power* (1982), *Victims Of The Future* (1984), the live *We Want Moore* (1984), *Run For Cover* (1985), *Wild Frontier* (1987) and *After The War* (1989). Frustrated with the music he was playing, Moore turned

FAR LEFT: Joni Mitchell, guitarist and singer-songwriter.
LEFT: Gary Moore, the Irish rock guitarist.
BELOW: Elvis Presley's early sessions at Sun Records featured the pioneering guitar sound of Scotty Moore, which went on to define the rock 'n' roll sound.

and Phillips invited Moore to play with a new singer called Elvis Presley. Moore subsequently toured and recorded with Presley from 1954 to 1958, as can be heard on Presley's *The Sun Sessions* (1976) and *Elvis 56* (1996), playing on Presley's hits 'Heartbreak Hotel', 'Blue Suede Shoes' and 'Hound Dog'. The band split up when Presley was drafted into the army, and Moore played sessions for Dale Hawkins, then briefly returned to Presley's band before working at Sun as a production manager. He released the solo album *The Guitar That Changed The World* (1964), and relocated to Nashville to run his own studio. He was reunited for the last time with Presley for his 1968 television special. In the 1970s Moore concentrated on production, but was coaxed into recording a solo album *Scotty Moore* (1976). In the 1980s Moore had a successful tape-copying service in Nashville. For the solo album *All The King's Men* (1997) Moore was joined by Keith Richards, members of the Band, Ron Wood and Jeff Beck. On Presley's Sun sessions he played a Gibson ES-295 hollow-body electric.

➤ *Gibson, Rock 'n' Roll*

to the blues for *Still Got The Blues* (1990), *After Hours* (1992), the live *Blues Alive* (1993), *Blues For Green* (1995) and *Back To The Blues* (2001). He tends to play Les Pauls, including Peter Green's 1959 Les Paul as heard on Fleetwood Mac's 'Need Your Love So Bad', and a Gibson signature-model Les Paul; he uses a Gibson ES-355 on *Back To The Blues*.

➤ *Gibson Les Paul, Gibson 335, Rock*

MOORE, SCOTTY

American, born 1931. Rock 'n' roll guitarist. Influenced by Chet Atkins, Merle Travis, Les Paul, Tal Farlow and BB King, Moore influenced Jimmy Page, Jeff Beck, Keith Richards and many others. He played sessions for Sam Phillips' Sun Records in the early 1950s

PAGE, JIMMY

British, born 1944. Rock guitarist. Influenced by Scotty Moore, James Burton, Bert Jansch and BB King. Page started his musical career as a session guitarist, and joined the Yardbirds before forming Led Zeppelin. Generally regarded as heavy rock, Zeppelin's music covers a wide range of styles. *Led Zeppelin I* (1969) shows their blues roots; *Led Zeppelin II* (1969) is regarded as one of the first heavy metal albums, but was followed by the acoustic-based *Led Zeppelin III* (1970). *Led Zeppelin IV* (1971) includes 'Stairway To Heaven', their best-known track, followed by *Houses Of The Holy* (1973), *Physical Graffiti* (1975), *Presence* (1976), the live *The Song Remains The Same* (1976) and *In Through The Out Door* (1979). The death of drummer John Bonham in 1980 effectively marked the end of the band, although Page reunited with Zeppelin singer Robert Plant for *No Quarter – Unledded* (1994). Later, Page toured with the Black Crowes, recording the album *Live At The Greek* (1999) under Jimmy Page & The Black Crowes, playing mainly Zeppelin material. He played a wide variety of instruments, including a Fender Telecaster and a Gibson Les Paul. For live performances of 'Stairway To Heaven' he played a Gibson 6- and 12-string, double-neck electric. Page has a signature-model Gibson Les Paul.

➤— *Fender Telecaster, Gibson Les Paul, Rock, Twelve-String Guitar*

PASS, JOE

American, 1929–94. Jazz guitarist. Pass started playing when he was nine, practising six hours a day at his father's insistence; he was influenced by Django

Reinhardt. He soon started playing with Tony Pastor's and Charlie Barnet's bands. In the 1950s Pass struggled with drug addiction, playing to support his habit. He recorded the acclaimed *Sounds Of Synanon* (1962) whilst in rehab. Finally cured in 1963, he resumed his musical career. He established himself as a band leader with *Catch Me* (1963) followed by *For Django* (1964), which acknowledges Reinhardt's influence, and *Simplicity* (1966). His growing reputation brought him work with Julie London, Chet Baker and Frank Sinatra. Pass teamed up with fellow guitarist Herb Ellis for *Jazz/Concord* (1972) and the acclaimed *Seven Come Eleven* (1973), shortly after playing with Benny Goodman and Oscar Peterson. The solo album *Virtuoso* (1973) features Pass playing unaccompanied improvizations on standards, with a spontaneity previously unheard. Pass had developed into an unrivalled all-rounder, able to play solo, duet with singers such as Ella Fitzgerald, and play in bands, covering a huge range of styles such as bebop, blues and latin. He wrote instructional books including *Joe Pass Guitar Method* (1970) and *The Joe Pass Guitar Method* (1977). Posthumous releases include *Resonance* (2000), *Joe's Blues* (1998) and *What Is There To Say: Joe Pass Solo Guitar* (2001). He played signature-models, an Ibanez JP20 and an Epiphone Emperor.

➤ *Jazz*

PASTORIUS, JACO

American, 1951–1987. Electric-fusion bass player. The son of a jazz drummer, Pastorius played drums, guitar, piano and saxophone as a teenager, and backed bands on the local South Florida circuit. Despite being self-taught, he landed a job teaching jazz at the University of Miami. His debut solo album *Jaco Pastorius* (1976) included a stunning version of Charlie Parker's 'Donna Lee'; Pastorius redefined the scope of the bass with chords, double stops and previously unexplored sounds and textures from the fretless bass – 'Portrait Of Tracy' made extensive use of harmonics. He made distinctive contributions to Pat Metheny's *Bright Size Life* (1976) and Joni Mitchell's *Hejira* (1976); he then joined Weather Report with whom he recorded *Heavy Weather* (1977), which featured the crossover hit 'Birdland', *Mr Gone* (1978), *8.30* (1979), *Night Passage* (1980) and

Weather Report (1981). He formed his own band Word Of Mouth and continued to play with other musicians, including the Django Reinhardt-influenced Bireli Lagrene on *Bireli & Jaco* (1986). He suffered from manic depression and alcoholism, and died from injuries sustained after being beaten up trying to enter a night club. He played Fender Jazz basses, one fretted, the other fretless.

➤ *Fender Jazz Bass*

ABOVE: *Jaco Pastorius was a brilliant bass player who redefined the instrument.*
ABOVE LEFT: *Jimmy Page, renowned for his lengthy and infinitely inventive guitar solos which dominate many of Led Zeppelin's songs.*

PAUL, LES

American, born 1916. Jazz, pop and country guitarist. Paul started playing guitar and harmonica as a child and was influenced by Django Reinhardt. He played country and jazz under different names; his versatility meant he could accompany Bing Crosby, the Andrews Sisters and Nat 'King' Cole. Despite being a proficient and versatile player, Paul is perhaps better known as the pioneer of multi-track recording, building the first multi-track recorder in 1946, and for his design of the Les Paul solid-body electric guitar, issued by Gibson in 1952. 'Little Rock Getaway' features multiple guitar parts created by changing the speed of the tape to alter the register and sound texture. With his wife (the singer Mary Ford) he had the hits 'How High The Moon' and 'Mocking Bird Hill' in the 1950s, again making use of his multi-track recorder to overdub multiple parts. By the early 1960s he had tired of the music business, and started to work with Gibson. He came out of retirement to duet with Chet Atkins on the country album *Chester & Lester* (1978), which won a Grammy. *Les Paul: The Legend And The Legacy* (1991) compiles the high points of his career. Unsurprisingly, he plays a Gibson Les Paul.

➤ *Gibson, Gibson Les Paul*

PEÑA, PACO

Spanish, born 1942, relocated to London in 1966. Flamenco guitarist. A traditionalist who sees his role as promoting flamenco culture, rhythms and traditional sounds, Peña started playing young, giving his first professional concert aged 12. He accompanied the top flamenco singers and dancers and in 1970 founded the 'Paco Peña Flamenco Company', consisting of

Professor of Flamenco at the Rotterdam Conservatory, and in 1997 was awarded 'La Cruz de Oficial de la Orden del Merito Civil' by the King of Spain. He favours a guitar built by Almerian Gerunvino Fernández.

➤ *Flamenco*

REINHARDT, DJANGO

Belgium, 1910–53. Acoustic jazz guitarist. Reinhardt started playing banjo and violin aged 12, later moving onto the guitar. A travelling gyspy, he had his fretting hand severely damaged in a caravan fire leaving him with only two working fingers on his left hand – his first and second fingers. Against the odds, over the course of a year Reinhardt adjusted his technique to compensate, and taught himself to play both blindingly fast runs and chordal accompaniments. In 1935 he formed a fruitful partnership with violinist Stephane Grappelli in the Quintet of the Hot Club of France. In 1946 Reinhardt went to America and toured with Duke Ellington, returning to France having assimilated the sounds of American contemporary jazz. An innovator and master improviser, Reinhardt would work artificial harmonics, octaves and sophisticated harmonies into his playing – he often used artificial harmonics in his solo in his own composition 'Nuages'. Influenced himself by Charlie Christian and Eddie Lang, Reinhardt has influenced a diverse number of players including Bireli Legrene, BB King, Julian Bream and Eric Johnson. Compilations of Reinhardt's recordings include *The Classic Early Recordings* (2000), *All Star Sessions* (2001) and *Paris And London 1937–1948* (2001). He played a Macaferri acoustic.

➤ *Harmonics, Jazz*

himself, two dancers, two singers and another guitarist – the company has since given concerts throughout the world. He signed to the Decca label, resulting in *The Art Of Flamenco Guitar* (1972), *The Flamenco World Of Paco Peña* (1978), from the BBC TV documentary *The World Of Paco Peña* and *The Paco Peña Flamenco Company Live At Sadler's Wells, London* (1980), amongst others. In 1981 he founded the Centre of Flamenco in Cordoba, which hosts an annual Festival Internacional de la Guitarra, a two-month celebration of the guitar with concerts and master-classes from flamenco and classical musicians such as John Williams, Ben Verdery and Serranito. In 1985 Peña was appointed the world's first

SAMBORA, RICHIE

American, born 1959. Rock guitarist. Sambora joined melodic-rock act Bon Jovi, formed by and named after singer Jon Bon Jovi. He co-writes much of the Bon Jovi material. The band enjoyed modest success with *Bon Jovi* (1984) and *7,800 Degrees Farenheit* (1985); lengthy tours and stronger songwriting made third album *Slippery When Wet* (1986) their breakthrough, staying at number one in the US charts for two months and spawning the hits 'Living On A Prayer', on which Sambora plays a Talk Box, and 'Wanted Dead Or Alive'. *New Jersey* (1988) consolidated their success. Whilst Bon Jovi took a sabbatical, Sambora recorded a solo album, *Stranger In This Town* (1991), which showed his blues roots and features a guest appearance by Eric Clapton on 'Mr Bluesman'. Bon Jovi regrouped for *Keep The Faith* (1992), followed by the greatest hits compilation *Cross Road* (1994). *These Days* (1995) saw the band broadening their songwriting style and features Sambora on electric sitar. Sambora released a second solo album, the acoustic-based *Undiscovered Soul* (1998), returning to Bon Jovi for *Crush* (2000) and the live *One Wild Night: Live 1985–2001* (2001). His main guitar has always been the Fender Stratocaster; Fender have two signature-model Richie Sambora Stratocasters.

➤— *Fender Stratocaster, Rock*

SANTANA, CARLOS

Mexican, born 1947. Latin/rock electric guitarist. As well as a guitarist, Santana is a singer and leader of the band named after him. Initially enjoying regional success, Santana reached a wider audience with their appearance at the original Woodstock festival in 1969. Their debut album *Santana* (1969) contains 'Soul Sacrifice' and 'Evil Ways'; *Abraxas* (1970) contains Santana's best known instrumental 'Samba Pa Ti' and a version of Peter Green's 'Black Magic Woman'. *Santana III* (1971) consolidated the band's success, while *Caravanserai* (1972) marked a departure into jazz-rock, as did his *Love Devotion Surrender* (1973) collaboration with John McLaughlin. *Amigos* (1977) marked a return to latin-rock and included the hit single 'She's Not There', originally played by the Zombies. Much respected by fellow musicians, Santana has worked with Herbie Hancock, Wayne Shorter, Stanley Clarke and Billy Cobham, and played on John Lee Hooker's *The Healer* (1989). *The Ultimate Collection* (1998) draws together the highlights from Santana's career, which enjoyed a new lease of life with the release of *Supernatural* (1999) containing contributions from contemporary musicians such as Lauryn Hill, Matchbox 20's Rob Thomas and Everlast and a collaboration with his contemporary Eric Clapton. *Supernatural* won eight Grammys. Santana plays Paul Reed Smith guitars.

➤— *Paul Reed Smith, Rock*

ABOVE: *Richie Sambora, who plays with Bon Jovi.*
RIGHT: *Carlos Santana - one of the most soulful players around.*
FAR RIGHT: *Joe Satriani, a great player as well as being a teacher to the stars.*

SATRIANI, JOE

American, born 1952. Rock guitarist. Initially a drummer, Satriani changed to the guitar the day Jimi Hendrix died. He is influenced by Hendrix, John McLaughlin and Wes Montgomery. A respected private teacher, Satriani taught Steve Vai, Metallica's Kirk Hammett and Primus' Larry LaLonde. After self-financing *Not Of This Earth* (1986), he achieved unexpected commercial success with *Surfing With The Alien* (1987), followed by *Flying In A Blue Dream* (1990), *The Extremist* (1992), *Time Machine* (1993), *Joe Satriani* (1995), *Crystal Planet* (1998), *Engines Of Creation* (2000) and *Live In San Francisco* (2001). Satriani often uses hammer-ons, pull-offs and slides to create fast, flowing and seamless phrases, as can be heard in the solo of the title track of *Flying In A Blue Dream* and in 'The Bells Of Lal (Part 2)' from the same album. He is also fluent in two-handed tapping as heard in 'Day At The Beach (New Rays From An Ancient Sun)' from *Flying In A Blue Dream*. His book *Guitar Secrets* (1993) compiles his tuition columns for US magazine *Guitar For The Practising Musician*. A very well-schooled musican, he uses his 'pitch-axis theory' in the bridge of 'Satch Boogie' from *Surfing With The Alien* as a device to change key and modality. He plays Ibanez Joe Satriani signature models.

➤— *Ibanez, Rock*

SCOFIELD, JOHN

American, born 1951. Fusion guitarist. Influenced by Jim Hall – his favourite guitarist – plus Steve Shallow, John McLaughlin and Mick Goodrick, Scofield studied at the Berklee College of Music in Boston. He recorded with Chet Baker and Gerry Mulligan, then joined Billy Cobham's band. He received greater exposure with Miles Davis, playing on *Decoy* (1983) and *You're Under Arrest* (1985). Early Scofield solo album *Shinola* (1982) is uncharacteristically laid-back; *Still Warm* (1986) sees him developing his own style – a mixture of bebop, rock and blues, with funk rhythms. His trademark sound was created with a digital chorus unit. *Blue Matter* (1987) and *Loud Jazz* (1988) continued to exploit funky grooves; *Time On My Hands* (1990) saw more of his bebop leanings. He collaborated with fellow guitarist Bill Frisell on *Grace Under Pressure* (1991) creating a wide range of textures, contrasting with *Quiet* (1996), which was played on an amplified nylon-string guitar. For *A Go Go* (1998) Scofield ditched his trademark stereo-chorus sound; *Bump* (2000) saw Scofield's jazz-funk compositions played with a wide range of textures and dynamics. He plays an Ibanez AS200.

➤— *Blues, Ibanez, Jazz, Rock, Soul*

SEGOVIA, ANDRÉS

Spanish, 1893–1987. Classical guitarist. A tireless campaigner for the classical guitar, Segovia sought to raise his instrument to the same stature as the piano and violin through performing and increasing the repertoire. Self-taught, Segovia revised Tarrega's guitar technique, plucking the strings with a combination of flesh and nail which helped him produce a wide range of tones. He greatly increased the repertoire of the classical guitar through transcriptions and revisions of JS Bach, Weiss, Handel and Tárrega, and by commissioning contemporary composers to write for the guitar, including Turina, Torroba, Villa-Lobos, Rodrigo, Ponce, Tansman and Castelnuovo-Tedesco. An influential teacher, he tutored John Williams, Julian Bream, Christopher Parkening, David Russell and many others; he also wrote didactic material. Segovia performed from 1909 into his nineties and recorded from 1927–77, collections including *Centenary Celebration* (1999) and *Five Centuries Of Spanish Guitar* (1989). His interpretative style was warm and romantic, deemed by later generations to be inappropriate in Baroque music. He worked with guitar-makers Ramirez, Hauser and Fleta to improve the tone and volume of the instrument. He was largely responsible

for instigating the production of the first nylon guitar strings in 1947 by Du Pont Chemical and Albert Augustine, a huge breakthough for classical guitarists.

➤ *Classical, Finger-Style, Nylon Strings*

SESSION GUITARIST

A session guitarist is a professional musician who gets paid to play guitar parts for an artist's studio or live sessions. They may be required to sight-read, follow chord charts or to play a couple of short solos. Famous session guitar players include Larry Carlton (Steely Dan and Joni Mitchell), Darryl Steurmer (Genesis) and Snowy White (Pink Floyd and Cliff Richard), while session-bass aces include Nathan East (Eric Clapton, Phil Collins and Diana Ross) and James Jamerson (played on a great many Motown records).

➤ *Lead Guitar Tips, Playing A Solo*

SIMON, PAUL

American, born 1941. Guitarist and singer-songwriter. Simon met the singer Art Garfunkel at school and they had a minor hit with 'Hey Schoolgirl' in 1957. Simon studied at Queens College in New York before collaborating again with Garfunkel in 1964. They signed to Columbia but their first album, *Wednesday Morning 3am* (1964), was a flop and Simon went to Europe to record *The Paul Simon Songbook* (1965). Meanwhile, a new folk-rock backing was grafted on to 'The Sound Of Silence' (a song from the first Simon and Garfunkel album), which became a US number one hit.

Simon hurriedly returned from Europe to record a number of similarly treated tunes with Garfunkel and the result was the highly successful *Sounds Of Silence* (1966), which boasted two more hits: 'I Am A Rock' and 'Homeward Bound'. Success continued with *Parsley, Sage, Rosemary & Thyme* (1966), the film soundtrack for *The Graduate* (1967, featuring 'Mrs. Robinson'), and the now legendary *Bridge Over Troubled Water* (1970). The duo split up in 1970, and Simon went on to pursue a successful solo career. His later recordings, such as *Graceland* (1986) and *The Rhythm Of The Saints* (1990), have a strong multicultural influence. He remains a highly influential songwriter.

ABOVE: Paul Simon – one half of successful folk rock duo Simon & Garfunkel and a respected solo artist in his own right.
RIGHT: Andrés Segovia, a classical master.

SOR, FERNANDO

Spanish, 1778–1839. Classical guitarist and composer. Sor studied harmony, counterpoint, singing, organ and violin in the Escolania monastery in Montserrat. Inspired by Moretti's guitar music, Sor made the guitar his main instrument. He joined Napoleon's army after the French invasion of Spain, then resumed his musical career in Paris. He lived in London from 1815 to 1823 where as a performer, teacher and composer his career blossomed – his *Cinderella* ballet was performed in London, Paris and Russia. Sor lived in Russia from 1823–27 and played for Russian high society and the Imperial Royal family. He then returned to Paris, where he often appeared on-stage with his peers Aguado and Costé, and wrote *Sor's Method For The Classical Guitar* (1827, English edition), which contained music and text. Sor recommended resting the lower body of the guitar on the edge of a table for stability, and plucking the strings with the pads of his fingertips, not the nails, while resting the fourth finger of the picking hand on the top of the guitar. He composed over 400 pieces for the guitar including themes with variations, sonatas, studies and fantasies. His published guitar works include *Complete Method* (Merrick), *20 Collected Studies* (Segovia) and six volumes of the *Complete Works* edited by Brian Jeffery. He worked closely with guitarmakers René-François Lacote in France and Luis Panormo in London – early nineteenth-century instruments had short scale lengths enabling the hand to cover a greater number of frets.

➤– *Classical, Finger-Style*

SUMMERS, ANDY

British, born 1942. Rock, blues, pop and jazz guitarist. Influenced by Django Reinhardt, Wes Montgomery, Barney Kessel and Kenny Burrell, Summers started playing jazz and rhythm & blues with Zoot Money's Big Roll Band, then dabbled with psychedelia in Dantalion's Chariot. He left to join the original Soft Machine then joined the Animals, playing on *Love Is* (1968). He studied classical guitar at the University of California, then returned to Britain where he joined Kevin Coyne, playing on *Matching Head And Feet* (1975), *Heartburn* (1976) and the live *In Living Black And White* (1976). Summers saw an early line-up of the Police in London then joined them, replacing the original guitarist.

A three-piece outfit, the Police were well-schooled and talented musicians who came to prominence on the coat-tails of punk and new wave, playing bassist-singer Sting's songs. The Police's reggae influences and use of space, plus their interesting harmonies, gave them a highly distinctive sound. Whilst Summers has played a variety of styles in his career, it is his textural work with the Police with which he is most associated – sparse, tasteful rhythm guitar parts which often demonstrate a mastery of effects such as chorus, compression and delay. *Outlandos D'Amour* (1978) included the hit singles 'Can't Stand Losing You' and 'Roxanne', which featured Summers' clipped rhythm guitar accompaniment plus the John Coltrane-influenced solo break in 'Peanuts'.

Regatta De Blanc (1979) ('White Reggae') included 'Walking On The Moon', which contains one of Summers' favourite guitar sounds, plus 'Message In A Bottle' which

starts with a guitar riff using ninths. Touring for 20 months consolidated the band's position as one of the world's top live acts. *Zenyatta Mondatta* (1980) includes a notable angst-ridden solo from Summers in 'Driven To Tears'. A richer, more overdubbed sound on *Ghost In The Machine* (1981) also sees Summers playing guitar synthesizer on 'Secret Journey'. *Synchronicity* (1983) included the massive hit single 'Every Breath You Take' with Summers' distinctive riff based on the Aadd9 chord and inspired by Bartók.

Whilst with the Police he collaborated with Robert Fripp on *I Advance Masked* (1982) and *Bewitched* (1984). He wrote soundtracks for the 1985 films *2010* and *Down And Out In Beverly Hills*. Since the Police split in 1986, Summers has pursued a solo career, mixing elements of jazz, world music and classical music in releases including *XYZ* (1987), *The Golden Wire* (1989) and *Mysterious Barricade* (1989). He collaborated with jazz guitarist John Etheridge on *Invisible Threads* (1994) followed by solo albums *Synaesthesia* (1995), *The Last Dance Of Mr X* (1997), *Green Chimneys* (1999) and *Peggy's Blue Skylight* (2000). With the Police he played a Fender Telecaster.

➤— *Blues, Fender Telecaster, Jazz, Rock*

TÁRREGA, FRANCISCO

Spanish, 1854–1909. Classical guitarist and composer. Tárrega studied harmony and composition at the Madrid Conservatoire and won first prize for both. He performed his first recitals on both piano and guitar, before dedicating himself to the guitar. He followed Sor's example by plucking the strings with the pads of the fingers as opposed to the nails, but playing a Torres guitar with a wider neck than early nineteenth-century instruments helped him develop classical guitar technique – Tárrega rested the guitar on the left thigh, which was raised by a footstool, thus freeing the picking hand from resting on the guitar top. He transcribed many works for the guitar, including pieces by Beethoven, JS Bach, Schumann and Chopin. He also transcribed works by contemporary Spanish composers Granados and Albeniz; on hearing one of these transcriptions Albeniz said he preferred it on guitar. Tárrega became Professor of Guitar at the Conservatoires of Madrid and Barcelona; he taught Emilio Pujol and Miguel Llobet. He wrote studies for classical guitar, including the popular intermediate piece 'Lagrima' ('Teardrops') and the advanced tremolo study 'Recuerdos de la Alhambra' ('Memories of the Alhambra), both of which are included on Narciso Yepes' *Tarrega: Guitar Works* (1976). His *Collected Works* (Gangi/Carfagna) are grouped into four volumes: *Preludes, Studies, Original Works* and *Transcriptions*.

➤— *Classical*

TAYLOR, JAMES

American, born 1948. Guitarist and singer-songwriter. Taylor's mother was a classical soprano who encouraged her child's musicality. He won a local talent contest at the age of 15 and, a year later, formed a band called the Fabulous Corsairs with his brother Alex. He became addicted to heroin and, at 17, committed

LEFT: Andy Summers – formerly of the Police.
ABOVE: The Police's 1983 album Synchronicity, *which includes some fine examples of Andy Summers' guitar work.*

himself to a mental institution for nine months. A move to London in 1968 resulted in his first album, *James Taylor* (1968), recorded with Paul McCartney and George Harrison for their Apple label. While it was not a commercial success, Taylor's unique musical personality was clearly there: a deep and introspective style that would have a profound influence on future generations of singer-songwriters. Commercial success did come a few years later with *Sweet Baby James* (1970), *Mud Slide Slim And The Blue Horizon* (1971) and *One Man Dog* (1972). Taylor married the singer Carly Simon, but the couple divorced ten years later. Taylor's success coincided with that of other singer-songwriters such as Carole King and Joni Mitchell. He continued to write and perform through the 1980s and 1990s, releasing *October Road* in 2002. Taylor plays a Yamaha acoustic.

➤ *Yamaha*

TAYLOR, MARTIN

British, born 1956. Jazz guitarist. Son of a jazz musician, guitarist and bassist William 'Buck' Taylor, Taylor started learning the guitar when he was four and joined his father's band when he was 12. His influences are Django Reinhardt, Ike Isaacs and pianist Art Tatum. After his first solo album *Taylor Made* (1978), he was asked to tour with violinist Stephane Grappelli, who played formerly with Django Reinhardt. Taylor ended up playing on over 20 albums with Grappelli including *At The Winery* (1980), *Vintage 1981* (1981) and *Together At Last* (1987). At the same time he pursued a solo career with *Skye Boat* (1981), *A Tribute To Art Tatum* (1984) and *Sarabanda* (1988). In 1990 he decided to concentrate on his solo career with *Do not Fret* (1991) and *Artistry* (1993). *Spirit Of Django* (1994) created a contemporary sound inspired by Reinhardt, *Portraits*

(1995) included three duets with Chet Atkins and *Nitelife* (2001) revealed a new smooth, funky sound. Besides being a fluent improvizer and expert accompanist, Taylor's ability to play solos which include a bass line, chords and melody simultaneously is legendary amongst guitarists. He plays a Yamaha Martin Taylor signature-model AEX1500 hybrid archtop.

➤ *Archtop, Yamaha*

TOWNSHEND, PETE

British, born 1945. Rock guitarist and songwriter. Townshend was a member of the Who. The anthemic title track of *My Generation* (1965) provided the band's third hit single, followed by *A Quick One* (1966) and *The Who Sell Out* (1968). Rock opera *Tommy* (1969) marked an ambitious departure and *Live At Leeds* (1970) is generally regarded as one of the most exciting live albums ever recorded. *Who's Next* (1971) featured 'Behind Blue Eyes', one of Townshend's best songs, and was followed by *Meaty, Beaty, Big And Bouncy* (1971), *Quadrophenia* (1973), *The Who By*

Numbers (1975) and *Who Are You* (1978). Townshend has also intermittently pursued a solo career with *Who Came First* (1972), *Empty Glasses* (1980), *All The Best Cowboys Have Chinese Eyes* (1982), *White City* (1985), *The Iron Man* (1989) and *Psychoderelict* (1993). The Who were one of the first bands to make 'auto-destruction' – that is, smashing up their instruments – part of their live act after Townshend accidentally broke the neck of his guitar whilst on-stage. Townshend is known more for his powerful rhythm-guitar work than his lead playing, such as the strummed acoustic-guitar intro of 'Pinball Wizard' from *Tommy*. His songs have been recorded by artists including Tina Turner, Elton John and David Bowie. In the Who, Townshend played a Gibson Les Paul and an SG through HiWatt amps and a Gibson J-200 acoustic.

➤ *Gibson Les Paul, Rock*

BELOW: *The American singer-songwriter, James Taylor.*
ABOVE: *Pete Townshend, the Who's inimitable songwriter and guitarist, takes off during Live Aid.*

VAI, STEVE

American, born 1960. Rock guitarist. Influenced by Jimmy Page, Jimi Hendrix and Eddie Van Halen, Vai was taught by Joe Satriani and followed a strict, dedicated 12-hour practice schedule. He studied at Boston's Berklee College of Music. Initially he worked for Frank Zappa as a transcriber, then joined Zappa's band playing 'impossible guitar parts' on *You Are What You Is* (1981), *Ship Arriving Too Late To Save A Drowning Witch* (1982), *The Man From Utopia* (1983) and *Them Or Us* (1984). He released the solo album *Flex-Able* (1984), including 'The Attitude Song' which showcases his pinch harmonics, fast picking and extreme vibrato-arm effects, three of his trademarks. He replaced Yngwie Malmsteen in Alcatrazz, releasing *Disturbing The Peace* (1985), joined David Lee Roth for *Eat 'Em And Smile* (1986) and *Skyscraper* (1988), then joined Whitesnake for *Slip Of The Tongue* (1989). His instrumental solo album *Passion & Warfare* (1990) showcases his formidable technique, highly fertile musical imagination and sense of humour. He formed the band 'Vai', releasing *Sex And Religion* (1993). Further solo albums are *Alien Love Secrets* (1995), *Fire Garden* (1996), *The Ultra Zone* (1999) and *Alive In An Ultra World* (2001). He plays a signature-model seven-string Ibanez Universe and a signature model six-string Ibanez JEM through assorted amps, including his signature-model Carvin Legacy Head.

➤— *Ibanez, Rock*

VAN EPS, GEORGE

American, 1913–98. Jazz guitarist. The son of Fred, a leading ragtime-jazz banjo soloist, Van Eps was influenced by Segovia, Eddie Lang and George Gershwin's piano playing; he influenced Earl Klugh, Joe Pass, Ted Greene, Charlie Hunter and many others. He played a custom seven-string Epiphone with an extra low string tuned to A, an octave below the fifth string. Seven strings enabled him to play bass, melody and chords at the same time, or independent melodic lines; he described his style as 'lap piano', also enabling him to use particularly rich harmonies in his solo arrangements. In New York during the 1930s, he played on many sessions and with the Ray Noble Orchestra and the Benny Goodman Orchestra; he was rumoured to have got on Goodman's blacklist for putting too sophisticated reharmonizations into jazz standards! After the Second World War he became one of the top Hollywood session guitarists and worked for Frank Sinatra and Peggy Lee. He recorded the solo albums *Mellow Guitar* (1956) and *Soliloquy* (1968). In the 1970s, he started to organize his harmonic ideas and concepts plus guitar fingering systems into book form, culminating in the highly influential text *Harmonic Mechanisms for Guitar, Vols 1–3*. In later years he performed with guitarist Howard Alden, with whom he recorded *Hand-Crafted Swing* (1992).

➤— *Jazz*

VAN HALEN, EDDIE

Dutch, born 1957, family relocated to the USA in 1969. Rock guitarist. Initially influenced by Eric Clapton, Van Halen reinvented the vocabulary of the electric guitar with pick-hand tapped notes, various kinds of harmonics and vibrato-arm 'abuse'; he influenced Steve Vai,

Joe Satriani, Steve Luckather, Kirk Hammett and many others. The instrumentals 'Eruption' from *Van Halen* (1978) and 'Spanish Fly' from *Van Halen II* (1979) showcase Van Halen's tapping technique. Further guitar innovations followed, such as the funk bass-influenced intro to 'Mean Street' on *Fair Warning* (1981) and the ethereal 'Cathedral' from *Diver Down* (1982), played with an echoplex. Van Halen reached a wider audience playing a trademark tapping solo on Michael Jackson's 'Beat It' (1983). *1984* (1984) confirmed Van Halen's mastery of melodic heavy rock with the hit single 'Jump'. Original singer David Lee Roth left to be replaced by Sammy Hagar, the new line-up releasing *5150* (1986), *OU812* (1988) and others. After fighting alcoholism, Van Halen returned with *Van Halen III* (1998) with new singer Garry Cherone, ex-Extreme. He is noted for his warm 'brown sound' created on early albums with a home-made 'superstrat' (a souped-up Strat-based guitar) through a customized Marshall head. Latterly, he plays his signature-model Peavey Wolfgang guitars through signature Peavey 5150 amps.

➤— *Rock, Superstrat, Tapping*

LEFT: Eddie Van Halen erupting.
ABOVE: Van Halen's 1986 album 5150.
FAR LEFT: Steve Vai, rock guitar wizard.

VAUGHAN, STEVIE RAY

American, 1954–90. Electric blues guitarist and singer. Influenced by Albert King, Albert Collins, Django Reinhardt, Lonnie Mack, Jimi Hendrix and his brother Jimmie Vaughan. Vaughan gained widespread exposure playing on David Bowie's *Let's Dance* (1983). With his bass and drums rhythm section Double Trouble Vaughan was signed to Columbia by legendary talent scout John Hammond. His acclaimed debut album *Texas Flood* (1983) mixed roughly half originals and half blues covers, a formula he generally continued through *Couldn't Stand The Weather* (1984) and *Soul To Soul* (1986). A below-par live album *Live Alive* (1986) suffered as Vaughan battled with drink and drugs; newly sober and straight, *In Step* (1989) marked a triumphant return to form. He died tragically in a helicopter accident. The posthumous releases overseen by brother Jimmie serve his legacy well, including *The Sky Is Crying* (1991), *Live At Carnegie Hall* (1997), *Greatest Hits* (1995), *The Real Deal: Greatest Hits 2* (1999) and *Blues At Sunrise* (2000). Vaughan's style included Albert King-style lead work as heard in the title track of *Texas Flood* and driving, swing rhythm guitar work as heard in 'Pride & Joy' from the same album. He played a Fender Stratocaster fitted with a left-handed vibrato system. Fender have a Stevie Ray Vaughan signature model.

➤ *Blues, Fender Stratocaster*

VEGA, SUZANNE

American, born 1959. Guitarist and singer-songwriter. Vega's parents divorced shortly after her first birthday, and she had no contact with her father for many years. Her mother married Ed Vega in 1960, and the family moved to New York City. The Vega household was musical and Suzanne was encouraged to take part in all kinds of creative activity; she studied dance and songwriting at the High School of Performing Arts in 1975 and became influenced by singer-songwriters such as Joni Mitchell, Woody Guthrie, Laura Nyro, Leo Kottke and Lou Reed. She developed a minimalist folk-rock guitar style (which she describes as 'circular'), often using open strings on the instrument, and built up enough courage to begin playing the folk-club circuit in 1977. She signed to A&M records and released her debut album, *Suzanne Vega* (1983), which featured the hit 'Marlene On the Wall'. Her second album, *Solitude Standing* (1987), featured another hit, 'Luka', a story about child abuse. Yet another Vega song, the *a capella* 'Tom's Diner', became a surprise hit in 1990 in a remixed

version by dance team DNA. Other notable Suzanne Vega albums include *Days Of Open Hand* (1990) and *99.9°F* (1992).

➤— *Folk*

WILLIAMS, JOHN

Australian, born 1941, based in Britain since 1952. Classical guitarist. John Williams should not to be confused with the American film composer of the same name. He was taught by his father Len Williams,

a respected teacher who founded the Spanish Guitar Centre in London. As an 11 year old, Williams impressed Segovia, who tutored him and encouraged him to pursue a musical education. He attended the Royal College of Music, studying piano and theory. Aged 17, Williams made his acclaimed professional debut in London on 6 November 1958, heralded by Segovia's proclamation that 'a prince of the guitar has arrived in the musical world'. Reviews praised his technique – he is a very controlled, precise and elegant player – but commented that he could be more expressive, a comment that some critics have echoed throughout his career. Williams toured extensively and highly successfully in professional terms until the early 1970s, then decided to tour in shorter bouts in order not to sacrifice his home life.

He made his recording debut for CBS with *CBS Records Presents John Williams* (1964) followed by *Virtuoso Music For Guitar* (1965) and *More Virtuoso Music for*

ABOVE: *Classical guitar maestro John Williams.*
RIGHT: *Suzanne Vega, the American songstress.*
FAR RIGHT: *Stevie Ray Vaughan – one of the finest of the white bluesmen.*

Guitar (1967). To mark the twenty-fifth anniversary of their association, CBS released the compilations *The Great Guitar Concertos* (1990) and *Spanish Guitar Favourites* (1990). Williams has also recorded with his peer Julian Bream on *Together* (1971) and *Together Again* (1974). Several contemporary composers' works have dedicated to him, including André Previn's 'Guitar Concerto' (1971); Stephen Dodgson has also written works for Williams including 'Partita' (1964) and 'Fantasy Division' (1969).

Williams has done much to cross musical boundaries, venturing into popular music with *Changes* (1971). Arranged and produced by composer-arranger Stanley Myers, this features Williams on electric guitar for the first time and includes Myers' 'Cavatina', later used as the theme for the film *The Deer Hunter*, a piece associated with Williams which he has recorded four times. The Height Below (1973), recorded with Beatles producer George Martin, similarly mixes elements of pop, classical and jazz.

He has recorded with jazz singer Cleo Laine, producing *Best Friends* (1976) and *Let The Music Take You* (1983). Williams co-founded the classical-rock fusion group Sky, recording *Sky* (1979), *Sky 2* (1980), *Sky 3* (1981), *Sky 4 Forthcoming* (1983), *Sky Five Live* (1983), *Cadium* (1983). Alongside his non-classical work he has also recorded classical albums including *Bach: Complete Lute Music* (1975), *Barrios* (1977), *The Baroque Album* (1988), *The Seville Concert* (1993, CD and video), *John Williams Plays Barrios* (1995) and *Schubert and Giuliani* (1999). He favours instruments built by Australian guitarmaker Greg Smallman.

➤ *Classical, Classical Guitar*

YOUNG, ANGUS

British, born 1959, family relocated to Australia in 1964. Rock guitarist. Influenced by blues players such as Elmore James and BB King as well as Chuck Berry and Eric Clapton, Young's British release *High Voltage* (1976) compiled selections from his band AC/DC's first two Australian releases, followed by *Dirty Deeds Done Dirt Cheap* (1976), *Let There Be Rock* (1977) and *Powerage* (1978). Through constant touring AC/DC built up a reputation as an exciting live act, captured on the live *If You Want Blood, You've Got It* (1978), featuring the crowd favourite 'Whole Lotta Rosie'. *Highway To Hell* (1979) took the band to a new level of commercial success. Singer Bon Scott died in 1980, but the band returned with new singer Brian Johnson on *Back In Black* (1980), then *For Those About To Rock* (1981) and they enjoyed even greater success. Box-set *Bonfire* (1997) pays tribute to the Scott era. AC/DC returned on form after a lay-off with *Stiff Upper Lip* (2000). AC/DC's image gimmick is Young dressing up as a schoolboy – which he still does in his forties! Young's and AC/DC's sound and approach has changed little over the years. The standing joke is that they have recorded the same album over and over. Young plays Gibson SGs through Marshall amps.

➤ *Blues, Gibson*

YOUNG, NEIL

Canadian, born 1945. Guitarist and singer-songwriter. Young started playing music at an early age, despite a succession of illnesses: diabetes, polio and epilepsy. He moved to Los Angeles during his early twenties, and with Steve Stills, formed the folk-rock band Buffalo Springfield. His first solo album was the

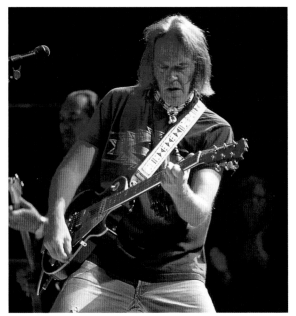

compositions cover a huge range of music from doo-wop to modern classical. His early influences included blues guitarists Johnny Guitar Watson and Guitar Slim and classical composers Varèse and Stravinsky. With the Mothers Of Invention he recorded *Freak Out* (1966), *Absolutely Free* (1966), *Lumpy Gravy* (1967) – once described as Zappa's favourite – and *We're Only In It For The Money* (1967). His songwriting is often highly satirical and displays his scathing sense of humour. Later, recording under his own name, as his music developed he employed guitarists such as Steve Vai to play the parts he could not play, although Zappa was an extremely accomplished guitar soloist in his own right, with a distinctive style. His guitar-soloing style is predominantly legato phrasing (i.e. using lots of pull-offs, hammer-ons and slides) over a two-chord vamp (a repeating chord progression), as heard in 'Black Napkins' from *Zoot Alures* (1976). He released two albums consisting entirely of guitar solos, *Shut Up 'N' Play Yer Guitar* (1981) and *Guitar* (1988). He stopped playing the guitar in order to concentrate on composing. He played a variety of guitars including a Gibson ES-5 Switchmaster, Gibson SGs and Fender Stratocasters.

>— *Fender Stratocaster, Gibson, Rock*

LEFT: Angus Young and his Gibson SG.
ABOVE: Neil Young, one of the world's most original songwriters.
BELOW: The multi-talented Frank Zappa.

melancholy *Neil Young* (1969), and his second, the critically acclaimed *Everybody Knows This Is Nowhere* (1969), introduced his now famous backing band, Crazy Horse. It also boasted some of his most popular songs, including 'Down By The River' and 'Cinnamon Girl'. He joined forces with Crosby, Stills and Nash while working on his *After The Gold Rush* (1970) album and, as a quartet, they recorded *Déjà Vu* (1970) and *Four Way Street* (1971), before splitting up in 1971. Young then released another solo album, *Harvest* (1972), which was to become his most commercial work, topping both the US and UK album charts and featuring the hit 'Heart Of Gold'. Later albums include the harrowing *Tonight's The Night* (1975), hard rock/rhythm & blues *Re-ac-tor* (1981), synthetic *Trans* (1983), bluesy *This Note's For You* (1988), abrasive *Arc* (1991) and acoustic *Harvest Moon* (1992). He is one of the world's most original, experimental and influential singer-songwriters, and as well as playing many acoustic guitars, he is associated with a Gibson Les Paul electric.

>— *Gibson Les Paul*

ZAPPA, FRANK

American, 1940–93. Rock guitarist and songwriter/composer. A multifaceted and prolific talent, easily misunderstood by the casual listener, Zappa's

INSTRUMENTS

CLASSICAL GUITAR

The classical guitar is a large acoustic guitar with a wide neck over which metal-wound silk bass strings and gut treble strings are usually strung. It was the first type of guitar to feature struts – pieces of wood attached to the inside of the body to improve volume and tonal response – and, to this day, is always played finger-style. The earliest guitar-like instrument was the pear-shaped *ud*, introduced to medieval Europe by the Arabs. This evolved into the European lute by the fifteenth century, the guitar-shaped *vihuela* by the sixteenth century, and the modern classical guitar by the nineteenth century. Well-known classical guitar players include Andrés Segovia, considered to be the father of modern classical guitar playing, John Williams, Liona Boyd and Julian Bream.

➤ *Classical, Flamenco Guitar, Lute*

FLAMENCO GUITAR

The flamenco guitar is similar to but slightly smaller than a typical Spanish classical guitar. It produces a louder, more penetrating sound than its classical relative, and many of today's top flamenco players tend to favour classical instruments for their more subtle, mellow tone.

➤ *Classical Guitar*

GUITAR, SEVEN-STRING

George Van Eps was a renowned jazz guitar player who could play melody, bass and chords, all at the same time on his instrument. The six-string guitar proved to have its limitations for his style, so he had the Epiphone guitar company make him a seven-string instrument with a low A string. This greatly expanded his range, and his unique technique inspired later seven-string jazz guitar players including Howard Alden, Bucky Pizzarelli and Ted Greene. Seven-string instruments have also been used more recently by Nu Metal artists Korn and Limp Bizkit.

➤ *Epiphone, Jazz*

GUITAR, TWELVE-STRING

These guitars have 12 strings arranged into pairs (courses) so that a six-string player can handle them easily. Six of the strings are tuned identically to those on a six-string instrument, while the other six are tuned as follows: the lowest four are usually tuned an octave above the conventional E, A, D and G strings, while the other two are tuned the same as the conventional B and E strings. Twelve-string guitars are capable of producing beautiful, rich chords. It is possible to simulate a 12-string effect by adding a slight delay and pitch shift to a six-string guitar signal.

➤ *Delay, Pitch Shifter, Tuning*

FENDER STRATOCASTER

Just over halfway through the last century a guitar was invented that would shape the sound of popular music for the next 50 years. Created in 1954 by a no-nonsense electrician called Leo Fender, the Stratocaster was designed to be the step-up from his bolt-together Telecaster with which he had entered the guitar market.

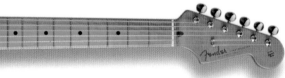

Still, it was nuts and bolts, not fine luthiery, that held his guitar together. But it did feature two major advances from the earlier Telecaster – a sprung through-body vibrato unit, and an extra pickup for smoother, more mid-range tones. Although the first guitars did not include mid-position settings to activate pairs of pickups together, this feature was added after players requested a five-way selector switch. The guitar was also contoured on the back, making it easier to play while standing, unlike the slab-bodied Telecaster. The earliest models had a one-piece maple neck with a 'skunk stripe' down the back to cover the truss rod, although after 1959, players could have the option of a rosewood fingerboard glued over the maple. In 1965 CBS paid $13.5 million for the Fender company, and several subsequent modifications were made to the Stratocaster; hence many collectors refer to vintage models as either pre- or post-CBS. Certainly, quality control did dip during the CBS years, although many 1970s Stratocasters are as highly prized now as the 1950s and early 1960s models have always been. The Stratocaster is the quintessential modern electric guitar, and is a design classic.

➤ *Fender, Fender Telecaster*

ABOVE: Roger McGuinn, famous for his use of the 12-string Rickenbacker.
CENTRE: The Fender Stratocaster.
LEFT: A classical guitar.

SUPERSTRAT

While the design of the Stratocaster is a true classic, owners envious of the high-power pickups and complex locking tremolo systems found on other more expensive instruments have often wanted to enhance their own guitars. This need for revision, and the 'bolt together' nature of the Stratocaster made it the ideal candidate for some radical customization in the hairspray-and-Spandex world of early 1980s California. The invention of what has become known as the 'superstrat' is credited to Californian guitar repairer Wayne Charvel who, after seeing his guitar-repair business succeed thanks to numerous Strat customizations, developed his own range of guitars. The Charvel guitar featured a Strat-type body with a 24-fret set neck, high-powered pickups, a Floyd-Rose tremolo system and an enhanced body shape. The Charvel company folded after only a short time, becoming the Jackson guitar company, with whom the superstrat is now firmly associated. The superstrat guitar was quickly adopted by rock and metal players such as George Lynch, Randy Rhoads and Eddie Van Halen. A range of Stratocaster models with similar, enhanced features is now available from Fender.

➤— *Fender Stratocaster, Jackson, Pickups, Tremolo Arm*

FENDER TELECASTER

The Fender Telecaster was the first production-made solid electric guitar, and since its birth in 1951 has rightly been hailed as a true innovation. Leo Fender wanted to call his guitar the Broadcaster, but was forced to change the name after Fred Gretsch sued – his firm made a drum kit with the same name. This led to a period of production in which the guitar had no name; these guitars, now known as 'no-casters', are as highly

prized by collectors as rare or misprinted stamps. Once the name Telecaster was settled upon, Leo Fender had the tricky job of convincing the public that his crude bolt-together guitar could really play. Sales were sluggish at first, but following endorsements from a few notable players, its popularity began to pick up. The Telecaster has always been associated highly with country music, and many of its first users played the guitar in a style reminiscent of a lap steel, the traditional accompaniment to country music.

The real secret of the Telecaster's enduring appeal is its tone, which stems from the 'ashtray' bridge unit, with through-body stringing and slanted rear pickup. This simple construction gives the distinctive 'frying-pan' tone that Tele players love, and which allows the guitar to cut through any band or orchestra setting. In the hands of rhythm guitarists like Keith Richards or Bruce Springsteen, the Telecaster has created some of the most elemental riffs in rock history; in the hands of country players like Albert Lee, Roy Buchanan or Danny Gatton, it has created some of the most startling solo virtuosity ever heard. The Telecaster was the first and, as some would have, the best electric guitar ever made.

>— *Country, Fender, Fender Stratocaster, Pedal Steel*

FENDER JAZZ BASS

Shortly after introducing the Jazzmaster, Fender developed another bass guitar intended to bring the Precision Bass up to date with a softer body and new pickups. In 1960 Fender unveiled the Deluxe Bass, soon afterwards renamed the Jazz Bass. This new Fender model featured a much slimmer and thinner neck than the Precision Bass had, updated and upgraded full-range bipole pickups, a groovy offset waist and, in 1966, a bound fingerboard and rectangular position markers. With features and styling almost directly lifted from the Jazzmaster guitar, this new bass guitar was the perfect foil to the Precision Bass. The flowing lines and slim look perfectly suited the 1960s and the Jazz Bass was soon adopted by the Californian musical community. Fender's simple marketing of one guitar and one bass for each of its three major lines (Tele, Strat and Jazz) proved to be their strength and by 1964, when they were purchased by CBS, Fender were almost succeeding in their ambition to be the premier manufacturer of guitars in the USA. The Jazz Bass is still in production, with Standard, 62 Reissue and 75 Reissue models currently available.

>— *Fender*

FENDER PRECISION BASS

The Precision Bass was developed in 1951 by Leo Fender in response to enquiries from dealers wanting to meet the demands of their customers for a bass instrument able to compete with the new and highly desirable Fender Telecaster. Bass players had become jealous of the Telecaster's portability and sound, so Leo Fender produced the 'P' or Precision Bass, a new, fretted bass guitar which needed far less concentration from the player to

ABOVE TOP: *The Fender Telecaster.*
ABOVE: *The Fender Jazz Bass.*
LEFT: *The human riff – Keith Richards (and his Telecaster).*
FAR LEFT: *A Superstrat with a Floyd-Rose tremolo system.*

ensure every note came out in tune (hence, the player could play with Precision). In 1951, the P Bass was very similar in body shape to the Telecaster, though this shape was modified in 1954 to include the flowing contours of the Stratocaster shortly after the introduction of Fender's flagship electric. The P Bass is fitted with one split single coil pickup. One half of the pickup is aligned to detect vibration from the E and A strings and the other half of the pickup detects vibration from the D and G strings. The two halves are offset to produce a deeper sound from the lower strings. Tone and volume control are set into the plastic scratchplate. The body is poplar wood and the neck is maple with a rosewood fingerboard. Many revisions of the P Bass have been produced by Fender including in 1970 the innovative fretless electric bass, but the standard P Bass remains for many the classic electric bass guitar.

>— *Fender*

BASS, FIVE-STRING

Most electric basses have four strings, tuned E, A, D and G, each an octave below the correspon-ding strings on a conventional six-string guitar. Some have an extra string tuned to a low B so the player can reach notes lower than the conventional E. This instrument is similar to a four-string instrument, but with a wider neck to accommodate the extra string. Nathan East, a top session bass player who has worked with artists such as Eric Clapton, Phil Collins and Barry White, is a five-string player.

>— *Eric Clapton, Six-String Bass*

BASS, SIX-STRING

Six-string bass guitars usually have a top C string and a low B string in addition to the other four strings you will find on a standard bass guitar. This means that a six-string bass player's range is extended to play both lower and higher notes than a conventional bass player. Of course, with every advantage there's often a disadvantage, and many bass guitarists find the wide necks of six-string instruments difficult to play. An early six-string bass guitar, the Fender VI, had each of the strings tuned an octave lower than those on a standard guitar.

>— *Five-String Bass*

GIBSON LES PAUL

Among all electric guitars the Gibson Les Paul is the most famous, and, among vintage guitar collectors, the most desirable. Developed in 1952 by Ted Macarty, the Les Paul is a descendant of Gibson's famous line of jazz guitars but with one important new feature: the 1952 Les Paul Standard was the very first solid-bodied Gibson guitar. Between 1952 and today the Les Paul has seen many changes. The guitar has always had its famous single cut away and carved top, but the addition of the Tune-O-Matic bridge in 1955, PAF pickups in 1957 and a new sunburst finish in 1958 led to the golden years of the Les Paul between 1958 and 1962. Guitars produced during this period are regarded as the most desirable of all Gibson guitars, and good examples change hands for many thousands of pounds. The Gibson Les Paul Standard is still in production and continues to sell very well. Gibson's close relationship with artists

ABOVE: The Fender Precision Bass.
RIGHT: The one and only Gibson Les Paul.
FAR RIGHT ABOVE: The renowned Gibson L5 from the Gibson Guitar Corp.
FAR RIGHT: Gibson Double Neck.

has led to a new range of custom shop models, replicas of guitars owned or customized by famous guitarists, and of course the highly regarded and desirable handmade copies of those first 1958 Les Paul Standard guitars.

➤— *Cut Away, Gibson, Jazz, Les Paul*

GIBSON L5

The Gibson Guitar Corp have been manufacturing guitars for well over 100 years, and the L5 is probably the most significant model from the early part of the last century. Introduced in 1922 by Gibson designer Lloyd Loar, the L5 was a 'Master Model', a guitar built by hand without compromise. Although production of this guitar seemed foolish in banjo-obsessed 1920s America it turned out to be a master-stroke, timed perfectly to anticipate the new popularity of jazz guitar. The L5 is the first F-hole guitar, a feature borrowed from the mandolin, which Gibson were also adept at producing. Compared with modern guitars the L5 seems almost ordinary, but at the time it represented the pinnacle of guitar production, with enhancements over previous models and new features such as the F-hole rather than an oval soundhole, a larger lower body, bound fingerboard and sleek, modern lines. The L5 is still in production as the L5-CES, a custom shop instrument with the modern additions of single humbucking pickup, volume and tone controls and inlaid fingerboard. A cut-away model was introduced in 1939, and this feature is still retained. Famous

L5 players include Wes Montgomery, Carl Kriess and Django Reinhardt.

➤— *Banjo, Cut Away, F-Hole, Gibson,*

GIBSON DOUBLE-NECK

During the late 1950s Gibson Guitar Corp and Fender were competing to produce the most innovative guitar designs. Amongst Gibson's new ideas were two double-necked instruments: the EDS-1275 Double Twelve, Gibson's first electric 12-string, and the EMS-1235 Double Mandolin. The EDS-1275 Double Twelve six- and 12-string double-neck has the most enduring image. It is a very large instrument made of two guitars joined together: a 12-string and a six-string. Both guitars have a standard 20-fret neck and a 24-note scale each with two Gibson PAF (Patent Applied For) pickups; each guitar has a standard three-position selector switch. An additional selector switch is used to switch between six- and 12-string or both. The price, weight and complexity of these instruments meant that Gibson were only able to sell 46 during the first four years of production. After 1961, some changes were made to the guitar and sales increased gradually until 1979, when even though the guitar was unadvertised, more than 450 guitars were sold, owing almost certainly to the use of the Double Twelve by Jimmy Page of Led Zeppelin who adopted it in 1978. His use of the guitar in the band's later years remains its most enduring image.

➤— *Gibson, Pickups*

GIBSON 335

In 1958 The Gibson company enhanced their range of jazz instruments with a new guitar called the ES-335, now known simply as the 335. This guitar was a development of earlier models the ES-350T and Gibson Byrdland, but featured a much thinner body and a radical 'semi-solid' construction, based around a solid maple centre block supporting the two humbucking pickups, Tune-O-Matic bridge and stop tailpiece. This centre block enabled the neck to be set into the body for additional mass leading to sustain, while the wings on each side could be left hollow, allowing for a rich jazz tone. This design enabled jazz guitar players to compete on the same stages as the new louder rock guitarists where before, the fully hollow jazz guitar had been unusable, suffering from feedback at high volumes. The guitar was an instant hit and was quickly adopted by BB King. Many players have used and endorsed the 335, from 'Mr 335' Larry Carlton, who named an album *Room 335* after his guitar, through to the Smiths' Johnny Marr, jazz guitarist Jeff Raines, and countless more.

➤ *Bridge, Gibson, Jazz, Pickups*

RICKENBACKER 360

Postwar Southern California was a productive place for guitar makers and designers with three of the most influential – Fender, Bigsby and Rickenbacker – all living within a short distance of each other. The Rickenbacker 360 is the least fussy and most popular of all Rickenbacker guitars, thanks in part to the adoption and promotion of Rickenbacker by the Beatles from 1964 onwards. The 360 model has a semi-acoustic body with a distinctive 'cateye' in the upper wing, two Rickenbacker pickups, tone and volume controls, and stereo outputs. The 360 guitar is famous for its all-maple construction; maple is a very dense wood producing a very bright tone when used in guitar making, so much so that an all-maple

guitar was considered too bright by Gibson when considering materials for their Les Paul. The 360 brought Rickenbacker to the eyes and ears of the world when used heavily by John Lennon throughout the Beatles' early years. George Harrison also used a 12-string model – the 320/12 – and famously inspired Roger McGuinn to buy one; the Byrds' sound was heavily dependent on the 360/12's sound. Other famous 360-users include Pete Townshend of the Who, Paul Weller, Tom Petty and John Fogerty.

➤ *Fender, Twelve-String Guitar*

ELECTRO-ACOUSTIC

An electro-acoustic guitar is an acoustic or semi-acoustic guitar fitted with a piezo-electric transducer (usually under the bridge saddle)

and an onboard preamplifier. When plugged into a suitable amp, this produces a crisp acoustic sound with plenty of sustain and little feedback. The Ovation Adamas and Balladeer models are perhaps the most famous examples of this type of guitar, but other respected models are also made by companies such as Wechter and Takamine. Some acoustic players feel these guitars sound too synthetic and prefer to mike up their acoustics the old-fashioned way.

➤— *Pre-Amp*

ARCHTOP

An archtop guitar is an instrument with an arched (curved) top and back. Such guitars, carved from solid pieces of wood, became hugely popular during the

1920s because they were louder than the previously used classical guitars. They featured f-shaped soundholes instead of round ones and, because of this, had a violin-like appearance. The most popular archtop during the 1920s was the steel-strung Gibson L5. This evolved into the Gibson Super 400 during the 1930s, the ES-175 during the late 1940s, and the ES-335 during the 1950s. Archtop guitars are the favourite instruments of jazz guitar players.

➤— *F-Hole, Gibson L-5, Gibson 335, Jazz*

ABOVE: Classical guitarist John Williams is here pictured playing an electro-acoustic guitar. Note the volume knob on the body of his guitar.
ABOVE FAR LEFT: The Gibson 335, great for jazz and rock 'n' roll .
LEFT: The 360, Rickenbacker's most popular instrument.

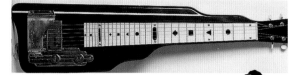

LAP STEEL

The lap-steel guitar differs from a conventional guitar mainly in the way it is played: it is held in the lap facing upwards and a steel bar is pressed against the strings. The lap-steel guitar is usually tuned in one of several open tunings rather than standard guitar tuning. It was originally invented in Hawaii but became popular in the United States in the first half of the last century. Some aspects of Hawaiian guitar playing were picked up and incorporated into blues, country , rock and pop.

➤⸺ *Bottleneck, Slide*

PEDAL STEEL

The pedal-steel guitar is like a Hawaiian steel guitar with pedals. Like its Hawaiian cousin, the pedal steel is played by sliding a steel bar up and down the strings, but the similarity ends there. By using a pedal-steel instrument's system of pedals and knee levers, a player can access a large number of different tunings.

➤⸺ *Lap Steel, Slide*

BANJO (FIVE-STRING)

A banjo is a guitar-like instrument with a round body used for a number of folk and country styles. The most common is the popular five-string banjo. There are many tunings used for this instrument, but the most popular is an 'Open G' tuning in which the open strings sound a G major chord: GDGBD. The fifth string is a short, thin string attached on the side of the neck, tuned to G an octave higher than the third string G. The fifth string is not always fretted and it often functions as a drone string, a feature that gives the five-string its unique character.

➤⸺ *Country, Folk, Lute, Mandolin, Tuning*

SITAR, ELECTRIC

In 1967, Vinnie Bell invented the Coral electric sitar, a small six-string guitar-like instrument producing a twangy sound that reminded people of its Indian namesake. It became an integral part of the 1960s psychedelic movement and appeared on hits such as 'Green Tambourine' by the Lemon Pipers, 'Band of Gold' by Freda Payne and 'Heartbreaker' by Gene Pitney. It was later revived by Pat Metheny, who used it with great

effect on 'Last Train Home', featured on his 1987 album, *Still Life Talking*. German maker Gunter Eyb introduced his own version of the electric sitar to the market in 1994, with a pointed headstock and tuner-equipped tailpiece.

➤— *Headstock, Tailpiece*

LUTE

The lute is a small pear-shaped instrument that was popular in Western music from the late Middle Ages to the end of the eighteenth century. Descended from the *ud*, an Arab instrument, the European lute had 12 strings arranged into six double courses tuned to the notes G, C, F, A, D, and G. It gradually evolved into a number of different stringed instruments including the *vihuela*, the guitar, the banjo, the mandolin and the cittern, an evolution that contributed to the lute's decline in popularity.

➤— *Banjo, Mandolin*

MANDOLIN

The modern mandolin, also known as the Neapolitan mandolin, is a small guitar-like instrument with a rounded body. It has eight strings arranged into four double courses tuned like a violin: G, D, A and E. Mozart, Vivaldi, Beethoven, Mahler and Schoenberg all wrote pieces for the mandolin. It has also become popular as a folk instrument in the US, Europe and Latin America. The mandolin has been used by many popular folk-rock bands, including Fairport Convention and Jethro Tull, and has appeared on folk-pop recordings from the Corrs and fusion albums by Al Di Meola.

➤— *Banjo, Lute*

ABOVE: A selection of mandolins, instruments popular in the folk genre.
ABOVE LEFT: A pedal-steel guitar.
ABOVE FAR LEFT: The Gretsch Electromatic – an electric lap steel.
CENTRE LEFT: The banjo is a traditional bluegrass instrument.
LEFT: A Coral electric sitar.

EQUIPMENT

HEAD

A head is a dedicated amplifier that uses a separate speaker cabinet to project the sound. Such amps can drive a number of speaker cabinets at the same time. The most popular heads include the Marshall JTM-45 (45 Watts), SLP (Super Lead Plexi – 100 Watts) and 30th Anniversary Head (100 Watts) models, and the Soldano SLO 100 (100 Watts), all of which have been used by Eric Clapton. Most modern heads have several channels, half/full-power operation and sockets for effects-loop connections.

➤— *Combo*

HEADSTOCK

The headstock is the structure at the end of a guitar's neck onto which the machine heads or tuning pegs are mounted. It is usually the part of the guitar that carries the manufacturer's name and logo plus any other significant details of the guitar model.

Headstocks vary greatly in design: some, such as those on the Fender Stratocaster and Telecaster guitars, have all of the machine heads mounted on one side while others,

including the Gibson Les Paul and ES-335 models, have three on one side and three on the other.

➤— *Fender Stratocaster, Fender Telecaster, Gibson Les Paul, Gibson 335*

CAPSTAN

Also known as a string post, the capstan is a round structure in a tuning head, usually made of steel, around which a string is wound. The whole structure is

ABOVE TOP: A Marshall JTM-45 head.
ABOVE: There are a variety of headstock designs.
ABOVE CENTRE: Guitar strings are wrapped around capstans.
FAR RIGHT: The truss rod reinforces an electric guitar's neck.
TOP RIGHT: The nut is the part of the headstock over which the strings pass.

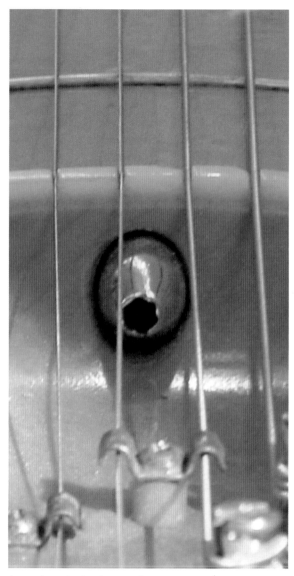

reach the machine heads or pegs. The strings rest on the nut, and all string vibrations occur between here and the guitar's bridge. The nut also sets the strings' height above the fingerboard. It is traditionally made out of bone or ivory but most cheap guitar models have plastic ones fitted. Some guitars have a 'zero fret' fitted just in front of the nut. In such cases, the fret sets the string height at the headstock end of the guitar.

➤— *Construction Materials, Headstock*

TRUSS ROD

 The truss rod is a metal bar used for reinforcing and adjusting a steel-strung guitar's neck. It can be adjusted to keep the neck straight if the tension changes when different gauge strings are used. One end of the truss rod is secured firmly to the heel (body end) of the neck and the other end is usually found beneath a cover-plate in the headstock, where it can be adjusted. Some guitars, notably Martin acoustics, have fixed truss rods that cannot be adjusted by the user.

➤— *Intonation, Repairs – Advanced*

housed on the headstock of the guitar. When putting a new string on a guitar, make sure it is wrapped tightly and neatly several times around the capstan to ensure the guitar stays reliably in tune, especially if the type of playing to be done includes bending a lot of notes.

➤— *Headstock*

NUT

The nut is a structure at the headstock end of the fingerboard that the strings pass over before they

FRET

Frets are metal strips placed across the radius of a guitar's fingerboard to mark out notes a semitone apart. They make it easy for a guitarist to find precise notes in scales and chords. Frets come in all shapes and sizes: some are narrow while others are wide; and some are flat at the top while others are rounded. Some bass players prefer fretless basses for their more fluid sound. Fretless six-string guitars, however, are rarely used in popular music.

➤— *Crown*

DOT MARKER

Most guitars have markers along the neck to help players navigate the fingerboard. The most common markers are dots behind the 3rd, 5th, 7th, 9th,

15th, 17th, 19th and 21st frets, along with two dots behind the 12th fret to highlight the notes one octave higher than those on the open strings. Other common markers are blocks (commonly found on Gibson and Ibanez guitars) and 'shark-tooths' (used on rock guitar models such as the Jackson Soloist). Markers are usually made out of abalone or plastic.

➤— *Fret*

CROWN

The crown is the top of a fret on the guitar fingerboard. Crowns vary in width and curvature, and these differences influence the tone of a vibrating

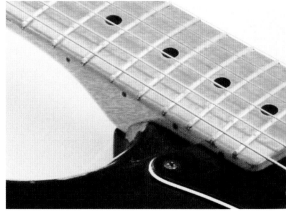

string: a thin crown tends to give a crisp treble edge to a string's tone, while a thicker one produces a more mellow sound that would appeal to a jazz player. Some crowns are rounded while others are flat, and these features also influence the tone of a guitar. A manufacturer will often stick to using a particular type of crown for their guitars: Fender electrics tend to have thin, rounded crowns while Gibsons usually have flat, wider ones.

>--- *Fret*

BELOW: A cut away, which allows access to the upper part of the neck.
BOTTOM FAR LEFT: Frets are metal strips placed across the radius of a guitar's fingerboard.
BOTTOM LEFT: The crown is the top of a fret on the guitar fingerboard.
TOP LEFT: Dot markers help the player to navigate the fingerboard.

CUT AWAY

This is a rounded area cut out of a guitar's body next to the neck so that a player can comfortably reach further up the neck. Guitars such as Gibson Les Pauls and Fender Telecasters have cut aways underneath the neck, while others, including the Gibson SG, Gibson 335, Fender Stratocaster and numerous Paul Reed Smith models, have cut aways above and below the neck. The advantage of the latter is obvious: with a double cut away you can easily reach high notes on the top and bottom strings of the fingerboard, giving a much larger range of notes to the virtuoso player. Popular acoustics made by Ovation and Takamine also have cut aways.

>--- *Fender, Gibson*

F-HOLE

F-holes are soundholes found on a number of acoustic and electric guitars. Early Gibson acoustic models, archtops such as the L-5 (first produced during the 1920s) and Super 400 (made during the 1930s), were among the first guitars to feature F-holes. A more recent model, the Gibson 335, introduced in 1957 and played by everyone from Chuck Berry to Noel Gallagher, is a semi-acoustic guitar with F-holes. Some guitars, such as the Gretsch Chet Atkins 1962 reissue model, have simulated F-holes painted onto the body as an ornamental decoration.

➤— *Archtop*

SOLID-BODY

A solid-body guitar is a guitar with a body that has no cavities other than those used for inserting pickups and other electrical components. Solid-body electric guitar prototypes were developed during the 1920s and 1930s when amplified acoustic guitars gave musicians too much feedback. One pioneer, Les Paul, built his own solid-body electric guitar, The Log, during the 1940s and took it to the Gibson guitar company. They eventually became interested and, in 1952, designed a guitar which they named after him: the Gibson Les Paul.

➤— *Gibson Les Paul, Les Paul, Semi-Solid*

SEMI-SOLID

During the late 1950s, Gibson introduced a range of semi-acoustic guitars that didn't suffer from the feedback problems that traditional electric-acoustic models produced. These guitars, including the ES-355,

ES-345, and the now famous ES-335, had thin hollow bodies with a solid centre block, with F-holes to let the sound out, and a design which increased sustain and greatly reduced feedback. Semi-solid guitars have been played by artists as diverse as Chuck Berry, Noel Gallagher, John Scofield, Larry Carlton, John Lee Hooker, BB King and Alvin Lee.

>— *Electro-Acoustic, Gibson, Solid-Body*

PICKUP SELECTOR

Most electric guitars have a selector switch that allows the player to choose whichever pickup is desired. The treble pickup (the one nearest to the neck) produces a brighter tone than the more mellow bridge pickup. A simple three-way switch on a two-pickup guitar, such as a Telecaster, allows you to switch between

HUMBUCKING PICKUPS

Humbucking pickups have two coils instead of just one. These coils are wired in such a way that any electrical hum produced by one is cancelled out by the other. The result is a fatter sound with less background noise. Humbuckers were originally launched by Gibson in 1955 and soon became a standard feature on their Les Paul, Explorer, Flying V, Firebird and SG guitars. This is one reason why these guitars contrast so sharply in tone with the clear, biting sounds produced by Stratocasters and Telecasters fitted with single-coil pickups.

>— *Pickups*

the two or even to use both at the same time. Stratocasters, however, have three single-pole pickups and are usually fitted with a five-way switch.

>— *Pickups*

ABOVE LEFT: A pickup selector on a Fender Stratocaster.
ABOVE: Humbucking pickups produce a larger sound than single-coil.
LEFT AND TOP LEFT: A semi-solid Guild and a solid-body Fender Stratocaster.
FAR LEFT: F-holes are ornamental soundholes.

PAF PICKUP

The Patent Applied For (PAF) humbucker pickup is perhaps the most well known and sought-after of all the Gibson electric guitar pickups. It was originally fitted to Les Paul guitars between 1957 and 1960, and earned such a reputation that rockers were even fitting them on to their Stratocasters many years later. Other respected humbuckers include Gibson's 'Velvet Brick' and the high-output Seymour Duncan Invader.

➤— *Pickups*

round-wound strings is the flat-wound string, which uses flat steel tape or ribbon instead of wire, and thus eliminates the grooves. This produces a mellow tone and feel, perfect for jazz musicians. Ground-wound strings use the same construction methods as ordinary round-wounds, but are flattened or ground down to produce a smooth surface.

STRINGS, BRONZE

Guitar strings were traditionally made from either wire or gut, but nowadays there are just two main types, steel and nylon. Bronze, or phosphor bronze, strings are of the steel variety and are usually used with acoustic guitars. The sixth through to the fourth string will typically be wound – a solid steel core with bronze wound around the outside – while the first and second strings, the lowest gauges, will be plain steel. There are various manners of winding available, all of which give the instrument a different feel and tone. Round-wound strings are the most common.

STRINGS, FLAT-WOUND AND GROUND-WOUND

The answer to the problem of the unwanted fret noise caused by the grooved, uneven surface of

STRING GAUGE

The gauge of a string is the technical term for its width or thickness, measured in thousandths of an inch. Typically, a set of six guitar strings will be referred to by the thickness of the first or highest string. Therefore a set of '10' gauge strings, considered to be the standard width for most electric players, will consist of a thinnest string of 0.010 inches and five further strings of varying gauges to give a corresponding tension across the neck.

STRINGS, GOLD

Most strings used on a guitar consist of a solid steel core and a winding of either silver or bronze alloys. Silver strings usually use stainless steel for their winding, as this resonates within the magnetic field of the pickup of an electric guitar, producing an electric tone. Gold or bronze wound strings are more typically found on acoustic guitars. Bronze wound strings do not allow as much magnetic resonance and thus require a different amplification method, usually based on piezo crystals.

LEFT AND BELOW: A selection of strings, of various gauges.
ABOVE RIGHT: The Patent Applied For (PAF) pickup.

cat gut, although traditionally a sheep's or pig's intestine would have been used. Nowadays, you can buy nylon equivalents which come in hard, medium or light gauges, and in ball end or loop varieties.

STRINGS, ROUND-WOUND

Over the nylon core of classical strings or the nickel core of steel strings, a wound loop of steel can be placed to increase the diameter of the string. The greater the diameter, the lower the note produced when the string is plucked under tension. The most common form is the round-wound variety. It is produced literally by spinning the core of the string as wire is fed out to cover it. The slight grooves between the windings of each thread of wire give the string an uneven surface, and can cause unwanted fret noise when sliding between notes.

➤— ***Ground-Wound Strings***

STRINGS, NYLON

Nylon strings are used on classical guitars. They produce a much softer tone than steel or bronze strings and create less tension on the guitar's neck. The first stringed instruments used strings made of stretched

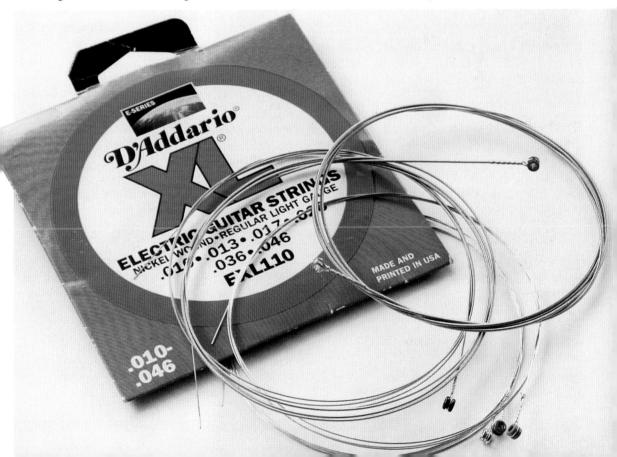

STRINGS, STEEL

Steel or nickel strings are used on electric guitars. The thicker gauges, normally reserved for the first, second and third strings, will consist of a solid steel core wound with nickel, steel or even gold. The highest three strings will be solid steel or nickel. The strings come in various thicknesses, or gauges, designed to be tuned up to the six notes of standard tuning, EADGBE. Each string can be tuned up to a whole tone higher than its intended note, but any more stretching may result in string breakage or neck damage.

STRING CLEANER

The more a guitar is played, the more dirt and grease will be deposited on the strings. There are three accepted ways of cleaning strings. The first is to use a soft cloth before and after you play and to keep your hands as clean as possible. The second is to raise the strings and 'snap' them back into position regularly, to help dislodge dirt build-up. You can also try removing strings and boiling them in water, although few players nowadays bother with this method. The last technique is to use a proprietary string cleaner, such as Fast-Fret, which employs a special liquid compound to reduce the build-up of grime and keep the string smooth.

➤— *Repairs – Simple*

acoustic guitars, such as the Gibson ES-335 and ES-355 models, also have F-holes. Acoustic guitar soundholes are usually surrounded by attractively decorated inlays made out of different woods, bone, plastic or abalone.

➤— *F-Hole*

SCRATCHPLATE

A scratchplate is a plastic plate fixed to the lower-front part of a guitar's body (underneath the sound-hole on an acoustic steel-string instrument) to protect it from wear and tear caused by the player's plectra or finger-picks. They can also serve an ornamental purpose and are sometimes adorned with intricate inlays, engravings and decoration. Some players do not have scratchplates on their guitars because they feel, with some

SOUNDHOLE

The soundhole is the hole in the front of the guitar body through which sound projects from the soundchamber. Most acoustic guitar soundholes are round, although some are oval (as on early Gibson acoustics), D-shaped (as on Maccaferri guitars), or violin-like F-holes (as on the Gibson ES350). Semi-

justification, that they compromise the tone of the soundboard. Classical and flamenco guitars do not have scratchplates.

BRIDGE

This part of the guitar, along with the saddle, transmits energy from the string vibrations to the body of the guitar. It also spreads the mechanical tension of the strings. There are two main types of bridge: a fixed bridge, which is glued to the top of the soundboard with the strings anchored to it; and a floating bridge, which is held in place only by the tension in the strings that pass over it. Both types of bridge are usually made of metal, or high-density woods such as ebony or rosewood that aid sustain and vibration transfer to the body. Floating bridges can be moved to adjust the intonation if necessary.

➤— **Saddle, Tailpiece**

TOP AND ABOVE: The scratchplate and bridge of a Rickenbacker 360.
ABOVE FAR LEFT: The soundhole of a Spanish guitar.
LEFT: Using string cleaner can increase the life of your strings.

SADDLE

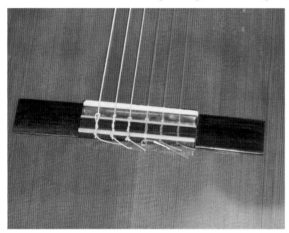 The saddle is the place on a guitar's bridge for supporting the strings. The distance between it and the nut determines the scale length (length of vibrating

open string) of a guitar. Acoustic guitars tend to have a one-piece saddle, made of bone or plastic, fixed at a slightly slanting angle so that the intonation of all six strings is correct. Electric-guitar saddles usually have six substructures, each with a groove over which a string passes. Some guitars have adjustable saddles that can be lowered or raised to alter their action.

➤ *Action, Bridge*

TREMOLO ARM

 A tremolo arm (also known a vibrato arm or whammy bar) is a mechanical arm attached to the bridge of an electric guitar that can alter the pitch of the strings; as the arm is depressed, the pitch of a note played drops, and when the arm is let go, the altered pitch returns to normal. Early tremolo arms tended to make guitars go out of tune but more recent ones, such as the Floyd Rose systems, are capable of greater pitch variations, locking the strings at the nut so they do not go out of tune.

B-BENDER

 A B-bender is a pitch-altering device that can pull up the B string (the guitar's second string) one whole step. It fits into Telecaster-styled electric guitars and can be used to simulate pedal steel and other guitar effects. The B-bender has been used extensively by well-known Telecaster players such as Danny Gatton, Steve Morse, Roy Buchanan and Jerry Donahue. Its instantly recognizable sound can be heard on many songs, including Led Zeppelin's 'All My Love' and The Eagles' 'Peaceful Easy Feeling'.

➤ *Fender Telecaster*

LEFT AND ABOVE LEFT: The saddles of an electric and a Spanish guitar.
TOP: The tremolo arm of a Gretsch 6120.
ABOVE: A B-bender can be used to simulate the sound of a pedal steel.

TAILPIECE

Some guitars have a tailpiece, which is a wooden or metal frame for holding the strings at the body end of the guitar. On such guitars the strings are fixed at the tailpiece and usually pass over a floating bridge attached to the guitar's body. The tailpiece was a prominent feature on archtop guitars, which first appeared during the 1920s and were hugely popular through to the late 1950s. Most modern guitars have their strings attached at a fixed bridge to pass over a saddle on or close to the bridge on the guitar's body.

➤— *Bridge, Saddle*

JACK PLUG

A 6 mm (¼ in) mono jack plug is the standard connection at either end of a typical guitar lead. One end plugs into a 6 mm (¼ in) jack socket on the guitar's body to take the signal out of the instrument, and the other end plugs into a 6 mm (¼ in) jack socket on an electronic device to deliver the signal into it.

BELOW: Jack plugs, which are the standard cable connection for most electrical effects and guitars.
BOTTOM: The decorative tailpiece of a Rickenbacker 360.

CAPO

A capo is a simple device that allows the pitch of the guitar's open strings to be changed. Taking the nut of the guitar as the zero fret, the open strings played at this zero fret will usually be tuned to E, A, D, G, B and E, starting from the sixth string. A capo uses a spring, lever or piece of elastic to hold a hard covered band over the guitar neck. This band can be placed behind any of the frets, thus creating a new position for the zero fret, or open string. If the capo is placed just before the fifth fret, the guitar will be raised in tuning by a perfect 4th. The new tuning of the open strings will therefore be A, D, G, C, E and A. The capo is typically used to help vocalists sing in a key that may be more suitable to their vocal range. Electric guitar players use them too, although this is slightly less common.

➤— *Open Tunings*

PLECTRA

A plectrum (plural – plectra or plectrums) is a device that allows you to pick an individual guitar string. For as long as there have been guitars, there have been plectra to go with them. Typically, they are held between thumb and first finger, and come in varying widths and shapes, ranging from heavy to light, even down to super light. Generally, light plectra are favoured by rhythm players, and heavier styles are better suited to the extreme attack needed for soloing. The angle at which the plectrum is held can also affect the sound of the note played, while techniques like pinched harmonics can be executed with just a tiny fraction of the plectrum visible between thumb and first finger. Some players use their own patented

plectra; for example, Brian May uses a sixpenny coin, while country and bluegrass players may well use small plectra (finger-picks) attached to each finger for rolling banjo-style guitar.

>— *Flat-Picking, Picking, Sweep-Picking, Thumb Pick*

STRAP

As guitar players moved from the back of the jazz or orchestra setting to the front of the stage, they found they had a problem: their guitars didn't stand

on the floor, so they needed to hang them around their necks. Straps nowadays come in a multitude of styles, ranging from simple nylon to leather, clear vinyl and elaborate mosaic embroidery. The majority of electric guitars have studs or strap buttons to fix a strap on the rear of the body and on the upper horn. Some acoustics and semi-acoustics feature strap buttons on the rear of the neck-to-body join.

>— *Strap Lock*

STRAP LOCK

Fitting your guitar with strap locks may be worthwhile to avoid an on-stage disaster. A strap lock replaces the simple strap buttons that are fitted as standard with a screw-in strap holder, preventing damage to precious instruments. For a small outlay, they're one of the best buys that a performing musician can make.

>— *Strap*

THUMB PICK

Thumb picks are often used by fingerstyle players who want to accentuate bass notes. A thumb pick fits over the end of the thumb, with the pick protruding to strike the strings. Some players use a thumb pick in conjunction with their fingers, while others use it along with other finger-picks for their other fingers.

>— *Finger-Style*

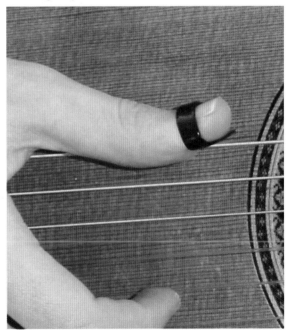

ABOVE: Using a thumbpick.
ABOVE LEFT: A guitar strap – an essential piece of kit for any guitarist.
TOP: An array of plectra.
OPPOSITE PAGE: A capo, and as demonstrated by James Taylor.

CASE

Every guitar needs at some time or other to be stored safely, away from damp, dirt and general destruction. There are a number of options for safely storing your guitar, and most dealers will supply one or the other with the instrument when it is sold. The most basic is a simple vinyl covering with a zip around the outer edge. This affords the guitar no structural protection whatsoever, but will at least make it easier to transport and keep it free of dust. Far more reliable is the gig bag, which is a hefty, padded nylon or cloth casing. A gig bag will usually also include straps so the guitar can be carried on your back, and outside pockets so you can store useful gadgets or spare strings. Lastly, a hard case is the heaviest but safest option for transporting your instrument safely. Some, such as the Gibson variety, come moulded to the shape of the instrument and include a silk cover for protecting its surface; others come in simple rectangular shapes, often lushly finished in foam and soft nylon padding.

FAST WINDER

Many players find changing strings quite a pleasant and therapeutic business, and once you have the technique down to a fine art, it is not overly time-consuming to change routinely all six strings. For some players, however, time is essential in performing a string change – particularly for professional roadies or guitar technicians who might have to change the strings of many guitars every day, or who might have to change a vital broken string in between the songs of a live set. A fast winder is a simple device that lets you quickly wind the capstan of the tuning peg with a single, smooth, easy turning action. Many players also prefer this technique, as it helps wind the string more evenly than turning the machine-head manually. Some roadies will even use converted power drills to wind on strings very quickly.

>— *Repairs – Simple*

FRET FILE

A fret file is a simple device for sanding down uneven or protruding frets on your guitar. It can also be used to smooth off the edges of badly finished or new frets at the edges of the guitar neck. There is an easy way of discovering if any of the frets are too high on the neck of your guitar, but first you must check that there are no other problems, such as a badly set action (string height) or a warped neck. Check the section on repairs to find out how to do this. To check your frets, play each fret on each string one at a time. A high fret will cause a buzzing sound when you play the fret below it. To file it down, use a fret file in a smooth easy action, working up and down the neck. Check frequently that you do not file too much off, or that you do not file down the surrounding frets too. A curved fret file can then be used to recreate the exact camber of the surrounding frets. Then restring the guitar and check again for buzzes along the neck. If in doubt about performing this kind of guitar surgery, take the instrument to your nearest dealer, who should be able to recommend a reliable guitar technician.

>— *Guitar Technician, Repairs – Simple*

CLEANING YOUR GUITAR

Keeping your guitar in good order is very important, and cleaning it every time you play is an essential part of this process. Firstly, always use a soft cloth to wipe down the strings after playing, and try pulling the strings away from the fingerboard and letting go a couple of times to dislodge any dirt build-up. This will dramatically extend their lifespan, and make the guitar much more playable the next time you pick it up. Secondly, use a non-abrasive cloth to wipe down the neck and body of the guitar, especially metal areas such as pickup covers and machine-heads, which can easily rust or tarnish if left damp or

LEFT: A guitar's case protects it from damage.
BELOW LEFT: A fast winder can save a lot of time when changing strings.
BELOW: Cleaning your guitar is a very important habit to get into.

unprotected. You can use any household spray polish on the lacquered body of your electric or acoustic guitar to remove grubby finger-marks and smears, and you can also use a similar cream or spray on the fingerboard. Make sure you clean the polish off thoroughly and work it well into the grain. Guitars with French-polish or oiled finishes (particularly classical guitars) will need to be cleaned with special oils and polish. If your guitar is of this type, ask your dealer what materials you should and should not use on it.

>— *Repairs*

CONSTRUCTION MATERIALS

The choice of woods used in guitar construction is essential to the final sound. Some makers have tried alternative materials: Dan Armstrong made some flashy Perspex electrics back in the 1970s; headless Steinberger guitars used graphite, as did the Parker Fly in the 1990s; and one British company, Alum, even turned out pressed aluminium-bodied guitars. But nothing beats the qualities of wood for sustain, resonance and natural strength.

The classic electric guitar, the Fender Telecaster, is simply two pieces of ash bolted together, while Gibson's famous Les Paul uses a heftier, more resonant mahogany body with a thin, arched maple top. As far as acoustic guitars are concerned, the harder the wood for the back and sides, the brighter the sound. Thin solid woods are best for acoustic resonance and strength. Traditionally, the back and sides of a guitar are made of a hardwood, such as rosewood, particularly the rare and expensive Brazilian rosewood. Alternatives include koa, mahogany, maple or bovinga. The neck will be made of a strong wood resistant to bending, such as mahogany or maple. The face or soundboard is always made of a softwood, such as Sitka or another kind of spruce. The soft wood of the face flexes to produce sound waves which the harder back and sides echo and amplify. Nowadays, plywoods and laminates are used on cheaper instruments as wood supplies become rarer and more expensive. Even the legendary Martin company now produces some laminate-bodied acoustics. Some makers are also championing the use of 'smart woods', cultivating a new ecological interest among guitar manufacturers as world supplies of choice hardwoods such as mahogany and rosewood become ever more depleted.

Maple

Maple is a hardwood commonly used in the manufacture of guitars, particularly the fingerboards and necks of Fender solid-bodies, such as the Telecaster or Stratocaster. The bodies of such guitars are typically made of ash or alder. Maple is a widely accepted alternative to rosewood for the finest quality resonance.

Korina

This is the trademark name for African limba wood, used on many Gibson models from the late 1950s onwards.

Rosewood

Rosewood is a heavy, expensive wood commonly used in the manufacture of guitar fingerboards. Some guitars in the Martin range come in all-rosewood bodies, and Fender famously made an all-rosewood Telecaster for George Harrison, later seen in the 'Get Back' television performance on the roof of Abbey Road studios.

➤ *Luthier*

CONSTRUCTION MATERIALS, OTHER

Mahogany

The inventor of the first Gibson solid-body, Les Paul, wanted a natural sustain of 25 seconds on the guitar. To achieve this, a heavy block of richly resonant mahogany was used for the body. These guitars are still known for their legendary sustain.

Spruce

Spruce is the wood most commonly found as the soundboard of good-quality acoustic instruments. It is a reasonably soft wood, giving plenty of natural projection to the final sound. Pine is a similar replacement.

Brass

The bridge or nut of a guitar has to be constructed of a very solid, durable material. Traditionally, this has meant the use of bone, ivory or even mother-of-pearl on high-quality instruments. Most production models use plastic equivalents. Some electric players choose to upgrade the plastic nut to a brass model. This gives better sustain, a brighter tone, and can increase tuning reliability.

Bone

Some players choose to upgrade the plastic nut of a modern acoustic guitar to ivory or bone. This gives better sustain and can increase tuning reliability.

Graphite

With the advent in the 1980s of high-performance rock guitars with locking tremolos and locking nuts, every factor of a guitar's build quality came under new scrutiny. Many players found the hard-wearing qualities of graphite gave the nut a much better sustain and tuning reliability than simple plastic alternatives. Other recent alternatives to bridge and nut materials include micarta and corion, very hard-wearing synthetic polymers.

➤ *Bridge, Nut*

REPAIRS – ADVANCED

Truss rod adjustment

Steel-strung acoustic and electric guitars have a steel truss rod fitted along the length of the neck underneath the fingerboard. This is held at tension to counteract the pull of the strings on the headstock. Its purpose is to maintain a slight bow in the neck to allow the string to vibrate at its widest point, while enabling the string height further up the neck to be as low as possible. The truss rod tension may need adjusting if the guitar has been left without maintenance for a number of years, or whenever a set of heavier or lighter strings are fitted.

Checking truss rod tension

Hold the guitar in the playing position and using both hands fret the first and seventh fret. Look carefully at the small gap between the top of the seventh fret and the bottom of the low E string. This gap (or relief) should be no more than 0.013 in and can be measured using a set of spark gap feeler gauges, or a ruler. Alternatively, a fairly good rule of thumb is to use a standard-weight business

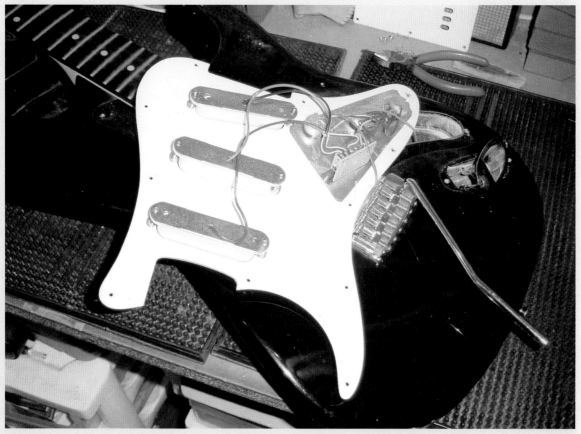

card. If the card can be slipped between the seventh fret and the string then the truss rod tension is satisfactory. Bass guitars require more relief. To adjust the truss rod it is necessary to find the adjustable nut at the end of the rod. On some Fender guitars this is a clearly visible 'bullet' behind the nut. Gibson and other guitars have a plate on the headstock, which must be removed. Some Telecasters and other similar guitars require that the neck be removed to gain access to the slotted key at the end of the neck. This job is best left to a repairperson.

If the neck has too much relief, the truss rod must be tightened by using the supplied key or wrench to turn the nut clockwise. Less than a quarter turn is required. As always, adjust and recheck until the correct adjustments have been made. A neck with too little relief requires that the truss rod be loosened slightly by turning the nut anti-clockwise. Again, use a very small adjustment and constantly recheck.

In general, always adjust the rod with the guitar tuned to concert pitch and in the playing position. Never force the adjustment. If the truss rod nut won't turn, the guitar should be taken to a repairperson. Too much tension can snap the rod, requiring that the fingerboard be removed to replace it.

Replacing a simple two-conductor Stratocaster-style pickup

Pickup replacement is a simple job that brings enormous benefits to the sound and value of your instrument. Replacement pickups of a much better quality than those fitted to most budget Far Eastern guitars can be purchased for around £30.

ABOVE: When replacing a pickup, first remove the scratchplate.
LEFT: Measuring the action of a guitar with a ruler.
ABOVE LEFT: Check for faults in the guitar's neck by looking along it.

To replace a pickup, first remove the strings and scratchplate screws. Store in a small bag for safe keeping. Trace the two conductors from the rear of the pickup to be replaced to the components on the underside of the scratchplate. Cut each wire carefully, leaving a small amount still attached to the guitar. This makes it much easier to identify the correct tags later on. Remove the height-adjustment screws and catch the two springs that will now be free. Remove the pickup from the hole. Assemble the new pickup and scratchplate using either the screws supplied or the original parts. Take the two conductors and trim 5 mm (0.2 in) of insulation from each. Carefully tin the bare ends with hot solder. Unsolder the remaining hot conductor from the underside of the pickup selector switch and make the tag ready for the new conductor. Solder the hot (white, or centre) conductor to the tag. Free the remaining ground wire from the rear of the volume control and replace with the new (black, or screen) ground wire. Attach the scratchplate to the guitar and refit the strings.

Note that some manufacturers use different colour coding, so check the instructions before fitting. Before replacing the scratchplate, test the new pickup by connecting the guitar to an amp and lightly tapping the polepices of the new pickup with a key or similar.

Fitting a replacement jack socket

The jack sockets are the part of your guitar most vulnerable to damage. Replacing a broken or worn socket is a simple job that can save a great deal of trouble.

Replacing a jack socket on a Fender-style guitar

Remove the two screws holding the recessed jack plate to the guitar then remove the old socket by releasing the nut holding the socket to the plate.

Cut away the ground and hot conductors as close as possible to the solder joints.

Trim and strip away 10 mm (0.3 in) of insulation from the cable, then strip 3 mm (0.1 in) of insulation from the centre conductor. Solder the screen of the cable to the tag connected to the ring of the socket. Solder the hot (centre) connector to the tag connected to the tip of the socket.

Replace the jack socket in the socket plate and attach to the top of the guitar.

➤ *Repairs – Simple, Truss Rod*

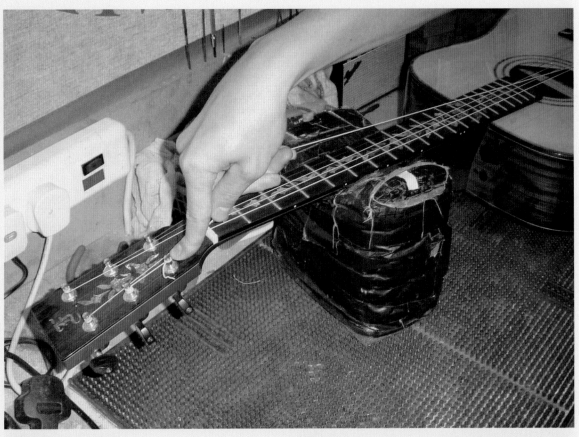

REPAIRS – SIMPLE

Broken String – Folk acoustic

Remove the broken string from the tuning machine. Ease a string-winding tool under the head of the bridge pin and use gentle downward pressure to lever the pin up and out of the bridge. Push the ball end of the fresh string into the empty hole and replace the pin. Note that the bridge pin has a groove in it to allow the string to pass by. The groove should face towards the soundhole.

Give the string a quick tug to ensure that the ball end is seated against the bottom of the pin, then pass the string through the capstan. There should be enough slack in the remaining string to allow it to be pulled about 7.5 cm (3 in) above the guitar. Use a string winder to wind neatly no more than four turns around the post. Plain strings may need more turns. Trim the excess string and tune.

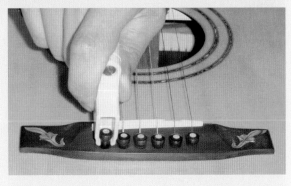

ABOVE LEFT: Before replacing the new pickup, it will need to be assembled.
LEFT: To replace a jack socket, it is necessary to first remove the jack plate.
ABOVE: When changing a string on an acoustic guitar, first remove the pin which holds it in place.
TOP: Once the new string has been inserted through the capstan, ensure enough slack has been left so that it can be wound around the post.

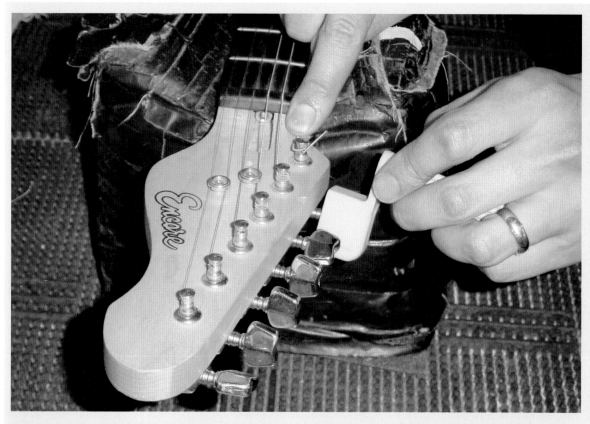

Broken string – electric, Stratocaster-style bridge

The fresh string is passed through one of six string holes from the rear of the guitar to emerge through the bridge. Tug the string to ensure it is seated correctly, then pass it through the tuning post and wind neatly three or four turns before trimming the excess.

Broken string – Spanish or classical-style

Pass the new string through the bridge in the direction of the bottom of the guitar until 5 cm (2 in) of string is showing clear of the bridge. Bring the short end up and over the bridge and pass from left to right under the string on the other side. Weave through the string from

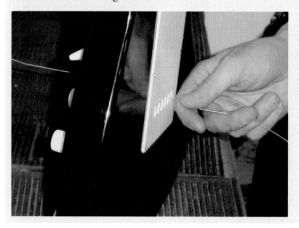

left to right until three turns are trapped between the string and the bridge and tug the free string to make the end tight. Pass the string through the hole in the tuning gear and neatly wind as many turns as possible onto the post. Plain strings must be passed twice through the post to minimize slipping.

Fretboard care – not for varnished fingerboards

Remove the strings and scrape rough dirt from the board with a clean cotton cloth until the wood is dry and clean. Take a piece of 000-gauge synthetic steel wool and gently rub over the length of the fingerboard. Take care not to press too hard – imagine you are brushing the coat of a dog. After a short time, the frets will become bright and the grain of the fingerboard will become clear.

Using your fingernail or a plectrum behind a thin piece of cotton or some kitchen wipes, remove residue trapped between the fret and fingerboard along the length of the neck. Wipe over the neck with a piece of clean cotton lightly dampened with prepared lemon oil or a very small amount of good-quality olive oil. Buff vigorously with
a cotton cloth until frets and fingerboard are glossy.

Intonation and string height adjustment

Check and, if necessary, adjust intonation and string height each time a new set of strings is fitted. If moving from different gauge, the intonation must be reset for each string. Correct string height is a matter of personal taste and dependent on the nature of your guitar.

String height – Fender-style bridge with individual saddles

Use the supplied hex wrench to raise or lower the height of each string saddle by turning the small height-adjustment screws in each saddle.

String height – Gibson-style ABS1 Tune-O-Matic bridge with adjustable pillars

Raise or lower the height of the bridge by turning the milled thumb wheel under the bass or treble sides. Some models have a slotted screw head on the upper surface of the bridge, requiring a screwdriver to adjust it.

String height – American-standard or Wilkinson-style bridge with fulcrum and pillars

Use the supplied hex key to raise or lower the bass and treble side of the bridge by screwing in or unscrewing each of the two retaining pillars at the front of the bridge.

Intonation adjustments

These must be made after string height has been adjusted. Lay the guitar down and connect to a good-quality electronic guitar tuner. Play the open E string and adjust using the tuner until the string is in tune. Stop the string at the 12th fret and note the pitch according to the tuner. This will indicate whether the intonation requires adjusting. If the tuner reads the same as the open string, then intonation for that string is perfect. If the tuner reads sharp or flat, the intonation will need adjusting.

For a flat string, using a screwdriver (or other tool) move the string saddle forward in the direction of the pickups. Adjust very slightly before checking the intonation, adjusting, rechecking etc., until both stopped and open strings read the same on the tuner. For a sharp string, follow the procedure as for a flat string but move the saddle backwards towards the bottom of the guitar.

➤ *Repairs – Advanced, Bridge, Capstan, Fret*

FAR LEFT: To change the string on an electric guitar, such as a Stratocaster, pass the new string through the rear of the guitar.
ABOVE FAR LEFT: Use a string winder to wind the string around the post.
LEFT: Secure strings on a Spanish guitar.
TOP: Fretboards should be cleaned with a piece of clean cotton moistened with lemon oil or olive oil.
ABOVE: Intonation adjustment on an electric guitar.

TUNER, ELECTRONIC

While many players still like to tune their instruments by ear, very few of us have hearing sensitive enough to pitch notes perfectly in unison with each other. The simplest answer is an electronic tuner, of which different kinds are available from anything between £10 and £1,000. The most basic types work by plugging the guitar into a single-input jack on the tuner, and will show via a needle display how near the tuning is to a selection of predetermined notes (usually E, A, D, G, B, E). These devices may also be fitted with an internal microphone to allow an acoustic guitar to be tuned. Many more elaborate tuners will show the exact note being played and the quarter or eighth-tone variations of it. These are called chromatic tuners, and come as standard in most multi-FX units.

➤ *Multi-FX*

A-B BOX

An A-B box is a signal router that allows an electric guitar player to connect one guitar to two amplifiers, or to switch between two guitars that are connected to one amplifier. This is very useful for live situations when a player wants to switch guitars or amps to get a completely different sound for a different song. Alternatively, an A-B box could be used by two players in a live situation. Such a box can be active (containing battery powered circuits) or passive (requiring no external power source).

FOOTSWITCH

A footswitch is a device that allows you to change guitar sounds during a live performance without having to stop playing. Many combo amps have channels with equalization and reverb settings that can be changed with a footswitch. There is also a wide variety of floor foot pedals that can allow you to introduce effects such as chorus, delay, tremolo, flanging, wah-wah and even guitar synthesis to spice up your soloing. More sophisticated live

players will often use a pedal board to control a large rack of devices including effects, filters and amps.

>— *AB Box*

TALK BOX

A talk box creates the impression of a speaking guitar by utilizing the guitarist's mouth cavity as a sound-shaping filter. A small amp sends sound along a plastic tube into the mouth and the guitarist mouths the words while playing the guitar notes. Talk boxes have been used by Peter Frampton, Joe Walsh and Richie Sambora.

E-BOW

The E-Bow (electronic bow) is a hand-held device used to create bowed sounds and endless sustain on a single string by creating a feedback loop. Manufactured by Heet Sound, it was invented by Greg Heet. The E-Bow first appeared in 1976, and is still available.

The E-Bow produces a magnetic field and, when held over the pickup, sets the string into vibration without it having to be plucked.

PRE-AMP

Many amplifiers and DI boxes contain what is known as a pre-amplifier, a device that can be used to generate extra signal gain. Such devices are often used

when acoustic instruments are amplified and when electric players need a bit more edge in their tone. The pre-amp passes the boosted signal to the amp's tone controls, which are used to change the guitar's bass, middle and treble characteristics, before the signal is amplified further by the more powerful main amplifier. Experiment with the pre-amp and main volume controls of a guitar amplifier and you'll be surprised at the number of completely different sounds you can find.

>— *DI Box, Electro-Acoustic*

TRANSISTOR AMPS

Early transistor (solid-state) guitar amps gained a bad reputation for their superclean sound, limited dynamic range and abrupt onset of harsh distortion. Modern designs however are vastly improved and aim to emulate the type of distortion produced by valve amps, with some models even including a valve in the pre-amp stage.

>— *Amp Simulator, Pre-Amp*

ABOVE FAR LEFT: An electronic tuner.

LEFT: Using a footswitch means that you can change sounds while playing.

ABOVE: An E-Bow can create endless sustain.

TOP: A Fender transistor amp.

SPEAKER

A loudspeaker or speaker is a device that converts audio-frequency signals into sound waves so you can hear them. There are many different types of speakers: woofers are large speakers capable of handling bass and sub-bass frequencies, while tweeters are small speakers that are excellent for high frequencies. Many speaker cabinets contain a range of different speakers to cover as much of the audio-frequency range as possible. Electric guitar combos and stacks do not use tweeters and consequently do not reproduce the very high frequencies that are generally thought to create an unpleasant guitar sound.

➤— *Combo Amps, Stack*

COMBO AMPS

Combo amps are a combination of amplifier and loudspeaker cabinet and tend to be more portable and convenient than an equivalent combination of separate amps and speakers. Whenever these two parts are built into one box the device may be called a combo rather than simply an amp. A combo amp is typically set out in two parts. At the top of the cabinet a pre-amp and power amp are combined. The amp may have one or two channels and some simple effects, such as reverb or a tremolo. A two-channel amp will offer one 'clean'

VALVE AMPS

Valve amps are the preferred choice of many guitarists as they respond particularly well to playing dynamics. The first guitar amps from the 1950s used valves, the prevailing technology of the time, and the basic circuitry has changed very little since. As their valves are driven into overload these amps produce the gradual onset of a smooth musical distortion, rich in low-order harmonics. The sound can go from clean, through progressive shades of crunch, up to full-on overdrive with plenty of sustain. The distortion can come from both the pre-amp valves and the power amp (output) valves, which is why some valve amps sound best when turned up loud. Modern valve amps may have several gain stages in the pre-amp for more overdrive, with a master-volume control to regulate the level through the power amplifier.

➤— *Pre-Amp*

FAR LEFT AND BELOW LEFT: A valve and a Fender valve amp, a popular amplifier amongst guitarists.
LEFT: Combo amps are a combination of amplifier and loudspeaker.
BELOW: A Marshall cab.

CAB (CABINET)

This box houses speakers that receive the output from an amplifier head. Cabs often contain several speakers, fitted in series or parallel, to improve the handling of the signal coming out of the amp. Large speakers are poor at handling high frequencies, while small speakers are not good for lows, so speaker cabinets often come fitted with twin-cone speakers that have a small speaker cone mounted in front of a larger one, and are driven by the same voice coil to give a good bass and treble response.

channel and one 'dirty' channel together with the ability to switch between them using either a button on the amp or a footswitch. The amp may also have other professional features such as an effects loop, a line out for recording, a connection for headphones or even a connection to play a CD player through it. Underneath the amp section is a box or 'cabinet' containing one or more loudspeakers. The speakers are matched to the amp. A reverb unit is sometimes fitted to the bottom of speaker cabinet, in a place furthest away from the amp so as to reduce interference.

Combos are often used for practice or at small gigs where a huge speaker stack is not needed to produce high volumes, though many major artists use them in conjunction with a PA system at their concerts. Famous combos include the Fender Twin Reverb (80-100 Watts), Roland Jazz Chorus (120 Watts), Mesa Boogie (60-100 Watts), Vox AC15 (15 Watts) and the legendary Vox AC30 (30 Watts).

➤— *Cabinet*

EFFECTS

MULTI-FX

Multi-FX is the name given to a combined effect constructed by using several individual effects types at the same time. A digital Multi-FX unit, either in the form of a stompable floor unit or rack-mounted box, usually features a range of individual effects that can be used singly or combined.

➤ *Effects*

CHORUS

Chorus is a shimmering, spacious sound that creates the perception that more than one instrument is playing, and is particularly effective in stereo. Working on the principle that two instruments playing in unison will be minutely out of time and out of tune with each other, chorus mixes a delayed signal with the original sound. The delay time changes constantly over a small range so that the sound is moving slowly in and out of pitch, this change (or modulation) being governed by an LFO (Low Frequency Oscillator). Chorus pedals usually have rate and depth adjustment controls.

➤ *Flanger, Phaser*

DELAY, ANALOGUE

Analogue delays first appeared in the 1970s and are the link between tape delay and digital delay. An analogue delay is an electronic device creating its repeats by using 'Bucket Brigade' technology, where a charge is passed along a series of capacitors like a chain of firemen passing buckets of water. The resulting sound is less pristine but warmer than a digital delay, though with the Bucket Brigade technology only short delay times are

possible. Typical analogue delay pedals include the Boss DM2 and the Electro Harmonix Memory Man as used by The Edge in U2's early days.

DELAY, DIGITAL

A digital delay samples and stores the guitar's sound and plays it back after a defined period. Each repeat is a clone of the original sound and, unlike tape and analogue delay, exhibits no signal degradation, thus producing a very clean sound. To provide variation among the repeats, some digital delays have facilities to reduce the treble content of the repeats, achieving a more natural sound. Some digital delays

slightly different timbre, generally getting duller and less distinct. This is due partly to the guitar sound being degraded slightly when recorded on to analogue tape. Classic tape delays include the Hank Marvin on the early Shadows' hits, Maestro Echoplex, Watkins (WEM) Copycat and the Roland Space Echo.

REVERB

Reverberation is the natural ambient sound of a room or space. Artificial reverberation (reverb) can envelop the guitar sound, putting a sense of space around it, making it sound distant, and increasing the perception of sustain. There are two basic methods of supplying reverb to the guitarist – spring reverb and digital reverb. Spring reverb is often built into older guitar amps. It creates the sound from the physical vibrations of a spring. Digital reverb can offer simulations of different-sized spaces, usually halls and rooms, and can mimic the sound of artificial reverb devices such as the reverb plates and chambers used in studios.

are capable of multiple taps – separate repeats generated at set intervals after the initial sound. The analogy is a water pipe with taps at different points along its length where water (a repeat) can be drawn off. Each replay head on a tape delay unit would generate a separate repeat so these were the original multitap machines. Some digital delays allow you to set the exact amount of delay time between the various taps, simulating the different replay heads of a tape delay, and can also create stereo effects like ping-pong delay, where the sound appears to bounce across the stereo image.

ROTARY SPEAKER (LESLIE)

A Rotary speaker is an electromechanical device that makes a sound similar to chorus. Most well known is the two-speed Leslie speaker, largely associated with Hammond organs, which relies on a rotating horn and drum to distribute the sound. Famous examples of a guitar through a rotary speaker include the lead guitar part from the Beatles' 'While My Guitar Gently Weeps' and the middle section from Cream's 'Badge' (both played by Eric Clapton).

➤— *Chorus*

DELAY, TAPE

Tape delay utilizes a continuous loop of magnetic recording tape driven by a motor in constant motion past a recording head and single or multiple replay heads. The signal from the guitar is recorded on to the tape, producing a repeat or echo as the tape passes the replay head (or heads). The delay time is dependent on the speed of the tape and the distance between the heads. Signals can also be sent back electronically from the replay head to the record head to create more repeats, a technique known as regeneration. This type of delay is characterized by a natural sound, each repeat having a

NOISE GATE

A noise gate can be used to silence low-level noise in the intervals when the guitar is not being played. This is useful in suppressing audible hiss and hum from noisy effects pedals. When the signal level falls below a threshold set by the user the gate closes, silencing the signal.

ABOVE LEFT: A Multi-FX pedal.
LEFT: A chorus pedal creates a shimmering, spacious sound.
ABOVE: A Yamaha digital delay pedal.

COMPRESSOR/LIMITER

Compressors are used in recording to control volume levels by automatically turning down louder signals, thus reducing the dynamic range. This makes quieter sounds louder and louder sounds quieter, producing a more consistent signal perceived to be louder overall. A limiter is a special kind of compressor that will not allow the signal to rise above a specific level – the sound will get no louder no matter how hard you pick. In guitar terms, a compressor can be used to give longer sustain, to shape the envelope of a note and add swell to slide parts.

➤— *Home Recording, Studio Recording*

FLANGER

Flanging, characterized by a prominent sweeping sound, can produce a series of effects, such as the whooshing 'jet taking off' sound and a metallic warbling reminiscent of sci-fi ray guns. It is a time-based effect, similar to chorus, in that a signal is mixed with a delayed copy of itself, the delay changing constantly. The delay range used by flanging is shorter than that used by chorus, and a flanger also usually has a resonance control that can feed some of the output back to the input, enhancing the peaks in the frequency response and making the sound more intense.

➤— *Chorus, Phaser*

TREMOLO

Tremolo, originally a feature of old Fender and Vox amps, creates cyclical changes in volume. The effect of this is a rhythmic pulsing or throbbing sound, or even a sense of the sound being chopped into pieces. The nature of the tremolo is governed by the shape of the waveform used to create it. A sine wave produces a gentle, smooth tremolo with the sound fading in and out, while a square wave creates the effect of the sound being turned on and off very quickly. The speed of the effect is variable, as is the depth of the volume change.

VIBRATO (EFFECT)

The electronic vibrato effect creates rhythmically timed small variations in pitch between sharp and flat. The effect usually has a speed control and a depth control to govern the amount of pitch change.

➤— *Tremolo Arm*

PHASER

A phaser has a characteristic swirling sound that can be varied with a speed (or rate) control from a slow, evolving tone colour enhancing a rhythm-guitar part, to a bubbling, underwater effect. It does this by creating equally spaced notches in the frequency range where sounds are eliminated. The notches are moved automatically up and down the frequency spectrum using an internal LFO (Low Frequency Oscillator), allowing us to hear the change in the frequency peaks between the notches. The MXR Phase 90 was heard extensively on the first two Van Halen albums.

ENVELOPE FOLLOWER/FILTER

An envelope-controlled filter can produce an automatic wah effect or a squelchy synth-like filter sound in response to the strength of the guitarist's picking. Hitting a note triggers a filter sweep, the tone being shaped directly by the level of the input signal.

Depending on the model, adjustments may include whether the sweep be triggered up or down, the sensitivity of the effect to the input signal, filter resonance and choice of filter type. Probably the most famous of this type of effect is the Mutron III, as used by funk bassist Bootsy Collins.

➤ *Wah-Wah*

DISTORTION

Distortion is a generic term for the sound produced by fuzz, overdrive and, indeed, distortion pedals, all of which demonstrate different aspects of the same kind of effect. More specifically, a distortion pedal produces a crunchier and grittier tone than an overdrive pedal.

➤ *Fuzz, Overdrive*

OVERDRIVE

An overdrive pedal is a kind of distortion pedal whose sound is closer to the natural, soft clipping of an overdriven valve amp and maintains the character of the original signal. The Ibanez Tube Screamer is a typical example, and was used by Stevie Ray Vaughan to boost the signal into his amp.

➤ *Distortion*

FUZZ

Fuzz, introduced to a mass audience by Keith Richards on 'Satisfaction', is a raspy, buzzy and fuzzy distortion. Fuzz is produced by clipping the tops off the rounded sine wave of the guitar signal, thus creating a square wave. Classic 1960s fuzz boxes include the Tone Bender and the Fuzzface, as used by Jimi Hendrix.

➤ *Distortion, Overdrive*

LEFT: A Boss distortion pedal.
BELOW: The Boss Super Overdrive.
FAR LEFT: Compressors are used to control volume levels.
BELOW LEFT: A Boss tremolo pedal.

OCTAVE SPLITTER

An octave splitter divides a note's fundamental frequency to create an extra note, often distorted, an octave (or two octaves) below, which is then mixed in with the original note. The effect, typified by the Octavia and the MXR Blue Box, can sound like two instruments played tightly in unison. The octave splitter has been replaced by the digital pitch shifter.

➤ *Pitch Shifter*

PITCH BEND

Pedal-operated pitch bend is a digital effect that can bend the input signal to a specified pre-set pitch, similar to extreme use of a guitar's vibrato arm. It can also add a harmony to the dry sound, with the pedal able to bend the harmony sound between two pre-set intervals, as featured by the Digitech Whammy pedal.

PITCH SHIFTER/HARMONISER

A pitch shifter can generate one or more notes at fixed intervals alongside your original note to create harmonies. One common use of pitch shifting is to use very small pitch shifts of, say, +/– eight cents (very small increments of pitch change – a cent is 1% of a semitone) to subtly thicken and widen a sound.

Since the early 1990s, newer models such as 'intelligent' harmonisers have become widely available. These are so-called because they analyse the note being played and respond with a different amount of pitch shift accordingly. This is typically used to toggle between major and minor thirds, based on a predetermined home key.

RING MODULATOR

A ring modulator can create strange atonal metallic timbres and bell-like sounds from a guitar signal. It works by combining two inputs (the guitar and a carrier signal created by an internal oscillator) into one output, creating a wholly new sound using the sum and difference of the signals.

WAH-WAH

One of the most recognizable guitar effects, wah-wah was originally intended to imitate the crying tone of a muted trumpet, but became an expressive tool in its own right when soloing or being used to create 'wack-wacka' funk rhythms. Basically a band pass filter with a variable resonant frequency, a foot-operated wah pedal shifts a peak in the frequency response up and down the frequency spectrum, emphasizing the higher frequencies when pressed down and the lower ones when brought back, the overall movement creating that classic wah sound. Wah-wah effects can also be produced automatically by an envelope follower.

➤— *Envelope Follower*

VOLUME PEDAL (SWELL PEDAL)

A volume pedal allows guitarists to control the volume of the sound with their foot. The pedal can

be used to swell in a note gradually so that its natural attack is not heard, creating a sound more akin to a bowed instrument like a violin.

➤ *Violining*

EFFECTS SEND/RETURN (FX SEND)

All good mixers have auxiliary send connectors for most of their channels. These connectors can be used to send a channel's signal into an external effects unit for processing and then feed the processed soundback into the mixer via a return port. The amount of signal going into the effects processor can be adjusted – and therefore the amount of effect in the mix – by using a control that is dedicated to this function. It is generally considered good practice to record instruments like acoustic guitars and saxophones dry (with no effects) and then apply effects to them later with sends and returns.

MID-RANGE

The mid-range part of the audio spectrum is the area between the bass and treble ranges. It is important for a recorded guitar to have enough mid-range to give it depth, but not so much that it becomes over-powering. Most mixers and guitar amps have separate

controls to allow you to increase or decrease the amount of bass, mid-range and treble in your guitar tone.

➤ *EQ*

TOP (TREBLE)

The treble region of the sound spectrum. A lot of guitar players with two pickups on their instruments use the more treble-sounding pickup for performing solos. This is because it produces notes with a crisper definition, which cut more clearly through a mix and make the solo audible above the rest of the band.

VIOLINING

Violining is an effect in which a guitar's volume control (or a volume pedal) is used to fade in the sound from nothing to create a soft attack to the note. Violining can be applied to individual notes to provide interesting nuances during solos, or to whole chords to get a mysterious, haunting fade-in effect. Auto-violining can be achieved using a noise gate with a slow attack value. Rock legends such as Gary Moore, Jimmy Page and Mark Knopfler have used violining to great effect.

LEFT AND ABOVE: The Cry Baby wah-wah pedal and Jimi Hendrix's Electric Ladyland (1968), on which he used the wah-wah sound to startling effect. TOP: Violining: the little finger adjusts the volume control while playing.

MANUFACTURERS

AMPEG

Ampeg was a New York-based company most famous for making a classic line of valve-powered amps in the late 1950s and 1960s, including massive power set-ups for rock goliaths like The Who and Pink Floyd in the mid-1970s. The company is also known for its Portaflex range of bass-guitar amps, which included a separate amp head within the speaker cabinet, a design that several other makers were to copy in the future. Ampeg also teamed up with guitar designer Dan Armstrong in the early 1970s to produce clear plastic-bodied guitars and basses. Apart from its distinctive visual appeal, the plastic body was meant to improve sustain. Famous users include Ronnie Wood from the Rolling Stones.

➤ *Marshall*

ARIA

During the 1970s and 1980s, an increasing number of guitars began to be made in the East, particularly Japan. Rising production costs meant that genuine American models were getting too pricey for beginners, while traditional quality control at even the biggest brands, such as Fender, was beginning to slip. Among the key names in the Japanese influx was Aria, a company based at the Matsumoko factory, where it turned out exceptional-quality copies of many traditional US brands, such as Stratocaster and the Les Paul. The Fender Strat has since become by far the most copied guitar

design of all time, with some of the Japanese copyists getting so close to the American original that it fell to the lawyers to settle things, usually in Fender's favour. Aria continues today to make a range of high-quality original instruments at its plants in Japan and Korea. Their acoustic guitars, which are often also based on copies of classic US marques, are nowadays widely praised too.

➤ *Epiphone, Fender, Gibson, Gretsch, Martin*

BOSS

Boss is an offshoot of Japanese electronics giant Roland that deals almost exclusively with guitar effects and similar products. In the earliest days of guitar effects, users needed one solid consistent design for a floor-based effects unit, and with the ubiquitous Boss range they found it. Their first individual stomp box was the CE-1 Chorus Ensemble, the first widely accepted modulation effect in popular music. The sound was made famous by bands such as the Police, Genesis and Bon Jovi. The design of these great pedals has remained the same for years now, with their simple Tonka-toy construction and colour-coordination for easy stage use. Other popular pedals include the DD-5 Digital Delay, the HM-2 Heavy Metal and the BF-1 Flanger. Other notable additions to the Roland and Boss ranges include the Dr Rhythm drum machines and their simple bass sequencers, such as the TR-808, which were later to form the backbone of electronic house music.

➤ *Delay, Flanger*

BURNS

During the 1960s, the UK-based Burns Company produced some of the best-loved British guitars ever. The classic Bison and Marvin models are still widely sought after and both are genuinely unique. Hank Marvin of the Shadows was a famous endorser and played the guitar widely, attracting sales and popularity both in the UK and in the US. Burns was bought out by the US Baldwin company in the 1960s and never regained its status in the market. Gaz Coombes of Supergrass is a well-known player of Burns guitars, using one of the 1990s reissues of the vintage Bison model.

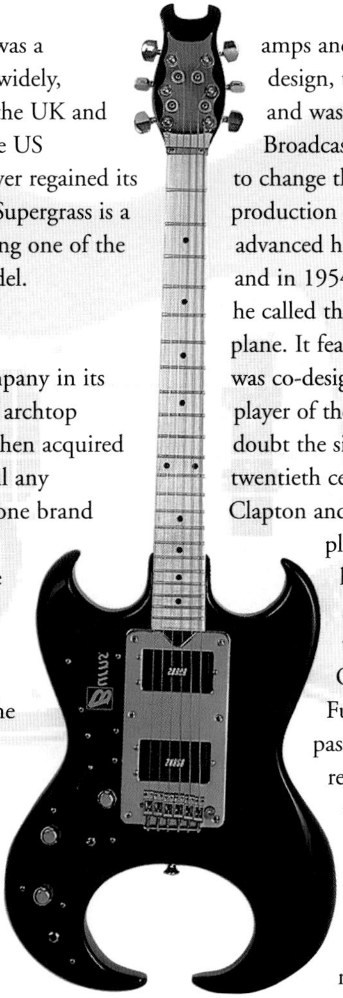

EPIPHONE

Until 1958 Epiphone was a company in its own right, producing a range of archtop acoustics and electric models. Gibson then acquired them, perhaps in an attempt to forestall any unwanted competition, and the Epiphone brand continued as a subsidiary of the Michigan-based guitar giant. Epiphone originals continue to be well regarded in their own right, especially from this 1960s period. The classic models include the Casino, based heavily on the slimline semi-solid Gibson ES330, the Sheraton and the Riviera, both of which used old-style trapeze tail-pieces and trademark mini-humbuckers. As the guitar market slowed down at the end of the 1960s, Gibson decided to move all Epiphone production to the Far East, where it remains today. Epiphone now produces a wide range of budget Gibson clones, including the Les Paul Standard and SG models. Paul Weller is a famous user of a 1964 Epiphone Casino.

>— *Gibson*

FENDER

Unlike the real old-time names such as Gibson and Martin, the Fender company was a relative newcomer to the world of musical-instrument production when it began making guitars in the 1940s. Clarence Leo Fender (1901–91) worked in his uncle's electrical shop and gradually became interested in the idea of electric amplification. In the mid-1930s he teamed up with a colleague, 'Doc' Kauffman, and started a business selling amps and lap-steel guitars. Fender's first original design, the Esquire, was first announced in 1949, and was launched on the market, as the Broadcaster, in 1951. Copyright reasons forced Leo to change this name to Telecaster, and the first production electric guitar in history was born. Leo advanced his designs further during the next few years and in 1954 came up with a three-pickup guitar which he called the Stratocaster, named after a Boeing jet plane. It featured a unique sprung-vibrato system that was co-designed by Freddie Tavares, a famous lap-steel player of the day. The Fender Stratocaster was without doubt the single most influential guitar design of the twentieth century – in the hands of players such as Eric Clapton and Jimi Hendrix, it would stretch guitar playing further than ever before. Leo Fender himself sold his business, which also made some of the finest guitar and bass amps in the world, to US corporation CBS in 1965. Quality began to deteriorate at the Fullerton, California plant, and several years passed before the Fender brand again drew the respect that it had during Leo's time. With the advent in the 1980s of so many high-quality Japanese copies, Fender introduced its own range of cut-price Eastern models under the Squier brand-name. Leo Fender himself went on to form another company, G&L, which continues to turn out exceptional US guitars based on his original design ideas. He died in 1991, aged 90.

>— *Fender Jazz Bass, Precision Bass, Stratocaster, Telecaster*

LEFT TOP: Ampeg is best known for its Portaflex range of bass-guitar amps, such as the one shown here.

LEFT CENTRE: An auto-wah effects unit from the classic Boss range.

LEFT: This hollow-bodied guitar is one of a number of models made by Japanese manufacturers Aria.

TOP: A Burns guitar.

ABOVE: A 1977 American Standard Fender Stratocaster.

GIBSON

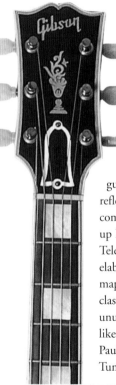

The Gibson company was set up in the early 1900s to make mandolins with a radical new carved-top technology, a feature that was to dominate their instrument design for the next 50 years. This arched-top design was far costlier to produce than the flattops of rivals such as Martin, but made Gibson guitars the most highly desirable instruments of the day, with classic archtops like the L5 and Super 400 among the most popular designs. Gibson have always been slow to accept change in the market, and it wasn't until the 1940s that they accepted flattop guitar design, after the success of the Martin Dreadnought models. The Gibson flattops quickly took off, however, particularly the heavy-bodied Jumbo models, such as the J-45 and the 'Super Jumbo' J-200.

It was even later that Gibson cottoned on to the solid-body electric guitar, teaming up with inventor and musician Les Paul to produce the first Gibson Les Paul solid-body in 1952. Les Paul made his first solid guitar, known as The Log, around 1940 from a simple slab of pine, parts salvaged from other guitars and his own electric pick-up. The first Gibson solid guitars, however, were pure class, reflecting the years of design tradition the company could boast of, and also showing up Leo Fender's crude bolt-together Telecaster. The original Les Paul had an elaborate gold finish, a sumptuous carved maple top, and a headstock based on their classic archtop models like the L5. The unusual trapeze tailpiece, which Les Paul liked, was soon discontinued, as was Les Paul's 'gold-top' finish. The patented Tune-O-Matic bridge was introduced in

1955, but it was not until three years later that the most prized models appeared: the 1958 Standard model, with a flame-top cherry-sunburst finish, and the classic Ted McCarty-designed PAF humbucking pickups. The glued-in neck and heavy body contribute to the guitar's legendary tone and sustain. Genuine 1958 models can fetch over £50,000 today. Famous owners include Gary Moore, Joe Walsh of the Eagles, Slash of Guns N' Roses and John Squire, formerly of the Stone Roses.

➤— *Archtop, Fender, Mandolin, Martin, Pickups*

GRETSCH

The company started by Fred Gretsch, of Brooklyn, New York, made archtop acoustic guitars from the 1920s onwards. But it was after tying

ABOVE: The head of a Gibson guitar.

RIGHT: The Beatles' manager, Brian Epstein, holding a Gretsch guitar.

FAR RIGHT: A customized Jackson Superstrat.

ABOVE FAR RIGHT: Steve Vai, a valued Ibanez customer.

itself in with country legend Chet Atkins that the company made some of its most famous and enduring designs, many of them named after their famous endorser. Famous users include George Harrison of the Beatles, who used a Gretsch Duo-Jet in the band's early days, before moving on to the Atkins-inspired models, the Tennessean and the Country Gentleman. Billy Duffy of the Cult and Dave Stewart of Eurythmics are also known for sporting the company's most ostentatious guitar, the White Falcon. Production of these guitars halted for a while in the 1980s, and it wasn't until 1990 that Fred Gretsch's great grandson began making Japanese copies of the original classics.

IBANEZ

Ibanez began making its own range of home-grown Japanese guitars in the 1960s, but the company really began to thrive when it started to copy US originals like the Stratocaster in the early to late-1970s. Unlike other companies from the east, Ibanez kept its eye on new models too, and became a real contender when the new wave of heavy-rock guitarists started to appear in the 1980s. With old makes too unreliable and lacking versatility, a new guitar was needed, one that is often referred to as the 'Superstrat', although this is an infringement of Fender's Stratocaster patent.

These guitars were designed for a new range of players from bands like Def Leppard, Iron Maiden and Saxon. Perhaps the most famous Ibanez user of all time is guitar wizard Steve Vai, who has several custom-designed models from the Ibanez stable. Vai also helped design a trademark seven-string guitar, to increase the potential of his phenomenally fast soloing. The Ibanez seven string has recently been rediscovered by a new generation of metal players, from bands such as Korn, Coal Chamber and Limp Bizkit, who use the extra string to give extra bass notes to their often radical playing.

Through the change in musical styles from the 1980s to the Nu Metal boom of the late 1990s, Ibanez has remained a major player in the rock guitar market.

➤ *Fender Stratocaster, Seven-String Guitar*

JACKSON/CHARVEL

More than any other company, Jackson, or Grover-Jackson as they are fully titled, were the leading name in the ultra-heavy-rock guitars of the 1980s. Commonly dubbed 'Superstrats', these guitars in fact have nothing to do with Fender's classic design of the 1950s. Instead of following the Stratocaster formula to the letter, Jackson increased the pickup capability, positioning a humbucker in the bridge position, fitted a Floyd-Rose locking tremolo for extra tuning stability and increased the length of the fretboard to 24 frets.

These guitars are also known for their downward-pointing headstocks and often lurid colour schemes. The first model the company made was the Soloist which, more than any other instrument, started the boom in what was to be called shred metal. Charvel is the brand-name the company uses for its Japanese-sourced instruments.

Shred metal is now out of fashion, but these guitars remain enduringly popular among die-hard rock fans.

➤ *Ibanez, Pickups, Superstrat, Tremolo Arm*

LUTHIER

A luthier is a guitar maker. Originally, the term was used only to describe classical guitar makers but now it is generally considered to apply to builders of all kinds of guitars and fretted instruments. Famous luthiers include C F Martin (founder of the Martin acoustic guitar company), Antonio de Torres (Torres classical guitars), Orville Gibson (Gibson), Mario Maccaferri (Maccaferri guitars, as used by Django Reinhardt), the Dopyera brothers (developers of National resonator guitars), Leo Fender (Fender), Charles Kaman (Ovation), Paul Reed Smith (PRS), Grover Jackson (Jackson), Ned Steinberger (Steinberger headless guitars) and Manuel Ramirez (Ramirez classical guitars).

MARSHALL

No logo is more synonymous with heavy rock and rock guitar playing than the gold-on-black Marshall stamp found on the front of their ever-popular amplifier heads and speaker cabinets. Pete Townshend windmilling madly in front of a huge stack of Marshall speaker cabinets became the image for a generation of rock fans in the 1970s. But like most musical ideas, it had humble beginnings. Jim Marshall, who still runs the company today, was a drummer who owned a music shop in 1960s London. He decided to remodel the classic bass amp of the day, the 4x10 Fender Bassman combo, into a cheaper British-made alternative. From the early days he decided to make separate amplifier sections, known as 'heads,' and speakers, or 'cabs', short for cabinets. With the well-tested method of 12AX7 valves in the pre-amp stage, the first Marshall amp, the JTM45, was born. These early models featured gold name-plates on a Plexiglas backing, and are often referred to as Marshall 'plexis'. The JTM45, running at 45 watts RMS, was soon joined by its bigger brother, the 100-watt JTM100, but distortion on these early amps was all natural – Jim didn't add a master volume, or a gain control, until 1975. So if you wanted to play dirty, you had to play loud. One of the most famous early Marshall recordings was Eric Clapton's outing with John Mayall's Bluesbreakers. At the time he was using a Gibson Les Paul and the most famous Marshall combo of them all, the 2x12 Bluesbreaker, and he reputedly deafened the

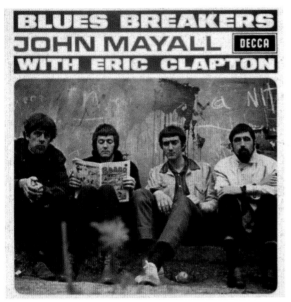

FAR RIGHT AND RIGHT: Famous users of Marshall equipment include Jimi Hendrix and Eric Clapton during his time with John Mayall's Bluesbreakers. BELOW: A Martin Dreadnought D-18 model.

engineers to get the harsh tone we hear on the record. Marshall equipment remains the mainstay of just about every serious rock guitarist's set-up, even with competition from newer companies like Mesa Boogie and Peavey.

➤ *Cab, Combo Amps, Head, Pre-Amp*

MARTIN

The Martin company, started by CF Martin in Nazareth, Pennsylvania in 1898, is responsible for the design of the acoustic guitar as we know it today. From the internal bracing structure to the ornamentation, the build of the headstock and the sound-hole, Martin acoustics are the template that every other maker has copied to this day. Using a soft, flattop on the guitar, usually spruce, gives it great sound projection, but the cross-bracing (or X-bracing) that Martin designed to keep the guitar sturdy without losing tone is the secret of these great instruments. Today almost every flattop acoustic uses the Martin X-bracing template. The most famous Martin design is their biggest-bodied model, the Dreadnought, named after a famous British battleship.

It features a wide body with square shoulders that is also deep, for good bass response. Compared to other designs of the day it is very large and boomy, perfect for vocal accompaniment and solo finger-style guitar. The classic Martin Dreadnoughts are the D-18 and D-28, but for a time in the 1930s they also made a heavily decorated model called the D-45. Martin guitars are referred to in a simple numerical code to show the body style and the level of decoration or ornamentation that the individual guitar has. Possible body styles are 'D' for Dreadnought, or '000', '00' and '0' in steadily descending body sizes. Ornamentation is measured by the second part of the guitar's name-tag, so '45' is the heaviest decoration, while '18' signifies the plainest model. The most visually stunning of all Martin guitars, the D-45, was first made for country star Gene Autry in 1932 and was reissued in 1970. Martin remains one of the most important names in acoustic guitar manufacture, in spite of competition from new kids on the block such as Taylor and Santa Cruz. Reflecting today's cost-conscious market, the cheapest Martin, the DXM, foresakes the traditional all-wood body and uses cheaper laminates.

➤ *Country, Soundhole*

MESA BOOGIE

US amplifier technician Randall Smith was looking for a new sound to suit the heavy, super-driven players of the early 1980s. He experimented with some of the old Fender models he had in his workshop and hot-rodded a 12-watt Fender Princeton combo with a 60-watt circuit. This vastly overdrives the pre-amp and leads to supersaturated but still harmonically sweet distortion. He lent the amp to Carlos Santana who said 'Wow, this really boogies!' And so Mesa Engineering and their now classic Boogie combo was born. Mesa Boogies remain high-quality amp systems, all valve-driven and often offering surprisingly low-output wattage, but with no shortage of classic Boogie wail.

➤ *Combo Amps, Distortion, Pre-Amp*

NATIONAL (DOBRO)

National is perhaps best known as the first major company to shift its focus from acoustic to electric instruments. But the company's origins were in resonator guitars, instruments with metal bodies and metal resonator cones, made of aluminium. These instruments first appeared in 1928. This design gave the guitar a louder sound than traditional wooden models, but made for a harsh and brittle metallic tone, which suited some styles of blues, particularly slide-guitar playing. A second company, Dobro, joined National in 1932, and the company began producing triplate resonators, or guitars with three metal cones that vibrated inside the body, thus amplifying the sound. The most

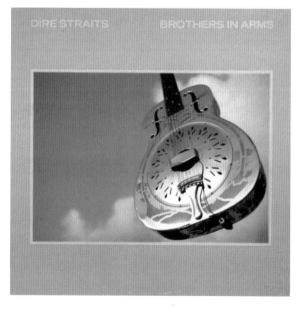

famous model, however, and the one that appears so famously on the cover of Dire Straits' *Brothers In Arms* album, is the National Style O, which features a single large resonating cone in the face of the guitar body, which is all made of pressed steel. The company also made lap-steel guitars and mandolins, and later made cheaper instruments under the Supra budget brand-name. National spotted early opportunities for the electric amplification of the guitar, but failed to capitalize on it in the way Rickenbacker, and later Fender, were to do so successfully. The company went bust in the 1950s but has since resurfaced, making resonator guitars to the original designs from the days of the Dobros.

➤— **Fender, Lap Steel, Mandolin, Rickenbacker**

OVATION

The Ovation company was started in the mid-1960s by Charles Kaman, who had made his name as an aerospace engineer. He tried to come up with a new answer to the problem of amplifying the traditional acoustic guitar, which until then had been done simply by placing a microphone in front of the soundhole while the guitarist played. This caused feedback and fluctuation in volume, and was difficult to master properly. Kaman invented a guitar which dispensed with traditional materials: it featured a back made of a Lycrachord plastic compound (until that time more often used in the aeronautics industry), and a pickup system consisting of piezo crystals. Piezo crystals generate small amounts of electricity when they are placed near a vibrating source, so placing individual piezo units under each string at the bridge created an acoustic pickup. Kaman found that the guitar needed to include an on-board pre-amp to amplify the signal from these piezo crystals before it reached the amplifier or PA system. The first Ovation was called the Balladeer and appeared in 1970 to instant acclaim. Within a very short time almost every famous acoustic guitarist was using an Ovation guitar, and the piezo pickup principle remains the industry standard to this day. Variations were made

OPPOSITE PAGE: The National Style O; as played by Mark Knopfler and as it appeared on the cover of Dire Straits' Brothers In Arms (1985). BELOW: A PRS guitar and the great Carlos Santana playing a PRS.

to the size of the lycrachord bowl at the back, to suit different styles of playing, and some Ovations even dispensed with traditional sound-holes altogether; models such as the Adamas use many small holes to amplify the acoustic tone. Ovation also moved into electric guitars, but these never really proved popular with the market.

By the late-1980s, the days of the Ovation were on the wane as more traditional instruments, made in Japan but still featuring Charles Kaman's piezo ideas, started to appear. Ovation guitars are still enduringly popular, however, especially the company's cheaper Celebrity range, which is made in Korea.

➤— **Electro-Acoustic, Pickups**

PRS – PAUL REED SMITH

The PRS guitar is the product of its inventor, the Maryland-based Paul Reed Smith. As the quest for new guitar development hotted up in the 1970s and 1980s, PRS became one of the biggest names in guitar design. The basic PRS template included a Strat-like body shape, contoured and shaped for even more perfect ergonomics than the Fender original, and better humbucking pickups, particularly in the bridge of the guitar, where long sustain and heavy drive in the style of the Les Paul were now considered essential. The first PRS guitars to hit the market in the early 1980s were an instant hit, especially at the professional end, for which their price tag was probably best suited. Today's PRS guitar comes in a huge range of body, neck, and pick-up options, making it a true performer's guitar for the modern guitar professional. Among its most famous endorsers is Carlos Santana.

RICKENBACKER

There may be some dispute over who first invented the idea of the electric guitar pickup, but this small US company was the first to bring an electric guitar to

steel electric guitar, and by 1937 even the staid Gibson Company was ready to launch its own electric model, the ES-150. Rickenbacker continued to produce a range of distinctive electric guitars, including some models from the noted German designer Roger Rossmeisl, but it wasn't until a young John Lennon picked up a Rickenbacker while playing in Hamburg that the company's future was assured. Lennon's first model was the short-necked 325, which featured three pickups, then later a Bigsby tremolo that Lennon had added himself. The Rickenbacker company were quick to exploit this connection and presented Lennon with a replacement for his old and by now battered 325 in 1964 when the band arrived to tour the US. At the same time they presented George Harrison with the first of what was to be one of their other most enduring models, – the 360 12-string electric. Harrison immediately took to his new guitar, which appeared on several Beatles hits over the next year. Roger McGuinn of US band the Byrds remembers seeing Harrison play his 12-string on television and dashing off to buy one for himself the next day. Since then, the chiming sound of these guitars has been heard on many classic tunes, with the opening chord to the Beatles' 'A Hard Day's Night' and the ringing intro to the Byrds' 'Mr Tambourine Man' being perhaps the best-known examples. This California-based company continues to produce high-quality instruments to the same specs as the original models, and has never dipped its toe into the budget or 'Korean-made' market.

➤— **Gibson, Pickups, Twelve-String Guitar**

STEINBERGER

The first model created by Ned Steinberger was a bass guitar, headless, with a narrow strip-like body made of moulded epoxy resin reinforced with carbon and fibreglass. It sounded fantastic, perhaps due to the special properties of the resin and carbon body, which has since been used by several other manufacturers looking for a new slant on traditional guitar design. The headless and bodyless guitar was something of a novelty item in the early 1980s, in spite of its eminent playability and great tone. Such guitars have since fallen from favour.

the market. Known as the Frying Pan because of its curious shape, the guitar first appeared in 1932, although it was some time before the unreceptive audience of the 1930s started to take it seriously. Sales had picked up by 1935, particularly for the company's plastic-bodied lap-

ABOVE: John Lennon sporting his Rickenbacker.
RIGHT: A headless Steinberger bass.
ABOVE RIGHT: A Taylor guitar.
FAR RIGHT: The classic Vox AC30 with a Fender Stratocaster.

shimmer. Later models were often fitted with Top Boost circuitry to drive the amplifiers even harder at the higher end of the tonal range. Top Boost first appeared as an add-on, with controls on the rear panel, and was later fitted as standard. Vox amps are still made today by Japanese electronics giant Korg, and are claimed to be every bit as good as the original classic British beat combo of yore.

➤— *Combo Amps*

TAYLOR

In 1974, Robert Taylor set up the Taylor company in California to produce guitars to compete with high-quality acoustic instruments from the likes of Martin and Gibson. Martins have always been seen as the workhorse acoustics at the pro end of the market, but many believe that their standards slipped during the 1970s, allowing several new luthiers a chance to enter the high-end market. Taylor traditionally use the very best tone woods available, and feature unique design elements, such as the NT neck join and new internal-bracing ideas. Similar to other US companies such as Santa Cruz, which was formed in 1976, many Taylor guitars are now considered as good as the old masters.

➤— *Gibson, Martin*

VOX

This unique British success story began when a company started by Tom Jennings and Dick Denny began manufacturing small combos for the UK market. Their first model, the AC15 appeared in1956, a two-channel amp with built-in tone circuitry. The unusual electrical design of the pre-amp stage of the AC15 made these amps inefficient, but capable of giving great harmonic overdrive when driven. The most famous model the company came up with was the higher wattage model with 2x12 speaker cabinet, called the AC30. The original featured six inputs, two for 'vibra-trem' to give that authentic 1960s

YAMAHA

Yamaha are one of the biggest and most successful musical-instrument companies in the world. For a while they were also the leading exponent of original guitar design from the East, with their Gibson-busting SG2000, first launched in 1973. The SG2000 had very much the look and feel of the classic Gibsons of the previous decade, and while US production costs were soaring, SG2000s were at least half the price of their US rivals. As Japanese production itself became more costly, the SG2000 was less of an attractive proposition and was shelved towards the end of the 1980s. Yamaha still make many guitars, both original and close copies of US originals. In particular, their Pacifica 112 model electric consistently wins buyers' awards for its unbeatable value.

➤— *Gibson*

TECHNICAL

HOME RECORDING

At some point, most guitarists will wish to make a recording of their playing. This does not necessarily have to involve the use of a commercial studio, as the quality of affordable home multi-track recording equipment is now so high that great results can be readily achieved.

The multi-track recording process

In multi-track recording, a song can be built up from separate tracks, each one being used to record a different instrument or musical part. Tracks can be recorded individually, or several can be recorded simultaneously. Any track can be subsequently erased without affecting any of the others.

The number of tracks used in multi-track recording was originally based on the number of parallel strips of equal width that a tape recorder's tape was subdivided into. A 4-track tape recorder with tape 2.5 cm (1 in) wide for example would have its tape subdivided into four

parallel strips each 6 mm (¼ in) wide, each one recordable and erasable independently of the other three. The concept was the same whether 8-, 16- or 24-track tape was being used. The majority of multi-track recorders used at home record on to a hard-disk drive rather than tape, but they still use the concept of tracks as a means of organizing the audio.

A multi-track recorder is traditionally connected to a mixer (or mixing desk) which not only routes the audio in and out of the recorder, but is also the nerve-centre connecting to the rest of the equipment in any studio. Signals can be recorded using microphones or, in the case of electric instruments, plugged directly into a mixer via a DI (direct injection) box or an amp/speaker simulator such as the Line 6 Pod. To build up a song, you can record each new track separately while listening through headphones or monitor speakers to the ones you have already recorded – a process known as overdubbing.

Once all the audio has been recorded, it needs to be mixed to create the final finished product. Audio is routed back through the mixer, each audio track being assigned to its own mixer channel where the volume, stereo panning and tone (EQ) can be set for each track, and effects such as reverb can be added.

Once a song is mixed to your satisfaction, it can then be recorded in stereo form using a master recorder (CD, minidisk, DAT, cassette) connected to the mixer's outputs.

Buying a home studio

There are several options available to the would-be home recordist. The first choice is whether to go for analogue or digital recording. Analogue recording is the traditional method that records audio in a linear fashion on to moving magnetic tape. In the world of home recording the reel-to-reel analogue tape recorder has been largely superseded by digital formats, but is still available in the form of the cassette multi-tracker, generically known as a portastudio after the original Tascam Portastudio. These multi-trackers with integral recorder and mixer can record four tracks of audio onto a compact cassette. They are inexpensive machines, ideal for someone on a tight budget who needs to use a multi-tracker as a musical sketchpad, but they cannot really compete with digital recorders in terms of sound quality and facilities.

Digital recording works by converting the analogue signal into a stream of numbers for storage. Its great advantage is the great many manipulations that can be applied to the audio in the digital domain, in particular non-linear editing in which sections of music can be recorded (something that could only be done with analogue recordings by taking a razor blade to the tape).

Digital hardware or digital software?

The choice of digital options is between hardware equipment or a computer-based system. Although you can pair a hardware digital multi-track recorder with a separate mixing desk to create a studio, many of the available hardware multi-trackers are in the convenient self-contained portastudio style with hard-disk recorder, mixer and effects all in one unit that in some instances may include onboard drum machine and CD burner. Computer recording involves the use of a computer, a software recording program (Cubase, Logic Audio, Pro Tools, etc.) and a soundcard which interfaces with the computer to convert the audio into digital form, which is then stored on hard disk. Computer-based packages do not necessarily have to be used with a separate physical mixing desk. They usually feature a virtual mixing environment with automation and integral software effects, so that once all the audio is in the computer, it can be mixed internally.

➤— *EQ, Studio Recording*

FAR LEFT: A cheap PZM microphone is very good for acoustic guitar work.
ABOVE LEFT: Drum machines provide simple help for any guitarist.
ABOVE: A four track analogue recorder and headphones.
BELOW: Even the Shadows made home recordings once.

STUDIO RECORDING

Even the most complex and expensive of bedroom or home recording setups cannot match the investment and manpower required to create the production values necessary in making a CD – especially one attractive enough to compete successfully in the gladiatorial commercial music marketplace. While there have been some notable success stories of Top 40 hit records having been made by a semi-professional musician using easily available equipment in a project studio, even these recordings must be completed or mastered in a professional facility.

The reason for this is that recording the song or music is just one third of the process involved in making a commercial recording. The other two processes, mixing and mastering, require skill and experience that very few, if any, people possess on their own. It is also necessary to finish the recording in a carefully designed environment created with the sole intention of ensuring that the audio being processed is able to be reproduced faithfully anywhere from a car hi-fi to a hi-tech sound system. Professional recording studios must therefore purchase

ABOVE: Mixing and mastering a track in a professional recording studio. With a reasonable computer, you can now do this at home.

RIGHT: Robert Fripp, inventor of 'Frippertonics', in his studio.

and maintain the most up-to-date equipment and provide separate rooms for performing and listening to the performance, known as 'live rooms' and 'control rooms'. The studio must also be staffed with highly qualified engineers and technicians, and the facility must be open 24 hours a day.

Access to a professional recording studio is the ambition of every band or artist. Record producers and record labels have their eye on costs and the speed in which a record can be made from beginning to end. In many cases the songs on an album are begun at home or on tour, often using a laptop computer, before being developed along with other band members using 'home' studio equipment, until the record company decides that the services of a multi-million pound facility need to be employed.

Computer or Hard Disk Recording

If you already own a personal computer it can be used as an inexpensive tool for recording simply by purchasing and installing additional software.

The guitar is connected to a computer's soundcard using an ordinary lead and computer software is used to stop and start the recording. As computers 'think' in numbers, the guitar's sound must be digitized. This is done using a process called sampling whereby the soundcard 'photographs' voltage received at its input. Each photograph is a permanent record of the sound at that moment in time and many thousands are taken; in the case of a CD-quality recording this would be 44,000, 100 times every second. These samples are converted into numbers and sent to the computer's central processor. The computer processes the numbers just like any other data, so when the sound is played back the result is a very high quality recording. This is known as digital recording and provides very flexible, high quality recordings. Not only is the sound digitally recorded but editing is also entirely digital, enabling parts to be copied and pasted many times or for edits to be undone. Parts from other recordings can be used in a new recording, and recordings made outside the computer can be incorporated into the mix.

The finished recording is saved to the computer's hard disk, and will take up a lot of space: typically one minute of CD-quality stereo recording uses 10 MB (megabytes) of hard disk space. Storing this much information used to

be very expensive, however it is now possible for manufacturers to produce extremely large hard-disk devices very cheaply. This development means that home personal computers are now powerful enough to be used without too much difficulty as complex recording and editing facilities, complete with the software tools required to create complex recordings. Once inside the computer the recording may be edited and processed just as if the user were using a conventional tape recorder.

Most recording software uses recognizable tape-recorder style controls in order to appear user-friendly. Because the sound has been digitized, it is possible for the computer to produce numerous special effects without the need for additional effects pedals or other equipment. Software may also be used to perform previously impossible tasks such as creating the impression that a different amplifier, microphone or even a completely different guitar has been used to create the recording.

Computer software may also be used to make multi-track recordings and recordings alongside MIDI sequences. In this way the recording may be made along with the sound produced by any MIDI equipped keyboard, module or drum machine etc. Using this technology it is easy to create very high quality recordings using techniques previously only available at expensive studios. However, if a personal computer is not already available it can be an expensive introduction to digital recording. Many people choose instead to use a purpose-built workstation such as the Zoom MRS1044 or Boss BR532. These all-in-one devices contain all the digital equipment necessary to create and produce high quality recordings including effects and even drum and bass machines etc. Workstations can be a third of the price of a computer and the necessary peripherals, but are not easily upgradeable and often use expensive storage media.

➤— *Home Recording, MIDI*

MIDI

Musical Instrument Digital Interface (MIDI) is a standard system that allows different electronic musical instruments to talk to each other. These instruments can send, receive and act upon MIDI information such as note value, patch data and controller data. A MIDI guitar can be used to control a wide range of other MIDI musical instruments, including synthesizers, sound modules and samplers. For a MIDI connection to work, the MIDI Out socket of a control instrument should be connected to the MIDI In socket of a slave instrument (the instrument you are controlling).

You can control a second slave instrument by connecting the MIDI Thru socket of your first slave instrument to the MIDI In socket of the second.

ACTION, SETTING OF

The 'action' of a guitar refers to the height of the strings from the fingerboard and determines how much pressure you have to put on the strings in order to play them. Most guitarists prefer a low-action set-up,

where the strings are set as close to the neck as possible to facilitate easy playing without causing fret buzz. The action can be adjusted by raising or lowering the bridge or saddle on the guitar or by altering the height of the nut or the frets. Adjust the action to suit your particular style of playing.

➤ *Intonation*

BINDING

Binding, or edge binding, is a protective strip fitted along the outside edges of the guitar soundbox where it joins with the sides of the guitar body. It also acts a decorative effect and can include materials such as mother-of-pearl or ivory.

➤ *Construction Materials*

EQ

EQ is short for equalization, a term describing the sound spectrum or parts of the sound spectrum of an audio signal. All audible sounds are pitched somewhere between 20Hz (the lowest) and 20KHz (the highest). An equalizer is a tone control that uses capacitors or other devices to cut or boost frequencies within this range. A parametric equalizer can be used to boost or cut one or two frequencies while a graphic equalizer can be set to act differently and independently on a whole number of different frequencies across the entire audio spectrum.

FREQUENCY

The frequency of a note relates to the number of vibrations per second. Frequency is usually measured in cycles per second, or Hertz (Hz). The human ear has a frequency range of 20Hz to 20KHz, and anything outside this range is inaudible. Low guitar notes produce low frequencies (the lowest open E string vibrates at 82.4Hz) while higher notes produce higher frequencies (the top open E string vibrates at 329.6Hz).

➤ *EQ*

GAIN CONTROL

The gain control on an amp or mixer is a control used to adjust the volume of an incoming signal. Different instruments have different output levels – guitars with active circuitry, for example, give out louder

signals than ones with passive circuitry, and microphones usually have very low outputs – and the gain control can be adjusted to suit whichever type of signal is coming into the amp.

INTONATION, SETTING OF

The intonation of a guitar is correct when the notes behind every fret of the fingerboard all have the right pitch when the guitar is in tune. To check the intonation of your guitar, tune it up accurately and then listen to each note on each string. If any notes on any string are out of tune, you should be able to make intonation adjustments on the bridge screw that controls the vibrating length of that string. If you have a floating bridge (a bridge that is only held in place by the tension in the strings), then you will need to adjust the position of the bridge.

➤ *Action, Bridge, Repairs*

AMP SIMULATORS

Amp simulators are able to imitate the sound of a traditional guitar amplifier. Guitarists often choose to use an amp simulator in an environment in which a normal amp could not be used, such as when practising or recording at home or in a professional studio. The simulator is able to recreate the sound of many different types and models of guitar amplifier, as well as the sound of effects pedals, microphones and loudspeaker cabs. This flexibility means that a guitar player can now choose an amp and speaker combination to suit the recording instead of relying on the equipment available at the time. Depending on which model you choose, an amp simulator can use digital effects (Zoom GMS 200) or digital modelling (Boss Amp Station, Johnson J Station) to create the amp sound. Modelling simulators (Line 6 POD, Roland VG88) use digital technology to recreate perfectly the sound of real amplifiers. Modelling means manipulating the sound of the guitar using a real digital recording of an amp or other device. The device holds digital descriptions of the effect on a guitar's sound that a particular amp or speaker may have. A small computer is used to combine that information with the sound of the guitar, with the result that the modeller is able to create the

BOTTOM FAR LEFT: All high-quality guitars are coated with a celluloid or hardwood finish, called binding.
BOTTOM LEFT: Gain control adjusts the volume of incoming signals.
BOTTOM RIGHT: A Marshall stack, combining an amp and speakers.
BELOW: An amp simulator, which can emulate the sound of an amplifier.

impression that a real amp, effects pedals and even microphones were actually used to amplify the guitar. The resulting sound is so lifelike that some players use a full-size digital-modelling amp complete with real speakers rather than a real amp when on stage.

➤ *Boss, Electro-Acoustic, Marshall*

STACK

A guitar stack has two or three parts: a head or amplifier without internal speakers and one or two large cabinets often containing four 30 cm (12 in) speakers. When these separate components are placed on top of each other, the height of the system can easily be 2 m (6 ft) or more, hence the term 'stack' simply meaning a stack of equipment. Stacks like these almost always incorporate a valve amp in the head. This is partly a legacy of traditional design based on the famous Marshall amp and speaker stacks that were a trademark of the heavy metal and rock scene in the 1960s and 1970s. A number of factors have led to the decline in popularity of the stack, particularly among semi-pro bands. These include advances in technology producing better-sounding and much more efficient solid-state amps, the requirement for venues to reduce noise pollution, and above all the sheer weight of three large boxes that makes using a stack system something of a labour of love.

➤ *Combo Amps, Marshall, Speaker, Valve Amp*

PA SYSTEM

 A PA system may be used to amplify the guitar without the need for a traditional back line combo amp or stack. Rack-mounted pre-amps and tone modules may be used connected to high-power fold-back (or monitor systems) and to the on-stage PA. This kind of set-up has significant advantages, particularly for bands or artists embarking on lengthy tours, as costs involved in carrying weighty and sometimes irreplaceable back-line guitar amplification need to be kept to a minimum. The use of a PA system combined with rack-mounted equipment means that the artist is able to rely on well-protected equipment performing consistently each night. The audience is often never aware that this production technique is being used; some bands even go to the trouble of carrying empty or low-powered speaker boxes in place of a back-line. On a smaller scale, acoustic guitarists can benefit from employing a small PA system instead of a guitar amplifier, as the acoustic player does

ABOVE: Humbucker pickups on a Rickenbacker guitar.
ABOVE RIGHT: A detachable, magnetic pickup for an acoustic guitar.
TOP RIGHT: A Gibson Flying V, complete with humbuckers.
FAR RIGHT: Single-coil pickups on a Fender Stratocaster.

not require the overdriven sound of a guitar amp, but prefers the detailed sound of a PA system instead. Another benefit is that microphones may also be used without the need for additional equipment.

➤── *Combo Amps, Gigging, Stack*

PICKUPS

Bug

A bug is a small transducer or microphone usually attached to the top of an acoustic guitar whenever a discreet but temporary way of amplifying the guitar is required. Because this type of device does not have any power source, the sound produced is not of a high quality. Bugs are inefficient and have largely given way to permanently installed pickup and pre-amp systems.

Humbucker

A humbucking pickup can detect a vibrating metal guitar string and translate the vibrations into energy. Humbucking pickups have two coils rather than one. The coils are wound and arranged in such a way that noise and interference detected by the pickup is rejected by way of phase cancellation. As a result the humbucking pickup is louder and deeper sounding than conventional single-coil pickups, and for this reason more popular with rock guitarists. Invention of the humbucking pickup is credited to Seth Lover of the Gibson Guitar Corp in 1955.

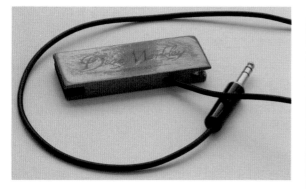

Microphones

A microphone may be used to pick up and transmit the sound of any guitar or amplifier to a recording device or PA system. In a studio the engineer may use a sensitive condenser microphone, but on stage a much less sensitive and more directional dynamic microphone is often used. Microphones may also be installed inside the acoustic guitar alongside a conventional piezo system to help the electro-acoustic sound.

Piezo

A piezo pickup strip may be laid under the bridge of an acoustic guitar and connected to a pre-amplifier. The

piezo pickup then senses any vibration transmitted through the bridge. This vibration causes small crystals within the pickup to create electrical energy that may be amplified and turned into sound. Piezo pickup systems are fitted to most electro-acoustic and some purely electric guitars.

Single-Coil

A single-coil pickup is a simple device constructed from a magnet and a very long piece of thin copper wire. Small voltages are created in the wire coil when the magnetic field of the magnet is disturbed. The single-coil pickup is used to detect the vibrations of a guitar string. The vibrations can then be amplified and turned into sound. The sound of the single-coil pickup is very bright, though the design also allows interference to be picked up very easily. However, many people prefer the sound of the single-coil to the humbucking pickup.

RADIUS

The radius of a guitar fingerboard can be described as the curvature of the neck from the high E string to the low E string. If you took a ruler and put a point at

one edge and a pencil at the other end and draw a circle, then cut out the width of the fretboard along the circumference of the circle, you would get the radius. Some guitars have completely flat fingerboards, and thus no radius.

➤— *Crown, Fret*

SHIELDING

Most electric guitars have their cavities lined with copper foil or electrical shielding tape to reduce the amount of interference that the internal circuitry picks up. They have their cables surrounded by further screening wires, again to reduce the amount of interference in the guitar's signal. All shielding and screening inside the guitar is connected to the earth side of the circuit. If your guitar appears to be very noisy, open it up and check to see if it is shielded and screened.

SIGNAL PATH

The signal path of a guitar in a recording or live situation is the complete path the guitar signal passes through before it hits the recorder or loudspeaker(s). To make sure you sound as good as possible, always use good-quality guitar leads and processors. If you use poor equipment, your guitar might end up sounding more lo-fi than hi-fi. When you process your guitar, think about which effects you use in which order and the impact that these effects will have on the sounds produced by the other effects, as well as your guitar.

➤— *Studio Recording*

ACTIVE ELECTRONICS

Some electric guitars use built-in battery powered circuitry to produce a consistently high-output signal. This is known as active electronics. Such circuitry improves a guitarist's signal-to-noise ratio and makes it easier to drive an amplifier into distortion. Active circuitry can also be used to change the tone of the guitar, to add special effects for more character or to spice up the sound. Many players, however, prefer a passive set-up – which only consists of the pickups, the volume and tone controls and the wires connecting them all up – and connecting them to the lead socket.

STEREO GUITAR OUTPUT

Some models of guitar feature stereo outputs. These twin outputs enable the guitarist to produce a wider and more versatile sound by splitting the output of the guitar between two amps. The earliest and most famous example of this is the Rickenbacker 360 guitar, produced in the 1960s and featuring both mono and stereo outputs. Guitars may also have two pickup systems; traditional magnetic pickups and acoustic piezo pickups may be combined to produce even more sounds One example is the Kramer Duo Pro electric guitar. This instrument features a bridge fitted with piezo-equipped string saddles as well as normal magnetic pickups. Through the use of a stereo guitar cable, the piezo pickup may be routed to an acoustic-guitar amplifier or PA system, while the regular magnetic pickups may be routed to a conventional back-line amp or system. This technique enables the guitarist to produce many different

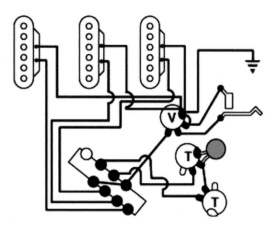

tones from one single guitar while retaining the look, feel and simplicity of an ordinary guitar. Another example is the Epiphone signature model 'BB King Lucille', featuring two jack sockets rather than one. Using these twin sockets, the output from the neck humbucking pickup may be routed to one amp, while the bridge pickup may be routed to another. Using the pickup selector switch, the guitarist is able to choose which amp to use for a particular song or solo.

➤— *Pickups*

WIRING

Stratocaster

The single coil pickups fitted to every Stratocaster use a very simple two conductor cable. On American and vintage models these are coded white for 'hot' and black for 'ground'. The five-way selector switch requires a jumper to enable the switching options, quality single conductor cable is used, as the short length means that the cable is easily damaged when applying heat. Two conductor screened cable is used for the connection between the jack socket and the rear of the volume control. This is the only place that screened cable is used in the Stratocaster. Volume and tone pots are 250K, the capacitor is a .05 mf ceramic.

Les Paul Standard

The Les Paul Standard is fitted with Gibson 490T and 490R pickups. These are two conductor pickups but unlike the Stratocaster the ground conductor is braided around the hot conductor forming a screen. A length of screened cable is also used to connect the jack socket to the switch. The specification for screened cable and humbucking pickups means that the Les Paul suffers much less from RF (radio frequency) interference and is one reason why it is a popular recording guitar. Volume and tone pots are 500K and the tone capacitor are .2 mf ceramic.

➤— *Repairs – Advanced*

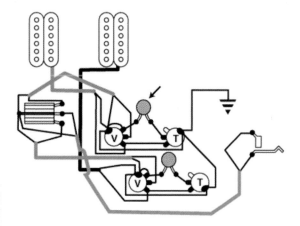

ABOVE LEFT: The radius is the upper curvature of the neck.
ABOVE: A Rickenbacker 360's stereo output.
ABOVE RIGHT: Wiring diagram for the Fender Stratocaster.
RIGHT: Wiring diagram for the Gibson Les Paul.

EARTH

In order to make sure that an electric guitar produces as little background noise as possible, earth connections are built into its electrical circuitry. These are usually achieved by connecting earth lines up to the metal casings of the volume and tone controls. If the guitar suddenly starts to hum, check to see if these connections are still intact. Earth connections and fuses are also fitted into most electronic sound-processing equipment, so that if a dangerously high voltage develops, it is carried safely to earth. Check if the earth circuitry is working correctly by using a ring mains tester, which plugs into a wall socket.

DI

Direct injection, also known as DI (or DI-ing), is when the output from a guitar is plugged straight into a sound system without going through a conventional guitar amp and microphone set-up. 'Direct boxes' such as the POD2 and Digitech Genesis 3 are recent creations designed to amplify and add effects to guitars, and send their outputs straight into a mixer or hi-fi system. Other guitar players DI their instruments by using computer effects-processing software to spice up the sound. Either way, the results are consistent, and it is much easier than miking up an amp every time you want to do some recording.

DI BOX

Acoustic and electric guitars create tiny voltages that must be amplified to be heard as sound. Long sections of cable such as those between a stage and a mixing desk are unsuitable for carrying these voltages because interference and other additional factors can spoil or distort the amplified sound. For this reason, microphones and other professional equipment are designed to produce what is called a balanced output, enabling current produced by the equipment to be carried over long sections of cable without interference. To enable a guitar or any other piece of unbalanced equipment to connect properly to a professional mixing desk, a device called a DI (Direct Injection) box is used. The DI box converts the unbalanced signal to a balanced signal suitable for transmission. The DI box may also have other useful features such as EQ, a ground lift and a pad switch. Some guitars are manufactured with the ability to produce a balanced output. A DI box is not necessary if the guitarist is using an amp and the engineer is using a microphone to pick up the sound of the speaker. However, many bass players use a DI in conjunction with an amp for increased flexibility.

➤ *Electro-Acoustic, EQ*

LEFT AND TOP: Two supreme guitarists: Frank Zappa and Jeff Beck.
ABOVE: A DI (Direct Injection) box.

THEORY

AURAL SKILLS

As well as practical playing skills, guitarists need to develop good aural abilities in order to become effective musicians. The main areas in which guitarists need to develop secure aural awareness are as follows:

Chord identification

Learning to recognize the sound of different types of chords is a very useful skill. Being able to distinguish by ear between major, minor, dominant and diminished chords is helpful not only for working out songs from recordings, but also as an aid to composing your own songs and chord progressions. As a guide, major chords sound bright, minor chords sound mellow, dominant chords have a slightly aggressive bluesy edge, whilst diminished chords sound rather dissonant.

Recognition of cadences

Cadences are musical 'punctuation marks' created by using a combination of chords that implies a resting place. A minimum of two chords have to be used in order to create the resolution. Cadences nearly always appear at the end of songs, however they also occur in other places during the course of a song, such as at the end of a phrase or verse.

The two most commonly used cadences are the perfect cadence (V to I) and the plagal cadence (IV to I). The perfect cadence creates a strong and complete ending to a phrase. In the key of C major it can be played as either G, or G7, to C. The plagal cadence is also often used to end a musical phrase, although its effect is more subtle than the perfect cadence. In the key of C major the plagal cadence is played as F to C. Recognizing the sound of cadences will greatly help you recognize the movement of chords within a progression. A knowledge of cadences is also a great aid in writing effective chord progressions.

RIGHT: Taking the time to develop your aural skills will enable you to create fantastic solos as well as playing better in groups.

Interval identification

An interval is the distance between two notes. Therefore, all melodic phrases are made up of intervals of one kind or another. As many tunes are constructed from the major scale, a good grounding in the intervals of the major scale will help when trying to work out the notes of a melody. The core intervals of the C major scale, for example, are as follows:

C to D	major second
C to E	major third
C to F	perfect fourth
C to G	perfect fifth
C to A	major sixth
C to B	major seventh
C to C	octave

The unique sound of each of these intervals can be learnt by either singing through the scale step by step, or by relating each interval to the start of a well-known melody. For example, the Christmas carol 'Away In A Manger' starts with a the interval of perfect fourth.

Rhythms and timing

It is important that a guitarist can recognize the time signature of a piece of music, as this is one of the most important factors in establishing its feel and groove. The most common time signatures in popular music are:

$\frac{4}{4}$ used in most pop and rock songs

$\frac{3}{4}$ used mainly for ballads and country music

$\frac{12}{8}$ often used in blues and jazz

Learning to keep time and maintain an even pulse in these time signatures is a basic prerequisite for becoming a good guitarist. Playing along with a drum machine, or even a metronome, can prove really helpful in developing these skills.

Reproducing phrases

The ability to pick up melodies, licks and riffs by ear is an essential skill for guitarists, whether you play electric or acoustic guitar. Traditionally, most electric and acoustic guitar players have learnt largely by this method of listening to recordings and then working out phrases and solos by ear. With the widespread availability in recent years of transcriptions for all styles of music, the emphasis on this approach has changed somewhat, but nevertheless the ability to hear a phrase and then reproduce it on the guitar remains a crucial one. A good level of aural awareness in this area will make learning riffs or songs much easier and quicker than relying upon working things out solely from TAB. Ability in this area will also help with creating solos, as it will enable a direct link between inventing phrases in your mind and being able to execute these ideas on the guitar. Finally, attention should be paid not just to the melodic aspect of aural recognition, but also to hearing rhythms: it is the rhythmic shape of a phrase that gives it its structure.

➤— *Chords, Improvizing, Intervals, Reading Music, Tablature*

READING MUSIC

Although notation for electric and acoustic guitarists is often written in TAB, this has the limitation of not including the rhythmic values, so knowing the sound of the music or listening to an accompanying audio version becomes necessary. However, treble clef notation does not have this limitation, making the ability to read music a useful asset – particularly if you intend to pursue guitar playing to a professional level, or are interested in classical guitar (where TAB is far less frequently used).

Learning to sight-read music

The first requirement is to look ahead in the score. Looking at a note only as you are about to play it will result, sooner or later, in a problem. By looking ahead you'll be prepared for anything difficult. The ideal place to get ahead is before you start: try to memorize the first bar, or more if you can. Then if you can keep looking ahead as you play, you'll always have a breathing space. Once you start playing the piece it is important to keep your eyes on the music. Avoid the temptation to look at the guitar fingerboard, as this may cause you to lose your place in the music. Just look at how a good touch-typist operates: by never looking at the keyboard.

Here are a few other essentials for reliable sight-reading:

* Look at the key signature and the time signature before you start: forgetting either of these will cause errors.
* Once you know the key of the piece, practice the key scale, then use this scale fingering when you play the piece. As you can rely on the scale you won't need to keep looking at the fingerboard to find where to put your fingers.
* Scan through the piece before you play it, trying to identify any awkward rhythms or combinations of notes. If there's time, take the difficult passages aside

and practise them separately.

▌ Avoid the temptation to play the piece too fast, especially if the first few bars look easy. Base your tempo on the speed at which you can perform the most difficult bar.

▌ Whatever happens, do not stop. All musicians make errors when reading music; it is just that the best ones do not let the audience know. The most important thing is to keep going and capture the overall shape of the music. It is far better to play a few wrong notes than to keep stopping or going back to correct errors.

➤— *Tablature, Treble Clef, Time Signature*

ABOVE: Being able to read msic is a useful skill, especially when learning new songs or jamming with new people; John Williams and the other members of Sky were all good sight-readers.

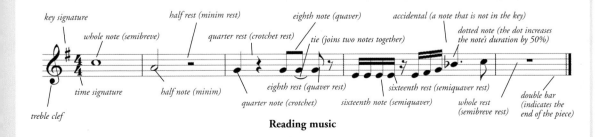

Reading music

TRANSPOSING CHORDS

To transpose a chord progression means to rewrite it changing its original key. The quality of the chords (major, minor, dominant) stays the same, as does their relationship to each other and to the key centre – only the pitch changes. Transposition is a useful skill to have because it means that you can change the key of a song to make it easier to play or to suit your voice if you intend to sing along.

There are two different methods that you can use to transpose chord progressions; both methods will give exactly the same result.

Identify the key of the original chord progression and work out the chord numbers within the key for each of the chords, then use the chord numbers to work out the chords in the new key. For example, Dm is the second chord in the key of C major; therefore when transposed to the key of D major it will become Em, because Em is the second chord in the key of D major.

Another way to transpose chord progressions is to change the root note of each chord by the interval of the key change. For example, if you transpose from C major to D major this is an interval of a whole tone. So you then move up all the other chords in the progression by the same interval. For example, Dm would move up a whole tone to become Em.

TABLATURE

Music for guitarists is often written in tablature (TAB) rather than standard music notation. TAB uses six lines to represent the six strings of the guitar. The numbers written on the strings indicate which fret to play at. A zero indicates that the string is played open.

➤— *Reading Music*

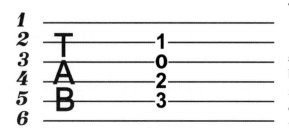

FRETBOX

This is a diagram indicating which strings and frets need to be used in order to play a particular chord or scale. Vertical lines represent the strings, and horizontal lines represent the frets, with (if the fingering starts above the first fret) the lowest fret number shown on the left-hand side. The numbers on the vertical lines show the fingering to be used for fretting notes. Open strings are indicated by a '0' above the relevant string, whilst strings which should not be sounded are indicated by an 'X'.

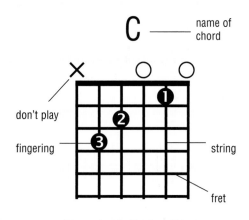

Example of a Fretbox Diagram

BOTTOM END

This is the slang term for both the bass region of the audio spectrum in a mix and the sound made by a bass guitarist in a band. A good, solid bottom end is essential to hold a mix together and complement the high and mid frequencies in a recording or live situation. It gives a mix a fuller, more complete sound.

➤— *EQ*

TONE

A tone (or whole tone) is an interval equivalent to two semitones. Two notes on a guitar string separated by two frets are a tone apart. The whole-tone bend (a bend such that a note is made to sound like the note two frets up on the same string) is probably the most common bend used by rock lead guitarists. In the whole-tone scale, each of the notes is a tone away from the next

(C, D, E, F♯, G♯, A♯, C in the key of C). Most western music is created out of scales with semitone, tone and tone-and-a-half (a tone plus a semitone) intervals.

➤— *Semitone*

SEMITONE

The smallest interval between two notes on a fretted guitar is called a semitone. Notes on either side of a fret are separated by a semitone. An interval of two semitones is called a tone.

➤— *Minor Second, Tone*

BAR/BAR-LINE

A bar-line is a vertical line drawn through a music staff or guitar tablature to mark off metric units. Each bar in a piece of music is the same length unless there are time signature changes within the piece. Many bands use a count-in of one bar when they play a song live to make sure they all start together. Bars in written music notation are usually numbered so that musicians can easily find a specific phrase or passage in the music they are playing.

➤— *Reading Music, Time Signature*

TREBLE CLEF

Music notation for guitar (particularly classical guitar) can be written on a staff of five lines in the treble clef (or G clef), which is indicated by the sign 𝄞.

Each line, and each space between the lines, represents a different note. For example, the bottom line corresponds to the E above middle C, the space above it to F. Temporary extra lines, known as leger lines, are used for any notes that are either too high or too low for a staff.

➤— *Reading Music*

TIME SIGNATURE

A time signature is a sign placed after the clef at the beginning of a piece of music to indicate its metre. Time signatures usually consist of two numbers, an upper one and a lower one. The upper number refers to the number of beats in each bar while the lower one indicates the value of each beat. Thus a signature of 4/4 means that there are four beats to every bar and each beat is worth a crotchet (or quarter note). Likewise, a signature of 6/8 means there are six beats to every bar and the beats are worth a quaver (or eighth note), and 3/2 means there are three beats to every bar and each beat is a minim (or half note).

➤— *Reading Music*

CODA

Most songs and compositions have a coda, a 'tail' or last part of the piece; an addition to the standard form or design. In popular music it is often referred to as the outro. If you see the instruction 'Al coda' in a musical score, it is a signpost telling you to go to the end section which starts with a coda symbol ⊕ and play from there. In addition you may come across 'Da Capo' (or DC) which tells you to go back and play from the beginning of the music, or 'Dal Segno', which instructs you to go back only as far as the 𝄋 sign and play from there.

➤— *Reading Music, Repeats*

REPEATS

If one bar of music is to be repeated then the symbol :∥ can be used. If the phrase to be repeated is longer than one bar, a similar symbol is used but with two slanting lines crossing the same number of bars as in the phrase, and with the number of bars written above it. For example: ✗.

To indicate that a section of music should be repeated, repeat marks are used. A double bar-line, followed by two dots on either side of the middle line of the staff indicates the start of the section; two dots on either side of the middle line of the staff, followed by a double bar-line, indicate the end of the section to be repeated. (If there are no dots at the start of the section, then repeat from the beginning of the piece). Repeat marks can also be used in chord charts. If the section is to be repeated more than once, the number of times it is to be played is written above the last repeat dots. This chord chart shows repeat marks being used in the second section:

∥⁴₄ C ∣ Am ∣ Dm ∣ G ∥: Am ∣ C :∥

If two sections of music are identical, except for the last bar or bars, repeat marks are used in conjunction with first-time and second-time directions.

$$|^4_4 \text{ C } | \text{ Dm } | \text{ Em } | \overset{1.}{\text{ F :}}\| \overset{2.}{\text{ G }} | \text{ C } \|$$

There are other methods of indicating that sections of the music are to be repeated. All have the aim of condensing the information as much as possible whilst retaining clarity and avoiding page turns:

D.C. (an abbreviation of Da Capo) means 'from the beginning'. For example, if the entire piece of music is to be repeated, D.C. can be written at the end of the music and this instructs the performer to play it again from the beginning.

D.S. (an abbreviation of Dal Segno) means 'from the sign': %
For example, if the verse and chorus of a song are to be repeated, but not the introduction, D.S. can be written at the end of the music with the sign (%) written at the start of the verse. This instructs the performer to start again from the sign.

- D.S. al Fine means repeat from the sign (%) until the word 'Fine' (which means 'end').
- D.C. al Fine means repeat from the beginning until the word Fine.
- D.C. al Coda means repeat from the beginning and then jump to the coda when instructed to do so.
- D.S. al Coda means repeat from the sign (%) and then jump to the coda when instructed to do so.
➤— *Coda*

MODES

Modes are scales formed by playing the notes of an existing scale starting from a note other than the original keynote. The most common modes played on the guitar are those of the major scale.

- The Dorian mode contains the notes of the major scale starting from its second degree;
- The Phrygian mode contains the notes of the major scale starting from its third degree;
- The Lydian mode contains the notes of the major scale

starting from its fourth degree;
- The Mixolydian mode contains the notes of the major scale starting from its fifth degree;
- The Aeolian mode contains the notes of the major scale starting from its sixth degree;
- The Locrian mode contains the notes of the major scale starting from its seventh degree.

Even though the major scale and its modal scales use the same notes, because they have different keynotes they do not have the same tonality. For example, while the major scale has a major third interval from the root to the third note and a major seventh interval from the root to the seventh note, in contrast, the Dorian modal scale has a flattened third interval from the root to the third note and a flattened seventh interval from the root to the seventh note – making it a type of 'minor' scale.

Using modes

Modal scales can be used for improvizing and for composing melodies. There are two different approaches that can be taken:

Advanced players sometimes use modal scales as chord scales (using a different mode over each chord). For example, the Dorian modal scale fits over the minor chord built on the second degree of the major scale (e.g. Dm in the key of C major).

Modes can also be treated as key centres in their own right, i.e. with a 'group' of chords to accompany each modal scale. For example, D Dorian modal scale could be used over a D Dorian minor key centre containing any of the following chords: Dm Em F G Am C.
➤— *Dorian Modal Scale, Locrian Modal Scale, Lydian Modal Scale, Major Scale, Mixolydian Modal Scale, Natural Minor Scale, Phrygian Modal Scale*

BOX SHAPE

Most guitarists normally learn scales as box shapes, which show the finger positions for notes in a particular region of the fingerboard. The pentatonic scale, for example, can be played using five box shapes that cover the whole neck, as can the major scale and the natural minor scale. Box shapes are often numbered, with the first finger position starting on the tonic note (first and last note) of the scale. Box-shape soloing is a term that describes solos carried out using a specific box shape or a number of box shapes for a particular scale.

➤— *Scales*

RIFF

 A short musical phrase that is repeated many times throughout a song. Riffs are typically one, two or four bars in length. Examples of well-known riffs can be heard in 'Satisfaction' by The Rolling Stones, David Bowie's 'Jean Genie' and 'Smoke On The Water' by Deep Purple.

➤— *Rhythm & Blues*

ALTERED SCALE

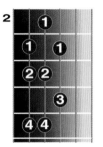 The altered scale is built from the seventh degree of the jazz melodic minor scale. For example, B is the seventh note in the scale of C jazz melodic minor, so the altered scale that is generated from this scale is the B altered scale. The B note becomes the keynote of the altered scale, and the remaining notes in the C jazz melodic minor scale make up the rest of the B altered scale.

The altered scale is widely used in jazz for improvising over altered dominant seventh chords (e.g. 7#11, 7#5, 7♭9, 7#9). The interval spelling is 1 ♭2 #2 3#4 #5 ♭7 8.

➤— *Improvization, Jazz*

BLUES SCALE

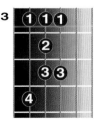 The blues scale forms the foundation of all blues guitar improvization. The scale is similar to the pentatonic minor scale, but with the addition of a ♭5 note. It is this note that gives the blues scale its distinctive blues flavour. The interval spelling is 1 ♭3 4 ♭5 5 ♭7. The C blues scale contains the notes C, E♭, F, G♭, G and B♭.

➤— *Blues, Pentatonic Minor Scale*

CHROMATIC SCALE

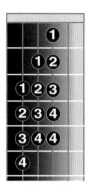 This is a 12-note scale that contains every semitone between the starting note and the octave. Because chromatic scales contain all 12 consecutive semitones they do not relate specifically to any particular key. When improvizing, notes from the chromatic scale can be chosen to introduce notes that are not in the key of the backing. Adding these 'outside' notes as chromatic passing notes within a solo can make it less predictable and create a feeling of musical tension.

➤— *Improvizing*

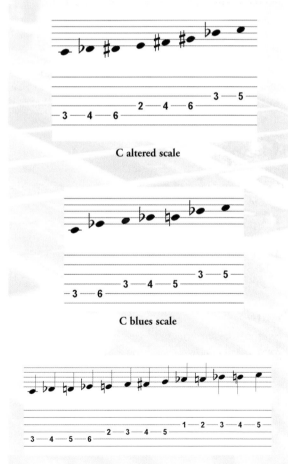

C altered scale

C blues scale

C chromatic scale

C country scale

C whole/half diminished scale

C half/whole diminished scale

C dorian modal scale

COUNTRY SCALE

This is a variation of the pentatonic major scale, but includes the minor third as well as the major third. It is often used in new country and country-rock.

>— *Country, Pentatonic Major Scale*

DIMINISHED SCALES

Diminished scales (also known as octatonic scales) contain eight different notes and are made up of alternating whole-tone and semitone intervals. Diminished scales can start with either a whole tone or a semitone.

♩ Diminished scales that start with a whole tone are described as whole/half diminished scales. These are generally used to improvize over diminished seventh chords. The interval spelling is: 1 2 ♭3 4 ♭5 ♭6 ♭♭7 7 8.

♩ Diminished scales that start with a semitone are described as half/whole diminished scales. These are widely used in jazz and fusion to create a sense of musical tension and colour when improvizing over dominant seventh chords. The interval spelling for this scale is: 1 ♭2 #2 3 #4 5 6 ♭7 8.

>— *Jazz*

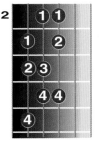

DORIAN MODAL SCALE

Dorian modal scales are minor scales that have a brighter, less melancholic sound than natural minor scales, which makes them suitable for use in jazz and soul music. Dorian modal scales are created by playing the notes of the major scale starting from the second degree. For example, the notes of the B♭ major scale are B♭ C D E♭ F G A B♭. The second note in the B♭ major scale is C, so

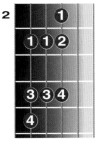

the C Dorian modal scale contains the notes C D E♭ F G A B♭ C. The interval spelling is 1 2 ♭3 4 5 6 ♭7 8.

➤— *Major Scale, Natural Minor Scale*

HARMONIC MINOR SCALE

The harmonic minor scale contains the same notes as the natural minor scale except that, in the harmonic minor scale, the note on the seventh degree is raised a semitone. This results in a large interval (of three semitones) between the sixth and seventh degrees of the scale, giving the scale a very distinctive and exotic sound. The interval spelling is 1 2 ♭3 4 5 ♭6 7 8. The harmonic minor scale is often used for improvizing in minor keys when the V chord is played as a dominant seventh.

➤— *Natural Minor Scale*

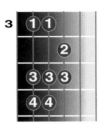

JAZZ MELODIC MINOR SCALE

The jazz melodic minor scale is constructed by taking the natural minor scale and raising the sixth and seventh degrees by a semitone. This gives it a much brighter, almost major tonality that is well suited to some forms of jazz music. It is known as the 'jazz' melodic minor to distinguish it from the traditional 'classical' melodic minor scale which is rarely used in popular music (and which uses the notes of the natural minor scale when descending). The interval spelling is 1 2 ♭3 4 5 6 7 8.

➤— *Jazz, Natural Minor Scale*

LOCRIAN MODAL SCALE

The Locrian modal scale is the mode that starts on the seventh degree of the major scale. For example, C is the seventh note in the scale of D♭ major, so the Locrian modal scale which is generated from the D♭ major scale is the C Locrian modal scale. The C note becomes the keynote of the Locrian modal scale, and the remaining notes in the D♭ major scale make up the rest of the C Locrian modal scale.

The Locrian modal scale is a minor scale with a diminished tonality, making it well suited to improvizing over half-diminished chords. The interval spelling is 1 ♭2 ♭3 4 ♭5 ♭6 ♭7 8.

➤— *Major Scale*

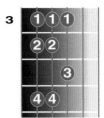

C harmonic minor scale

C jazz melodic minor scale

C Locrian modal scale

LYDIAN DOMINANT MODAL SCALE

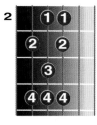

This is a variant of the Lydian modal scale, but containing a ♭7 interval. For this reason, the Lydian dominant scale is also known as the Lydian ♭7 modal scale. The scale can also be considered as a mode starting from the fourth degree of the jazz melodic minor scale. The interval spelling is 1 2 3 ♯4 5 6 ♭7 8.

➤— *Jazz Melodic Minor Scale, Lydian Modal Scale*

LYDIAN MODAL SCALE

The Lydian modal scale is created by playing the notes of the major scale starting from the fourth degree. For example, the notes of the G major scale are G

C Lydian dominant modal scale

C Lydian modal scale

C major scale

A B C D E F♯ G. The fourth note in the G major scale is C, so the Lydian modal scale that is generated from the G major scale is the C Lydian modal scale which contains the notes C D E F♯ G A B C. The interval spelling is 1 2 3 ♯4 5 6 7 8. When compared to the tonic major (the major scale with the same starting note), the only difference is the inclusion of the ♯4 note in the Lydian modal scale.

The Lydian modal scale is often used in jazz, fusion and soul music.

➤— *Jazz, Major Scale, Soul*

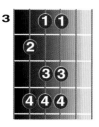

MAJOR SCALE

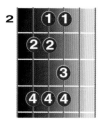

The major scale is one of the most important scales in music as all other scales and all chords are normally analyzed in relation to it. The major scale has a very bright and melodic sound and is used as the basis for the majority of popular melodies.

Major scales are constructed using a combination of tones (T) and semitones (S) in the following pattern: T T S T T T S. The C major scale, for example, is constructed in the following way:

C	to the 2nd note	(D)	=	whole tone
D	to the 3rd note	(E)	=	whole tone
E	to the 4th note	(F)	=	semitone
F	to the 5th note	(G)	=	whole tone
G	to the 6th note	(A)	=	whole tone
A	to the 7th note	(B)	=	whole tone
B	to the octave	(C)	=	semitone

➤— *Major Chords*

MIXOLYDIAN MODAL SCALE

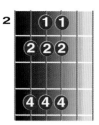

The Mixolydian modal scale is created by taking the notes of the major scale starting from the fifth degree. For example, the notes of the F major scale are F G A B♭ C

D E F. The fifth note in the F major scale is C, so the Mixolydian modal scale that is generated from the F major scale is the C Mixolydian modal scale which contains the notes C D E F G A B♭ C. The interval spelling is 1 2 3 4 5 6 ♭7 8. When compared to the tonic major (the major scale with the same starting note), the only difference is the inclusion of the ♭7 note in the Mixolydian modal scale. Consequently, the Mixolydian modal scale has a much more bluesy sound than the standard major scale; it is widely used in blues and rock music.

➤— *Major Scale, Modes*

NATURAL MINOR SCALE

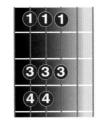

The natural minor scale has a very soulful and melodic sound and is widely used in rock and blues-based music. Natural minor scales are constructed using a combination of tones (T) and semitones (S) in the following pattern: T S T T S T T. The C natural minor scale is constructed in the following way:

C to the 2nd note	(D)	= whole tone
D to the 3rd note	(E♭)	= semitone
E♭ to the 4th note	(F)	= whole tone
F to the 5th note	(G)	= whole tone
G to the 6th note	(A♭)	= semitone
A♭ to the 7th note	(B♭)	= whole tone
B♭ to the octave	(C)	= whole tone

The interval spelling is 1 2 ♭3 4 5 ♭6 ♭7 8.

➤— *Blues, Rock*

PENTATONIC MAJOR SCALE

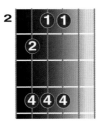

The pentatonic major scale is a five-note scale, made up of the 1st, 2nd, 3rd, 5th and 6th notes of the major scale with the same keynote. It is a very useful scale for improvizing in major keys: as it contains fewer notes than the standard major scale there is less chance of any of the notes clashing with the accompanying chords. The

pentatonic major scale is widely used in country, blues and rock music.

➤— *Major Scale*

ABOVE: Tal Farlow and George Benson jazzing it up with modal scales.

C Mixolydian modal scale

C natural minor scale

C pentatonic major scale

C pentatonic minor scale

C Phrygian major modal scale

C Phrygian modal scale

Whole-tone scale

PENTATONIC MINOR SCALE

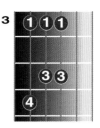

The pentatonic minor scale is a five-note scale, made up of the 1st, 3rd, 4th, 5th and 7th notes of the natural minor scale with the same keynote. It is a very useful scale for improvizing in minor keys: as it contains fewer notes than the standard natural minor scale there is less chance of any of the notes clashing with the accompanying chords. The pentatonic minor scale is the most widely used scale for improvizing in rock music. The interval spelling is 1 ♭3 4 5 ♭7 8.

➤— *Natural Minor Scale*

PHRYGIAN MAJOR MODAL SCALE

The Phrygian major modal scale is the mode that starts on the fifth degree of the harmonic minor scale. In practice, it can be considered as a variation of the Phrygian modal scale, but with a major (rather than flattened) third. It is most commonly used in flamenco and heavy metal music. The interval spelling is 1 ♭2 3 4 5 ♭6 ♭7 8.

➤— *Phrygian Modal Scale*

PHRYGIAN MODAL SCALE

The Phrygian modal scale is created by taking the notes of the major scale starting from the third degree. For example, the notes of the A♭ major scale are A♭ B♭ C D♭ E♭ F G. The third note in the A♭ major scale is C, so the Phrygian modal scale that is generated from the A♭ major scale is the C Phrygian modal scale, which contains the notes C D♭ E♭ F G A♭ B♭ C. The interval spelling is 1 ♭2 ♭3 4 5 ♭6 ♭7 8. The Phrygian modal scale is quite unusual in that it starts with a semitone interval between the first two degrees. This gives it a Spanish sound; it is widely used in flamenco and heavy metal music.

➤— *Major Scale*

WHOLE-TONE SCALE

Whole-tone scales are constructed using only whole steps. Between any note and its octave there are six whole steps, therefore the whole-tone scale contains six different notes. Whole-tone scales are rarely used as key scales, but instead tend to be used for improvizing over dominant altered chords (such as 7#5). The interval spelling is 1 2 3 #4 #5 ♭7 8.

>— *Augmented Chords*

CHORD CHART

This is the most commonly used method of notating a chord progression. Each bar is indicated by a vertical line (with two lines at the end).

| $\frac{4}{4}$ C | F | Em/G7/ | C ‖

Chords are indicated by chord symbols. Where two or more chords occur within a single bar, the division is shown by a dot or diagonal line after each chord to indicate another beat. If no such signs occur then the bar can be assumed to be evenly divided between the chords that appear within it.

>— *Chords, Fretbox*

TRIADS

Triads are basic three-note chords that are also the building blocks of all other chords. There are four basic triads: a major triad is the first, third and fifth notes of the diatonic major scale (C, E and G in the key of C); a minor triad is the first third and fifth notes of the natural minor scale (C, E♭

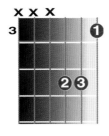

and G in the key of C); an augmented triad is a major triad with a sharpened fifth note (C, E and G# in the key of C); and a diminished triad is a minor triad with a flattened fifth note (C, E♭ and G♭ in the key of C). All of these basic chords can be extended; a major seventh chord,

for example, is a major triad with a seventh note added (C, E, G and B in the key of C).

>— *Major Scale, Natural Minor Scale*

OPEN CHORDS

These are chords in which open strings are used as part of the chord. They are normally, but not exclusively, played at the nut end of the fretboard. They are more often used in acoustic than electric guitar playing.

BARRE CHORDS

These are chords in which no open strings are played – instead the first finger lies flat across all the strings. Barre chord shapes are just open-position chords re-fingered, thereby leaving the first finger free for holding the barre. The advantage of barre chords is that once you have learned one shape, you can use it for all of the 12 different keys simply by moving it up or down the neck to change the pitch. This can be especially useful when playing rhythm guitar. As barre chords do not involve open strings they can sound great with distortion,

ABOVE: A barre chord – these chords are useful because a single hand postition can be used for all of the 12 different keys, simply by moving it up or down the neck of the guitar.

and are well suited for use with punchy rhythmic techniques (like staccato). The most common barre chords are the 'E' and 'A' shapes based on the E and A open chords respectively.

When playing a barre chord, ensure that the first finger is close to, and in line with, the fret rather than at an angle to it.

➤— *Distortion, Partial-Barre Chords*

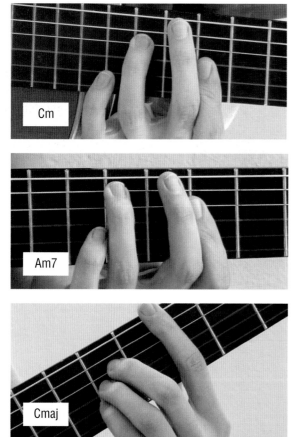

Cm

Am7

Cmaj

Em

PARTIAL-BARRE CHORDS

These are chords in which the top two, three or four strings are fretted with the first finger. The first finger must lie flat across the strings in order for them to sound clearly; any other fingers that are used should fret strings with their tips. Partial-barre chords are sometimes used in place of full-barre chords in order to achieve a crisper and lighter sound.

➤— *Barre Chords*

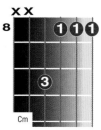

Cm

CHORD INVERSIONS

The term 'inversion' is widely used simply to refer to any chord in which a note other than the root is placed as the lowest note in the chord.

- 1st inversion is where the root is displaced from the bottom of the chord to the top, and the third becomes the lowest note.
- 2nd inversion is where the fifth becomes the lowest note.
- 3rd inversion is where the extension of the chord (e.g. the seventh) becomes the lowest note.

Inversions are normally notated as 'slash chords'.

➤— *Chord Chart, Slash Chords*

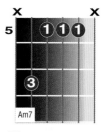

POWER CHORDS (FIFTH CHORDS)

These are chords that have no third, being made up of just the root and fifth. For example, C5 includes the notes C and G (the first and fifth notes of the C major scale). The root note of the chord is often doubled an octave higher to give a stronger sound. A fifth chord is not defined as either major or

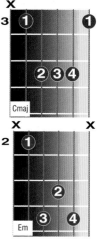

Am7

Cmaj

Em

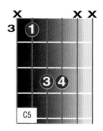

C5

minor as there is no (major or minor) third included within the chord.

Fifth chords are frequently used in heavy metal and rock music, with the sound of the chord often filled out by the use of distortion effects. Because of their solid and strong sound, fifth chords are often referred to as 'power chords'.

➤— *Metal, Rock*

SLASH CHORDS

These are chords in which the lowest note is not the root note of the chord. The chord symbol is written with a diagonal line (slash) after it and with the bass note following the line. For example, if the C major chord is to be played with the note E in the bass it would be written as C/E. This method of specifying the bass note can be used to describe chord

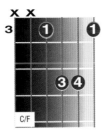

inversions, but it can also describe any chord type, including those in which the bass note does not appear in the original chord. C/F (above) is C major with the note F in the bass.

➤— *Chord Inversions*

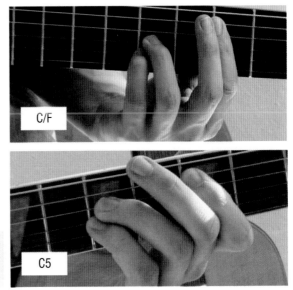

ABOVE: Power chords, or fifth chords, are popular in heavy metal music; here the boys from Iron Maiden power one out.

ROOT POSITION CHORDS

These are chords in which the lowest note that is played is the root note – i.e. the note that gives the chord its pitch name. For example, C is the root note of all types of C chords. Therefore, any C chord that is played with C as the lowest note will be in 'root position'.

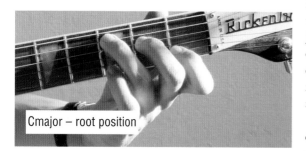

Cmajor – root position

Cmajor

C6

Cmaj7

MAJOR CHORDS

Major chords are made up of the 1st, 3rd, and 5th notes of the major scale with the same starting note. However, when played on the guitar, some of the notes are normally repeated at different pitches to give a fuller sound – rather than just playing three strings. For example, in the fretbox of C major illustrated, the chord contains only the notes C, E and G (the 1st, 3rd and 5th notes of the C major scale), but notice that both C and G notes are repeated on different stings at a different octave.

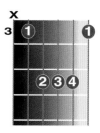

Major chords give a bright, strong sound and, of all chord types, are the most commonly used in many styles of music.

➤— *Major Scale*

MAJOR SIXTH CHORDS

These are extensions of major chords. They are formed by adding the sixth note of the major scale (with the same starting note) to a major chord. For example, C6 contains the notes C, E and G (the notes of C major) plus the note of A (the sixth note of the C major scale). The interval spelling is therefore 1 3 5 6.

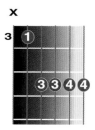

Major sixth chords have a very bright cheery sound. They are often used in jazz-swing, jump-jive and rock'n' roll. They can be used in place of major chords to add an extra sense of lightness to a chord progression.

➤— *Major Chords*

MAJOR SEVENTH CHORDS

These are extensions of major chords. They are formed by adding the seventh note of the major scale (with the same starting note) to a major chord. For example, Cmaj7 contains the notes C, E and G (the notes of C major) plus the note of B (the seventh note of the C major scale). The interval spelling is therefore 1 3 5 7.

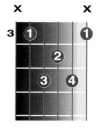

Major seventh chords have a luscious sound, and they are often used to add a feeling of romance to ballads and love songs.

>— *Major Chords*

MAJOR NINTH CHORDS

These are extensions of major seventh chords. They are formed by adding the ninth note of the major scale (with the same starting note) to a major seventh chord. For example, Cmaj9 contains the notes C, E, G and B (the notes of Cmaj7) plus the note of D (the ninth note of the C major scale). The interval spelling is therefore 1 3 5 7 9.

Major ninth chords have a soft and delicate sound that makes them highly suitable for use in ballads and romantic songs.

>— *Major Seventh Chords*

MINOR CHORDS

Minor chords are made up of the 1st, ♭3rd and 5th notes of the major scale with the same starting note. However, when played on the guitar, some of the notes are normally repeated at different pitches to give a fuller sound – rather than just playing three strings. For example, in the fretbox of C minor illustrated, the chord contains only the notes C, E♭ and G (the 1st, ♭3rd and 5th notes of the C major scale) but

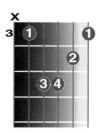

Cmin

notice that both C and G notes are repeated on different strings at a different octave.

Played alone, minor chords have a mellow and mournful sound, and songs that consist solely of minor chords will inevitably have a melancholic sound. However, when mixed with other chord types within a progression, minor chords can act as a useful balance and contrast to the natural brightness of major chords.

➤— *Major Scale*

MINOR SIXTH CHORDS

These are extensions of minor chords. They are formed by adding the sixth note of the major scale (with the same starting note) to a minor chord. For

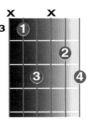

example, Cm6 contains the notes C, E♭, and G (the notes of C minor) plus the note A (the sixth note of the C major scale). The interval spelling is therefore 1 ♭3 5 6.

Minor sixth chords sound very distinctive; their tonality is quite different from that of other minor chords, because of the inclusion of the major sixth interval within the chord. This distracts from the normal mellowness of the minor chord and results in a somewhat jarring edge to the sound. Minor sixth chords are often used in jazz ballads, such as Gershwin's 'Summertime'.

➤— *Jazz, Minor Chords*

ABOVE: Paul Simon uses a lot of minor chords in his music, resulting in his melancholy, folk-influenced sound. Listen to any of Simon and Garfunkel's classic songs and you'll see what we mean!

MINOR SEVENTH CHORDS

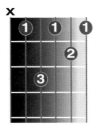 These are extensions of minor chords. They are formed by adding the ♭7 note of the major scale (with the same starting note) to a minor chord. For example, Cm7 contains the notes C, E♭ and G (the notes of C major) plus the note of B♭ (the ♭7 note of the C major scale – i.e. the note that is one fret below the seventh note B). The interval spelling is therefore 1 ♭3 5 ♭7.

Minor seventh chords have a gentle, mellow sound, making them well suited to soul and blues-based music.

➤— *Minor Chords*

MINOR SEVENTH FLAT 5 CHORDS

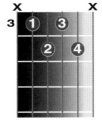 These are commonly referred to as 'half-diminished chords'. Their interval spelling is similar to that of diminished seventh chords, except that they contain a ♭7 note rather than a ♭♭7. The interval spelling is 1 ♭3 ♭5 ♭7.

Minor seventh flat 5 chords naturally occur on the seventh degree of the major scale. For example, Bm7♭5 contains the notes B D F A which all come from the C major scale. However, in practice minor seventh flat 5 chords are more often used in minor-key progressions – normally followed by a dominant seventh chord, and then the tonic minor (IIm7♭5 – V7 – Im). The sound of minor seventh flat 5 chords is quite unresolved, and so they are rarely played for very long before being followed by a more standard chord.

➤— *Dominant Seventh Chords, Major Scale*

MINOR NINTH CHORDS

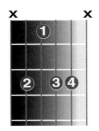 These are extensions of minor seventh chords. They are formed by adding the ninth note of the major scale (with the same starting note) to a minor seventh chord. For example, Cm9 contains the notes C, E♭, G and B♭

(the notes of Cm7) plus the note D (the ninth note of the C major scale). The interval spelling is therefore 1 ♭3 5 ♭7 9.

Minor ninth chords have a suave, mellow sound. They are often used in soul and funk music.

➤— *Minor Seventh Chords, Soul*

Cm6

Cm7

Cm7♭5

Cmin9

MINOR-MAJOR SEVENTH CHORDS

These are formed by adding the seventh note of the major scale (with the same starting note) to a minor chord. For example, Cm/maj7 contains the notes C, E♭ and G (the notes of C minor) plus the note B (the seventh note of the C major scale). The interval spelling is 1 ♭3 5 7. Minor-major seventh chords can therefore be seen as variants of minor seventh chords, but instead of using the ♭7, minor-major seventh chords include the 'major seventh' note.

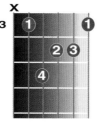

When played individually, minor-major seventh chords have a rather dissonant sound, and so they are rarely used for more than a short time within a chord progression. Instead they are used as passing chords, normally to create chromatic links between other chords. They fulfil this useful function well, and have been used to good effect in songs such as the Beatles' 'Michelle' and Led Zeppelin's 'Stairway To Heaven'.

➤— *Minor Seventh Chords, 'Stairway To Heaven'*

Cm/maj7

Cm/maj9

MINOR-MAJOR NINTH CHORDS

These are variations of minor ninth chords. They are constructed in the same way, but include a major 7th note (rather than a ♭7). The interval spelling is 1 ♭3 5 7 9. They have a unique and rather enigmatic sound and are rarely used, except in jazz and film music.

➤— *Minor Ninth Chords*

SECOND, MAJOR

A major second is the interval between the first and second notes of the diatonic major scale (e.g. C–D in the key of C). It could also be described as the interval between two notes one diatonic scale degree apart. If you play a tonic note anywhere on a guitar, a major second is two frets up from that note on the same string. If you transpose a major second note up an octave, it becomes a ninth interval in relation to the original tonic note.

➤— *Aural Skills, Major Scale, Tone*

SECOND, MINOR

A minor second is the note between the first and second notes of a diatonic major scale. Play a tonic note anywhere on a guitar – a minor second is one fret up from that note on the same string. It is present in the Phrygian mode (E F G A B C D E), which is used extensively in flamenco guitar music. Play the first four notes of the Phrygian mode (E F G A) forwards and backwards and to get an instant feel for this Spanish-sounding interval.

➤— *Aural Skills, Phrygian Modal Scale, Semitone, Triads*

THIRD, MAJOR

The major third is the interval between the first and third notes of the diatonic major scale (e.g. C–E in the key of C) or it could also be described as the interval between two notes, two diatonic scale degrees apart. The third determines that a scale or chord that contains it is major. Play a fretted note on a guitar string and then play the note four frets up on the same string; those two notes are a major third apart. The major triad is a chord or arpeggio consisting of the first, third and fifth notes of the major scale (1, 3, 5, or C, E, G in the key of C).

➤— *Major Scale, Triads*

THIRD, MINOR

The minor third note is the note between the second and third notes of the diatonic major scale (or a note a semitone lower than third, e.g. E♭ in the key of C). The minor third determines that a scale or chord that contains it is minor; it is the third note of the natural minor scale. Play a fretted note on a guitar string and then play the note three frets up on the same string; those two notes are a minor third apart. The minor triad is a chord or arpeggio consisting of the first, flattened third and fifth notes of the major scale (1, flat 3, 5, or C, E♭, G in the key of C).

➤— *Natural Minor Scale, Triads*

FOURTH, AUGMENTED

An augmented or sharpened fourth is the note between the perfect fourth and fifth notes of the diatonic scale (or a note a semitone higher than a perfect fourth). It is this note that gives the Lydian mode (C, D, E, F♯, G, A, B, C in the key of C) its distinct character. The lydian mode has been used extensively by top rock and jazz soloists including Steve Vai, John McLaughlin and Frank Zappa.

➤— *Diminished Fifth, Lydian*
Modal Scale

FOURTH, PERFECT

A perfect fourth is the interval between the first and fourth notes of the diatonic major scale (e.g. C–F in the key of C), or it could also be described as the interval between two notes, three diatonic scale degrees apart. The fourth interval is particularly important to guitar players, because it is used for standard guitar tuning: E A D G B E; with the exception of the B string, each of the other strings are tuned a perfect fourth apart. The perfect fourth note is also known as the subdominant note in a major scale, and blues and rock progressions commonly feature chords based on this note.

➤— *Perfect Fifth*

FIFTH, AUGMENTED

An augmented or sharpened fifth is the note between the perfect fifth and sixth notes of the diatonic major scale (or a note a semitone higher than a perfect fifth note). It is used to create the augmented chords (e.g. C, E, G♯ in the key of C) that were used by rock 'n' rollers such as Chuck Berry, Eddie Cochran and the Stray Cats, and it is also used in jazz and classical music. An augmented triad can be seen simply as a major triad with a sharpened fifth note.

➤— *Augmented Chords*

ABOVE: Always an incredibly inventive composer, Frank Zappa often wrote in the Lydian mode using the augmented fourth interval.

FIFTH, DIMINISHED

A diminished or flattened fifth is the note between the perfect fourth and fifth notes of the diatonic major scale (or a note a semitone lower than a perfect fifth). It is used to create diminished chords (e.g. C, E♭,

G♭ in the key of C) and scales, and is also used as a 'blue note' in blues guitar solos. A diminished triad can be seen as a minor triad with a flattened fifth note.

➤— *Diminished Chords*

FIFTH, PERFECT

A perfect fifth is the interval between the first and fifth notes of the diatonic major scale (e.g. C–G in the key of C), or it could also be described as the interval between two notes four diatonic scale degrees apart. This is one of the most important and widely used intervals in popular and classical music. It is an essential ingredient in the basic major- and minor-chord triads (C, E, G and C, E♭, G in the key of C respectively) and it is also known as the dominant note in a major scale, one of the most likely places to look for a primary chord or key change in any key.

SIXTH, MAJOR

The major sixth is the interval between the first and sixth notes of the diatonic major scale (e.g. C–A in the key of C), or it could also be described as the interval between two notes five diatonic scale degrees apart. The major sixth chord (identified by a 6 suffix after the key name) is a major triad with the sixth note of the major scale added (1, 3, 5, 6, or C, E, G, A in the key of C).

➤— *Major Scale, Major Sixth Chords, Triads*

SIXTH, MINOR

A minor sixth note is between the fifth and sixth notes of the diatonic major scale (or a note a semitone lower than the sixth, e.g. A♭ in the key of C). A minor sixth chord (identified by an m6 suffix after the key name) is made up of a minor triad plus a sixth note (1, ♭3, 5, 6 or C, E♭, G, A in the key of C).

➤— *Major Scale, Minor Sixth Chords, Semitone, Triads*

SEVENTH, MAJOR

The major seventh is the interval between the first and seventh notes of the diatonic major scale (e.g.

LEFT: Jazz guitarists like John McLaughlin often use extended jazz chords, such as elevenths.

C–B in the key of C), or it could also be described as the interval between two notes, six diatonic scale degrees apart. The major seventh chord (identified by an M7 suffix after the key name) is made up of a major triad with the seventh note of the major scale added (1, 3, 5, 7 or C, E, G, B in the key of C).

> *Aural Skills, Major Scale, Major Seventh Chords, Triads*

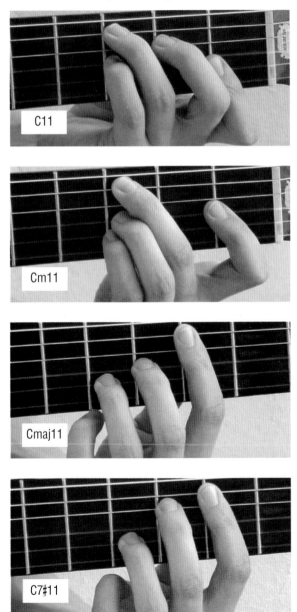

C11

Cm11

Cmaj11

C7#11

SEVENTH, MINOR

The minor seventh is the note between the sixth and seventh notes of the diatonic major scale (e.g. B flat in the key of C). The minor seventh chord (identified by an m7 suffix after the key name) is made up of a minor triad plus a flattened seventh note (1, ♭3, 5, ♭7 or C, E♭, G, B♭ in the key of C). Along with the seventh and dominant seventh chords, it is used widely in jazz music and is the first chord of the highly popular II, V, I chord progression (Dm7, G7 and Cm7 in the key of C).

> *Jazz, Major Scale, Minor Seventh Chords, Triads*

ELEVENTH CHORDS

There are four main types of eleventh chords:

- Dominant eleventh – made up of the 1st, 3rd, 5th, ♭7th, 9th and 11th notes of the major scale with the same starting note. For example, C11 includes the notes C, E, G, B♭, D and F.

- Minor eleventh – made up of the 1st, ♭3rd, 5th, ♭7th, 9th and 11th notes of the major scale with the same starting note. For example, Cm11 includes the notes C, E♭, G, B♭, D and F.
- Major eleventh – made up of the 1st, 3rd, 5th, 7th, 9th and 11th notes of the major scale. In practice, this chord type is rarely used in popular music.

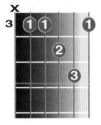

- Dominant seven sharp eleventh – made up of the 1st, 3rd, 5th, ♭7th, 9th and #11th notes of the major scale. For example, C7#11 includes the notes C, E, G, B♭, D and F#.

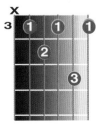

In practice, the ninth note is normally omitted when playing eleventh chords on the guitar.

> *Dominant Seventh Chords, Ninth Chords*

THIRTEENTH CHORDS

 There are three main types of thirteenth chord:

♦ Dominant thirteenth – made up of the 1st, 3rd, 5th, ♭7th, 9th, 11th and 13th notes of the major

C13

Cm13

Cmaj13

Cadd9

scale with the same starting note. For example, C13 includes the notes C, E, G, B♭, D, F and A.

♦ Minor thirteenth – made up of the 1st, ♭3rd, 5th, ♭7th, 9th, 11th and 13th notes of the major scale with the same starting note. For example, Cm13 includes the notes C, E♭, G, B♭, D, F and A.

♦ Major thirteenth – made up of the 1st, 3rd, 5th, 7th, 9th, 11th and 13th notes of the major scale. For example, Cmaj13 includes the notes C, E, G, B, D, F and A.

In practice, it is not possible to play all seven notes of a thirteenth chord on a guitar, therefore some notes, normally the 9th, 11th, and sometimes the 5th, are omitted. Leaving out these notes also results in a more well-defined sound.

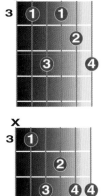

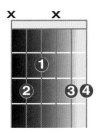

ADD CHORDS

 These are chords in which an extension is added without any intermediary notes being included. For example, Cadd9 involves adding the ninth note (of the C major scale) to the C major triad. The notes that make up the chord would therefore be C E G D (1 3 5 9). Notice that, unlike C major9, in Cadd9 the seventh note is not included – instead the ninth note is simply added to the basic triad.

➤— *Major Ninth*

ALTERED CHORDS

 These are chords in which the fifth and/or ninth has been 'altered' – i.e. either raised or lowered by a semitone. The distinctive sound of altered chords creates a temporary sense of dissonance within a chord progression. Altered chords are most commonly used in jazz music, where they are employed either to create a

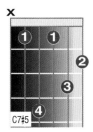

C7#5

chromatic effect or to aid the introduction of a modulation. Some altered chords do occasionally feature in rock music, the most notable being the 7#9 chord – widely referred to as 'the Hendrix chord'. Here are some examples of commonly used altered chords. Interval spellings:

C7#5:	1	3	#5	♭7
Cm7#5:	1	♭3	#5	♭7
C7#9:	1	3	5	#9
C7♭5♭9:	1	3	♭5	♭7	♭9

>— *Jimi Hendrix, Rock*

AUGMENTED CHORDS

These are major triads in which the fifth note is sharpened. For example, C major comprises the notes C, E and G (the 1st, 3rd and 5th notes of the C major scale), so C augmented is made up of the notes C, E and G# (1st, 3rd and #5th of the C major scale). The chord symbol is C+. Augmented chords have a very strident sound, so they tend to be used to create dramatic accents within, or more often at the end of, a chord progression.

>— *Whole-Tone Scale*

DIMINISHED CHORDS

These are either three-note chords, known as diminished triads, (made up of the 1st, ♭3rd and ♭5th notes of the major scale with the same starting note) or four-note chords, known as diminished sevenths, (made up of the 1st, ♭3rd, ♭5th and ♭♭7th). The double flattened seventh interval (♭♭7) is simply the ♭7 note (used in the minor seventh chord) lowered by one fret. For example, C diminished (C°7)

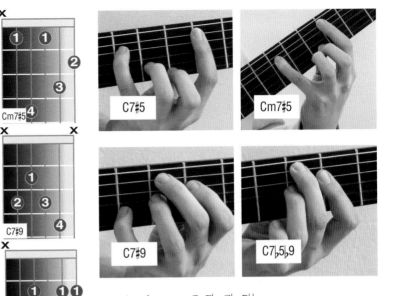

contains the notes C, E♭, G♭, B♭♭.

Diminished chords have a uniquely dissonant sound and are often emphasized to create a disturbing or unsettling effect. Alternatively they can be used as passing chords to link together two other chords within a progression.

>— *Minor Seventh Chords*

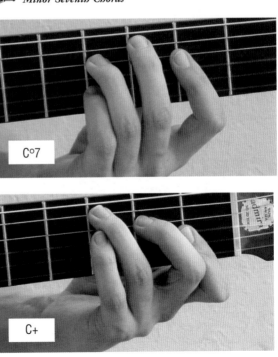

DOMINANT SEVENTH CHORDS

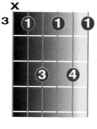

These are based on major chords but with an extra note added. The note to be added is one fret lower than the seventh note of the major scale (with the same starting note). For example, C7 contains the notes C, E and G (the notes of the C major

chord) plus B♭ (the ♭7 note of the C major scale). The interval spelling is 1 3 5 ♭7.

Adding the ♭7 note gives dominant seventh chords a very hard-edged, bluesy sound. Consequently, dominant seventh chords are essential chord types in rhythm & blues, rock 'n' roll and other blues-derived musical forms.

➤— *Major Chords, Blues*

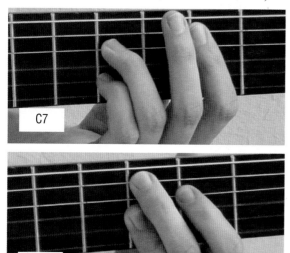

C7

DOMINANT NINTH CHORDS

These are extensions of dominant seventh chords. They are formed by adding the ninth note of the major scale (with the same starting note) to a dominant seventh chord. For example, C9 contains the notes C, E, G and B♭ (the notes of C7) plus the note of D (the ninth note of the C major scale). The interval spelling is therefore 1 3 5 ♭7 9.

Dominant ninth chords have a rich bluesy sound. They are often used in blues, jazz and funk music in place of standard dominant seventh chords. Ninth chords are very often used with slides, because the fingering makes them suitable for sliding into from a fret above or below.

➤— *Blues, Dominant Seventh Chords, Jazz, Slide*

C9

SUSPENDED CHORDS

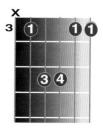

These are commonly known as 'sus chords'. Sus chords have quite an ethereal and unfinished sound, so a major or minor chord normally follows in order to create a sense of resolution. There are two types of sus chords: sus2 and sus4. Both can be considered as variations of major or minor chords, because in both sus chords the minor or major third of the chord is replaced with the required sus note.

✦ To work out a sus2 chord, replace the third of a major or minor chord with the second note of the major scale with the same starting note. For example, the C major triad will become Csus2 by

Csus2

Csus4

replacing the E note with a D note.

🎵 To work out a sus4 chord, replace the third of a major or minor chord with the fourth note from the major scale. For example, the C major triad will become Csus4 by replacing the E note with an F note.

Interval spellings:

🎵 Suspended second chords are numbered 1 2 5, because they contain the first, second and fifth notes of the major scale with the same starting note.

🎵 Suspended fourth chords are numbered 1 4 5, because they contain the first, fourth and fifth notes of the major scale with the same starting note.

➤― *Major Chords, Minor Chords*

BELOW: The late great John Lee Hooker, who influenced countless guitarists.

C

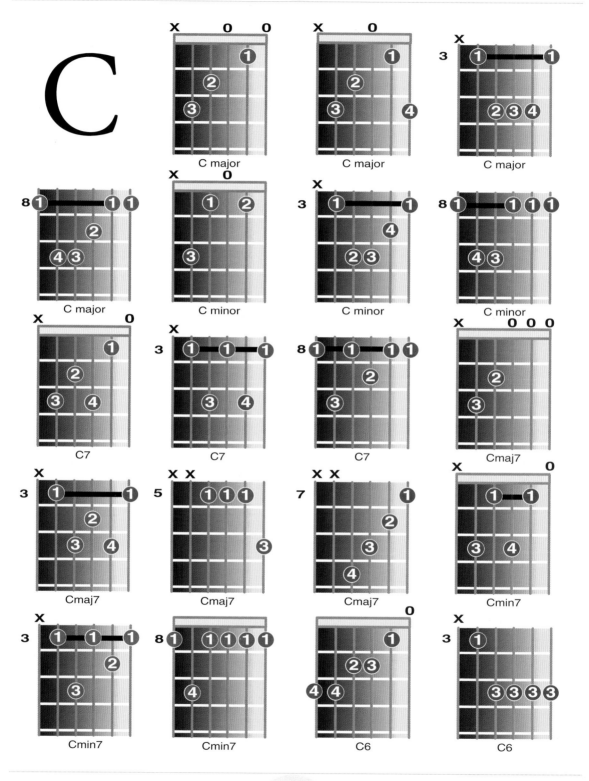

C major   C major   C major

C major   C minor   C minor   C minor

C7   C7   C7   Cmaj7

Cmaj7   Cmaj7   Cmaj7   Cmin7

Cmin7   Cmin7   C6   C6

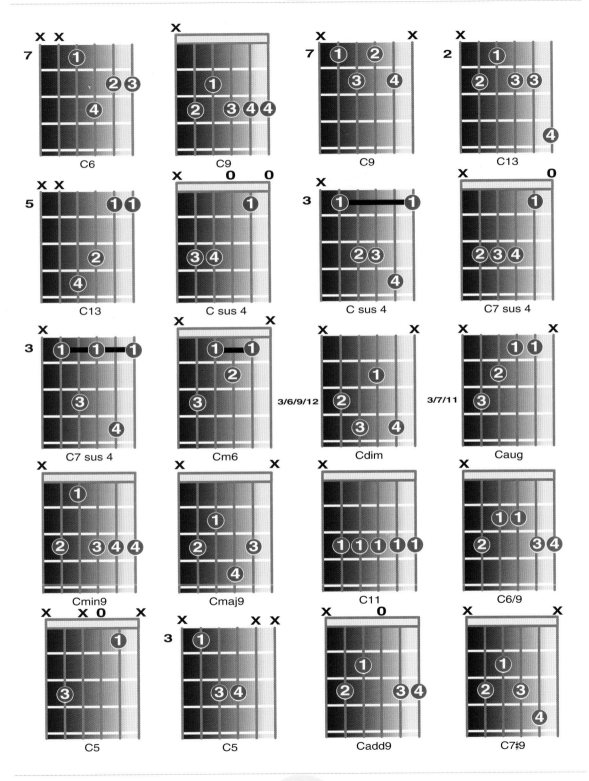

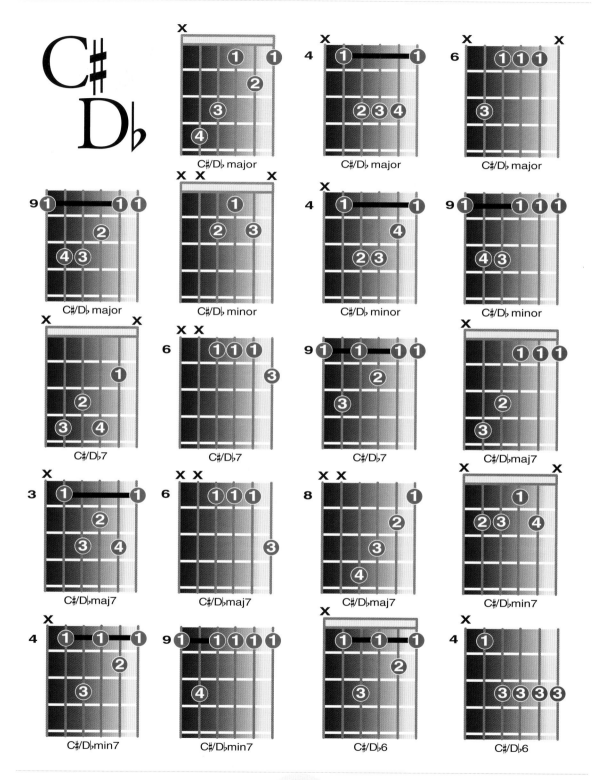

C#/Db major

C#/Db major

C#/Db major

C#/Db major

C#/Db minor

C#/Db minor

C#/Db minor

C#/Db7

C#/Db7

C#/Db7

C#/Dbmaj7

C#/Dbmaj7

C#/Dbmaj7

C#/Dbmaj7

C#/Dbmin7

C#/Dbmin7

C#/Dbmin7

C#/Db6

C#/Db6

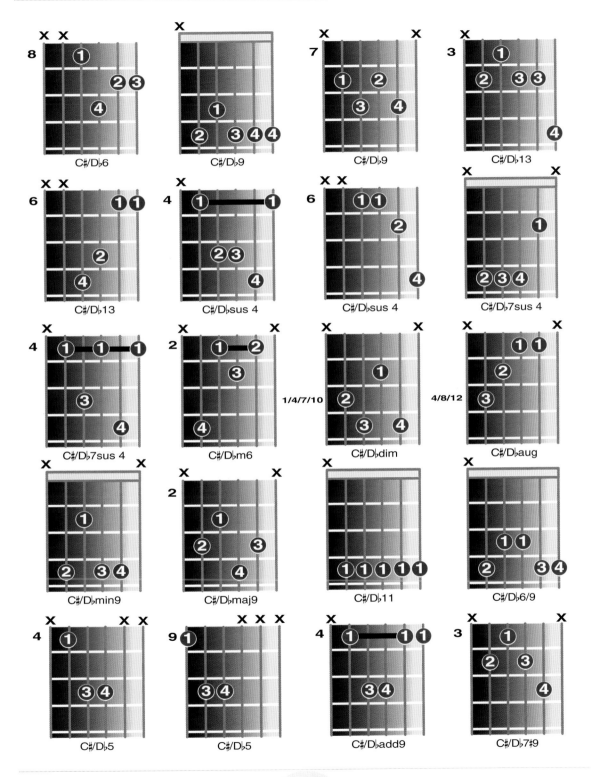

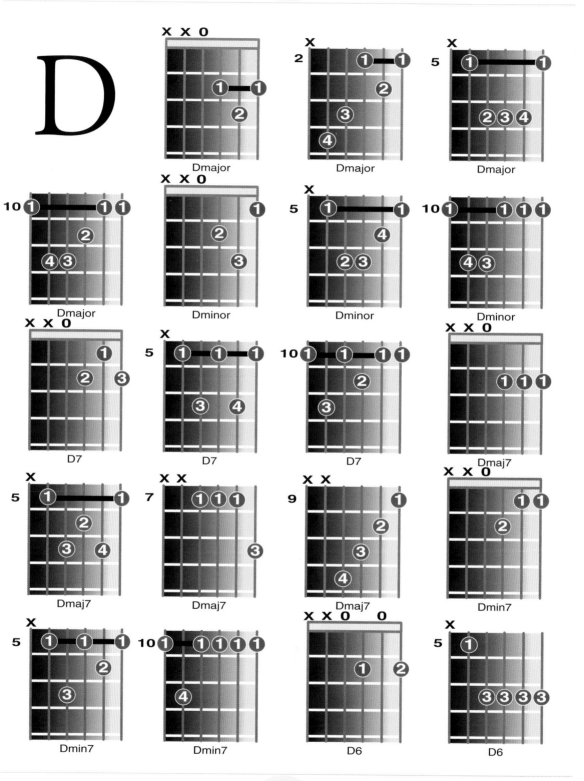

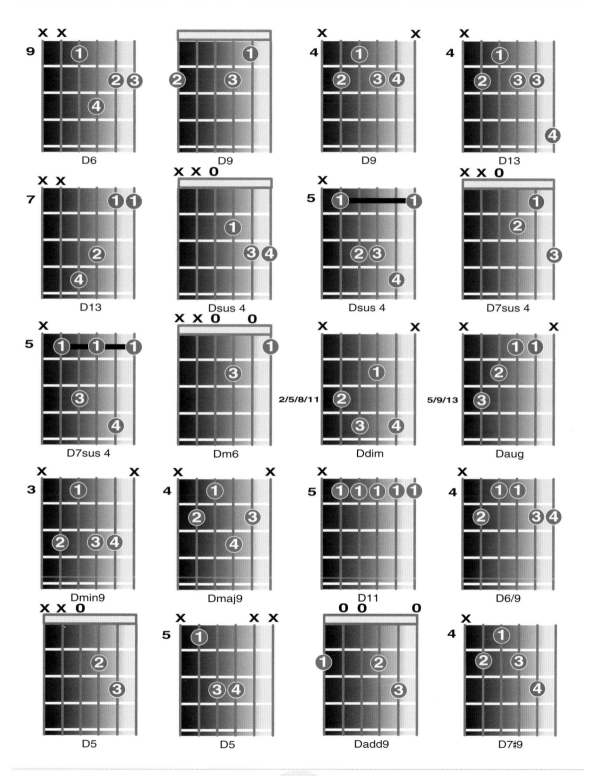

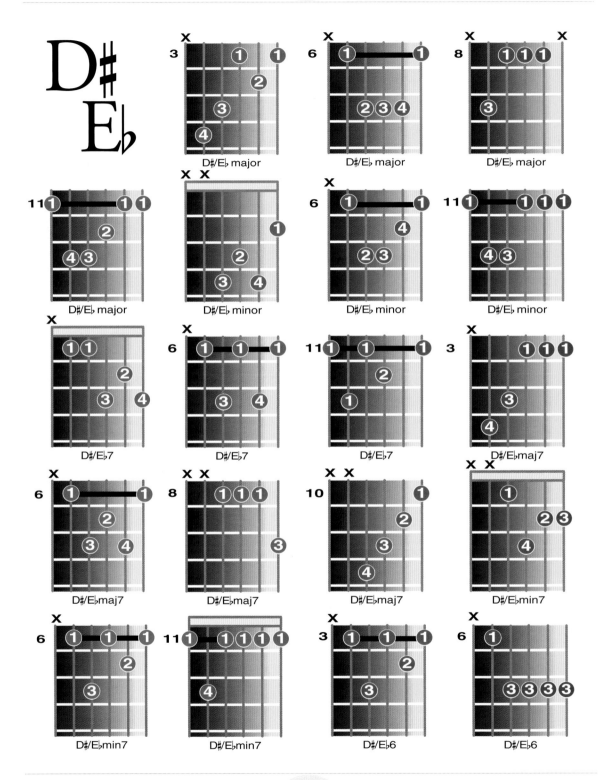

D#
E♭

D#/E♭ major

D#/E♭ major

D#/E♭ major

D#/E♭ major

D#/E♭ minor

D#/E♭ minor

D#/E♭ minor

D#/E♭7

D#/E♭7

D#/E♭7

D#/E♭maj7

D#/E♭maj7

D#/E♭maj7

D#/E♭maj7

D#/E♭min7

D#/E♭min7

D#/E♭min7

D#/E♭6

D#/E♭6

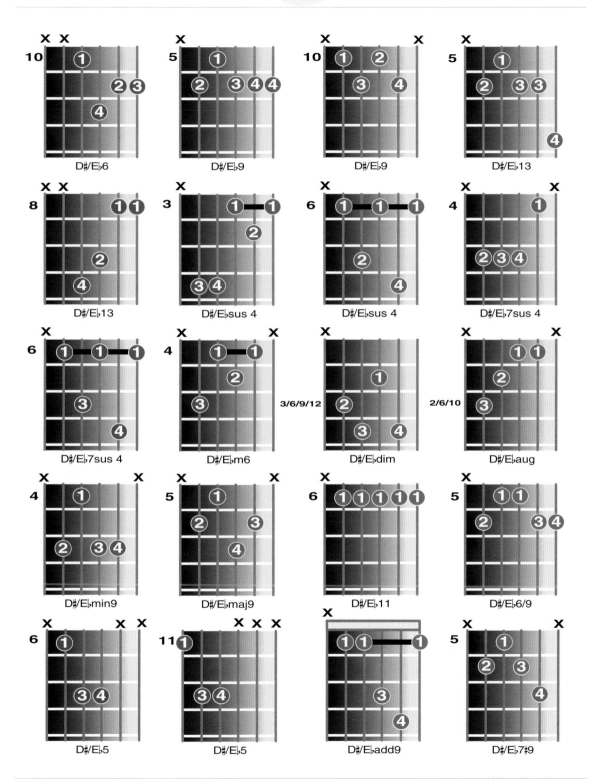

D#/E♭6

D#/E♭9

D#/E♭9

D#/E♭13

D#/E♭13

D#/E♭sus 4

D#/E♭sus 4

D#/E♭7sus 4

D#/E♭7sus 4

D#/E♭m6

3/6/9/12   D#/E♭dim

2/6/10   D#/E♭aug

D#/E♭min9

D#/E♭maj9

D#/E♭11

D#/E♭6/9

D#/E♭5

D#/E♭5

D#/E♭add9

D#/E♭7#9

E

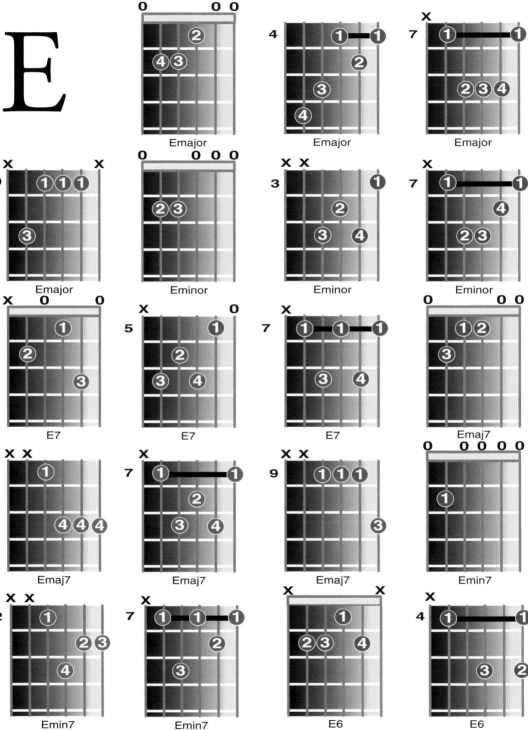

Emajor

Emajor

Emajor

Emajor

Eminor

Eminor

Eminor

E7

E7

E7

Emaj7

Emaj7

Emaj7

Emaj7

Emin7

Emin7

Emin7

E6

E6

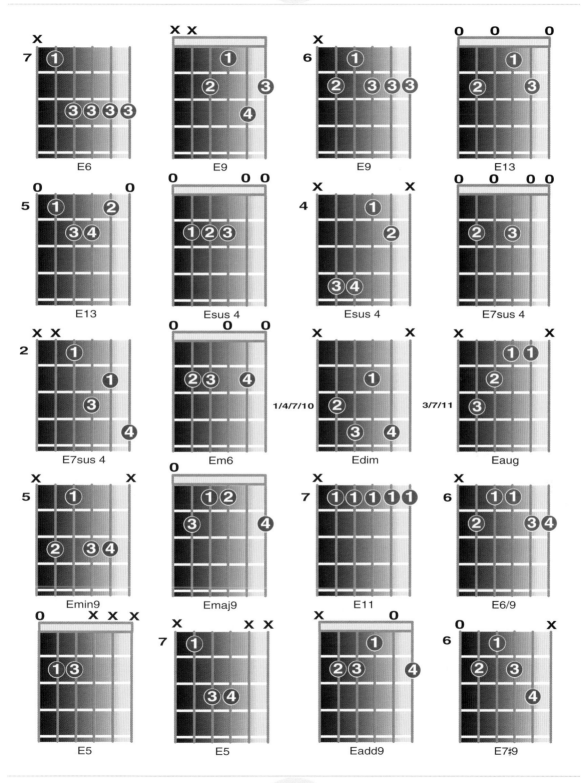

E6

E9

E9

E13

E13

Esus 4

Esus 4

E7sus 4

E7sus 4

Em6

1/4/7/10 Edim

3/7/11 Eaug

Emin9

Emaj9

E11

E6/9

E5

E5

Eadd9

E7#9

F

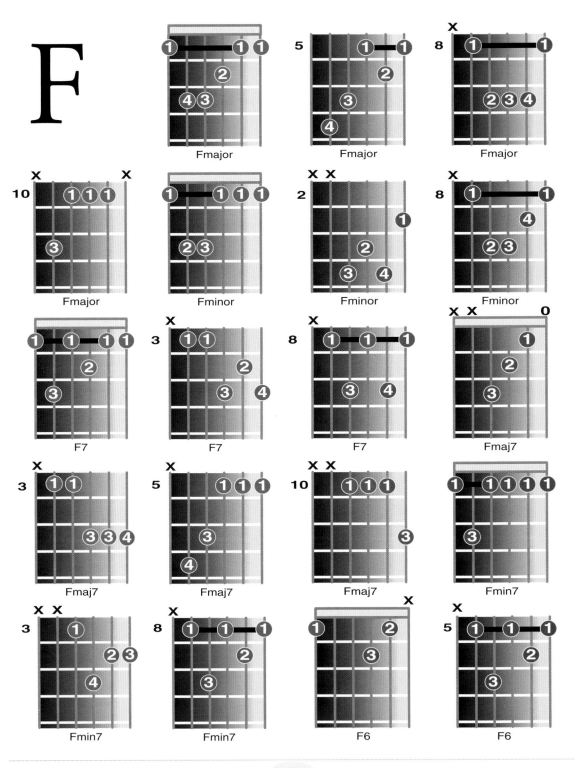

Fmajor

Fmajor

Fmajor

Fmajor

Fminor

Fminor

Fminor

F7

F7

F7

Fmaj7

Fmaj7

Fmaj7

Fmaj7

Fmin7

Fmin7

Fmin7

F6

F6

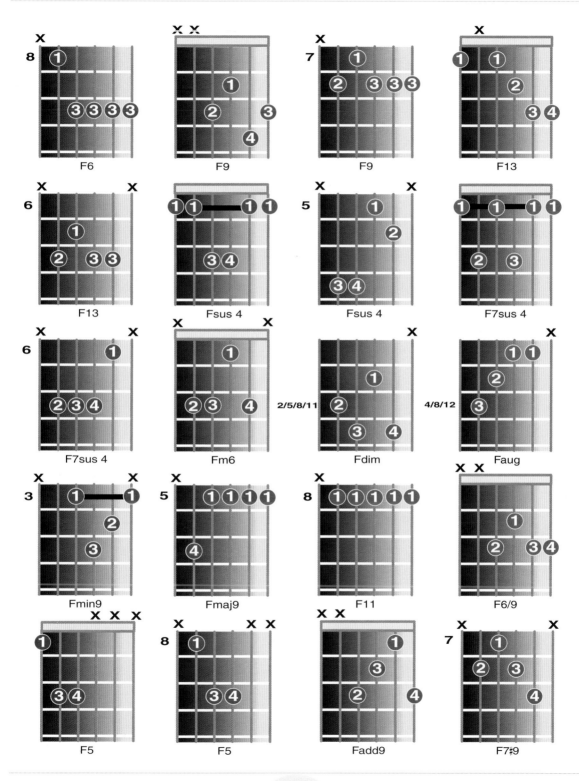

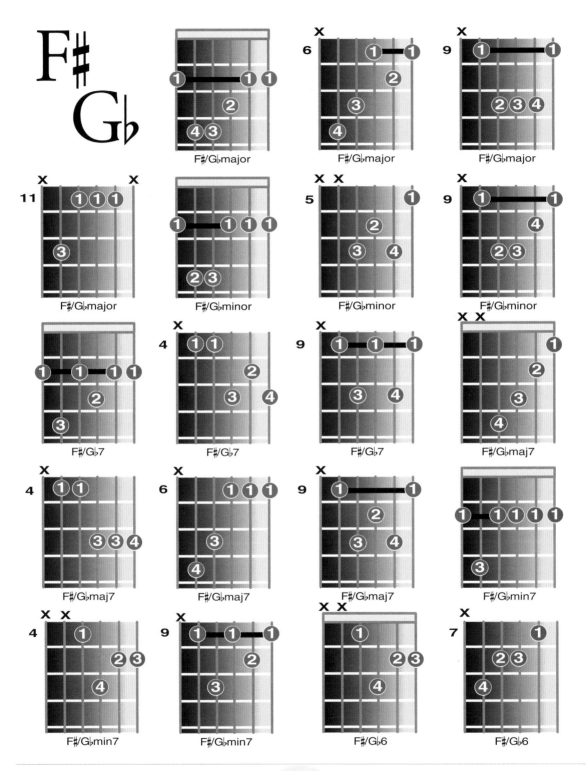

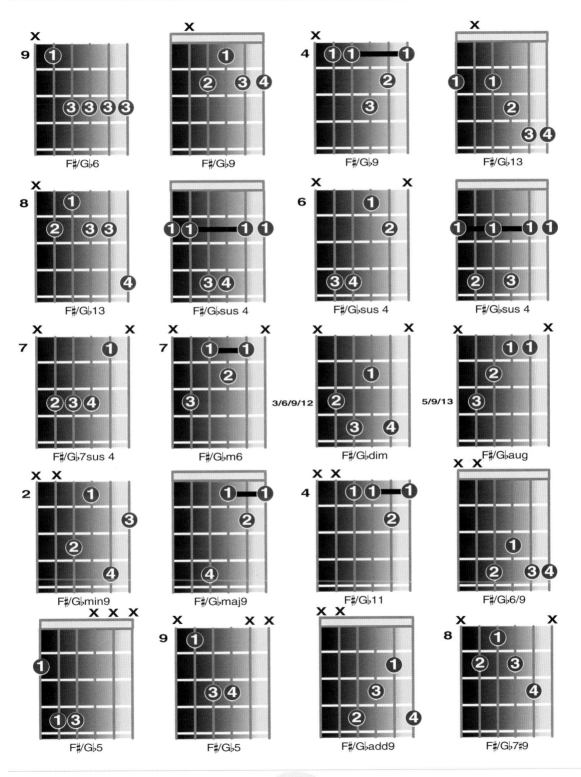

F#/Gb6

F#/Gb9

F#/Gb9

F#/Gb13

F#/Gb13

F#/Gbsus 4

F#/Gbsus 4

F#/Gbsus 4

F#/Gb7sus 4

F#/Gbm6

3/6/9/12 F#/Gbdim

5/9/13 F#/Gbaug

F#/Gbmin9

F#/Gbmaj9

F#/Gb11

F#/Gb6/9

F#/Gb5

F#/Gb5

F#/Gbadd9

F#/Gb7#9

G

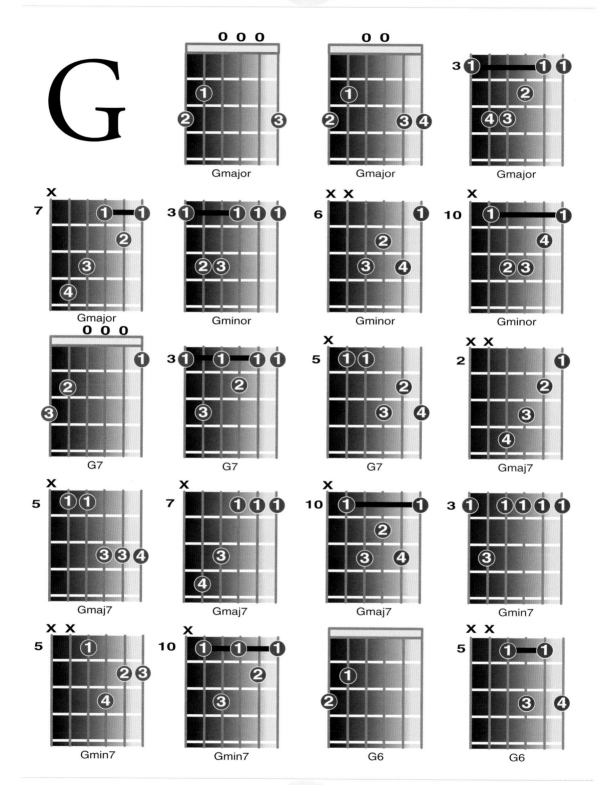

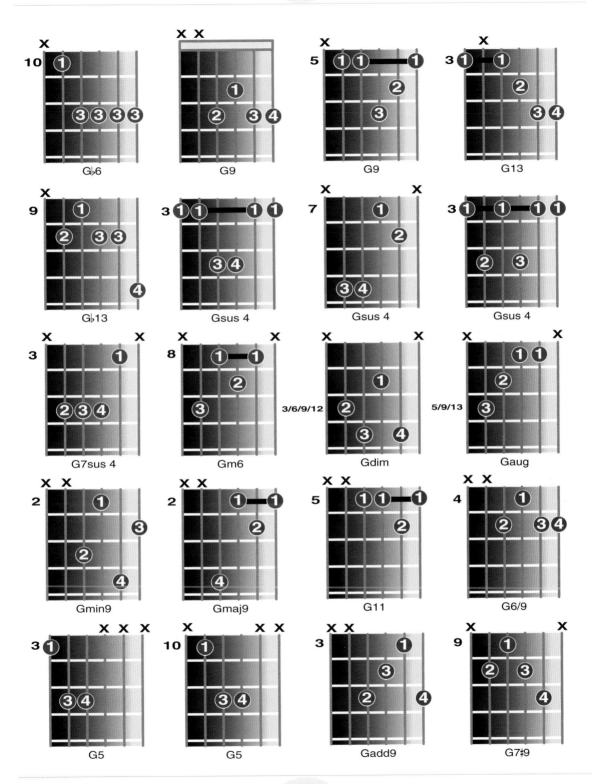

G♭6

G9

G9

G13

G♭13

Gsus 4

Gsus 4

Gsus 4

G7sus 4

Gm6

3/6/9/12   Gdim

5/9/13   Gaug

Gmin9

Gmaj9

G11

G6/9

G5

G5

Gadd9

G7♯9

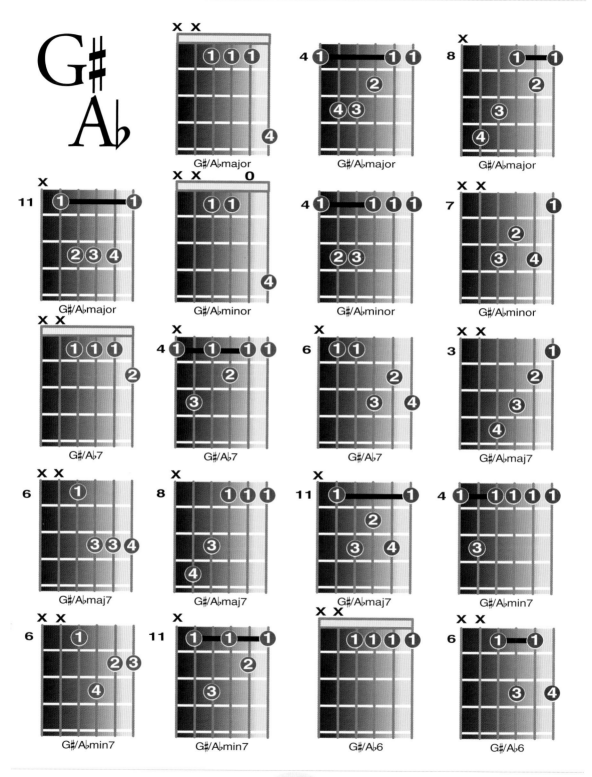

G#
A♭

G#/A♭major

G#/A♭major

G#/A♭major

G#/A♭major

G#/A♭minor

G#/A♭minor

G#/A♭minor

G#/A♭7

G#/A♭7

G#/A♭7

G#/A♭maj7

G#/A♭maj7

G#/A♭maj7

G#/A♭maj7

G#/A♭min7

G#/A♭min7

G#/A♭min7

G#/A♭6

G#/A♭6

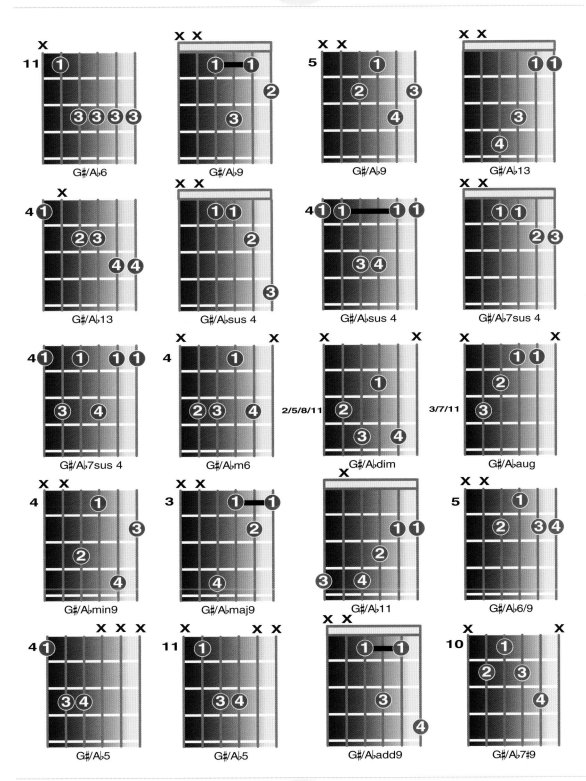

A

A major

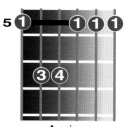
A major

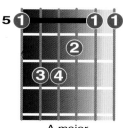
A major

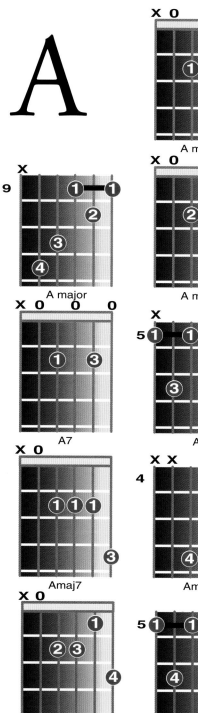
A major

A minor

A minor

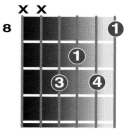
A minor

A7

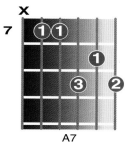
A7

A7

Amaj7

Amaj7

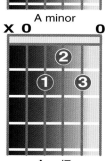
Amaj7

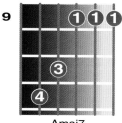
Amaj7

Amin7

Amin7

Amin7

Amin7

A6

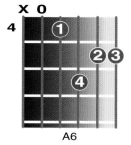
A6

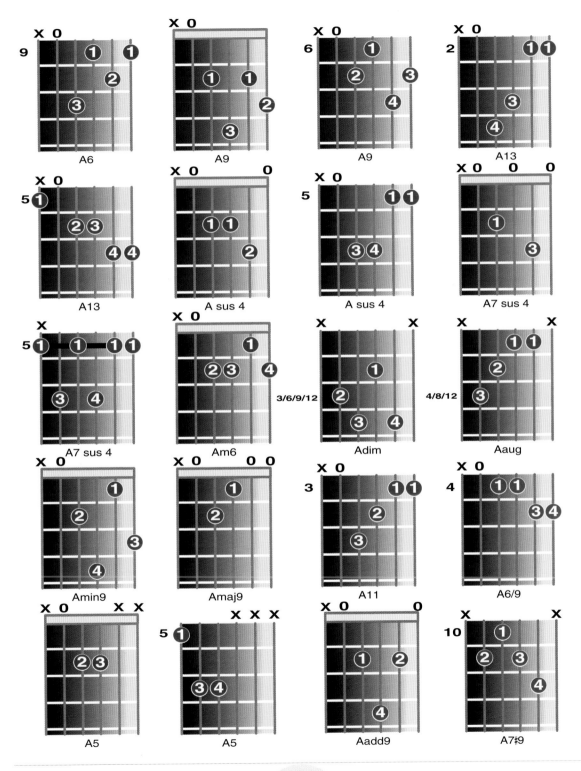

A6

A9

A9

A13

A13

A sus 4

A sus 4

A7 sus 4

A7 sus 4

Am6

3/6/9/12 Adim

4/8/12 Aaug

Amin9

Amaj9

A11

A6/9

A5

A5

Aadd9

A7#9

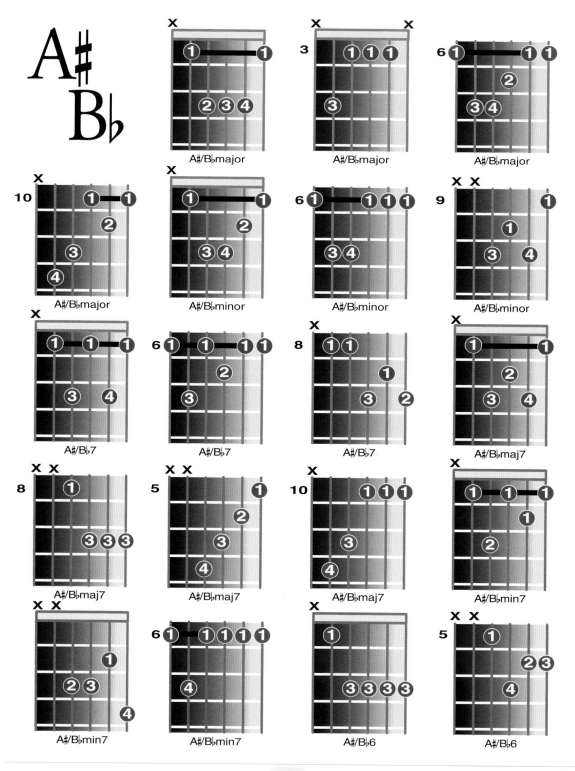

A# B♭

A#/B♭major

A#/B♭major

A#/B♭major

A#/B♭major

A#/B♭minor

A#/B♭minor

A#/B♭minor

A#/B♭7

A#/B♭7

A#/B♭7

A#/B♭maj7

A#/B♭maj7

A#/B♭maj7

A#/B♭maj7

A#/B♭min7

A#/B♭min7

A#/B♭min7

A#/B♭6

A#/B♭6

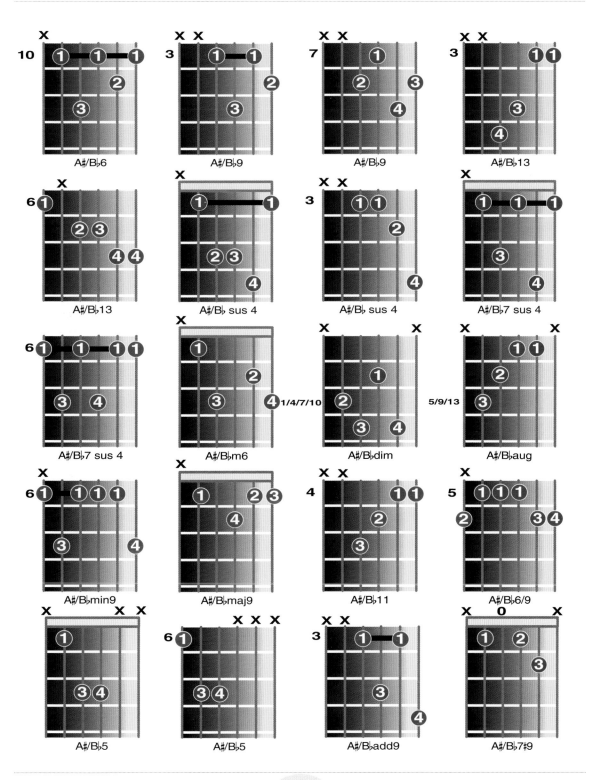

B

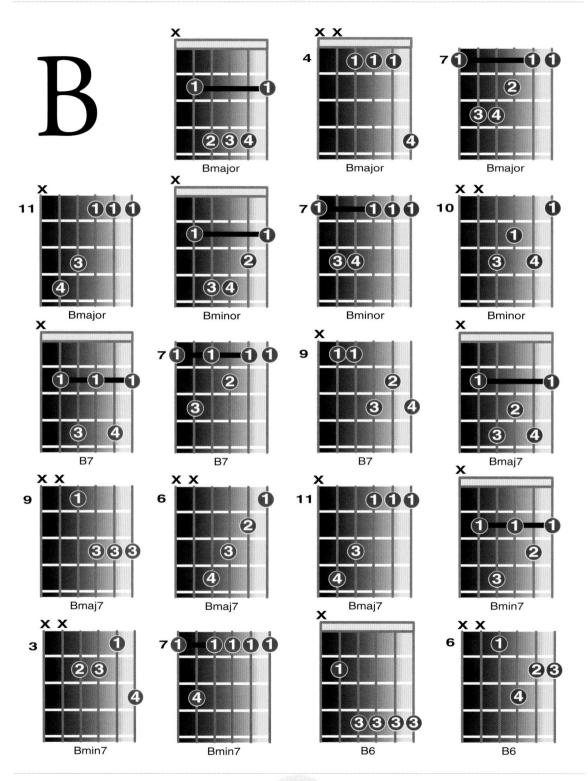

Bmajor

Bmajor

Bmajor

Bmajor

Bminor

Bminor

Bminor

B7

B7

B7

Bmaj7

Bmaj7

Bmaj7

Bmaj7

Bmin7

Bmin7

Bmin7

B6

B6

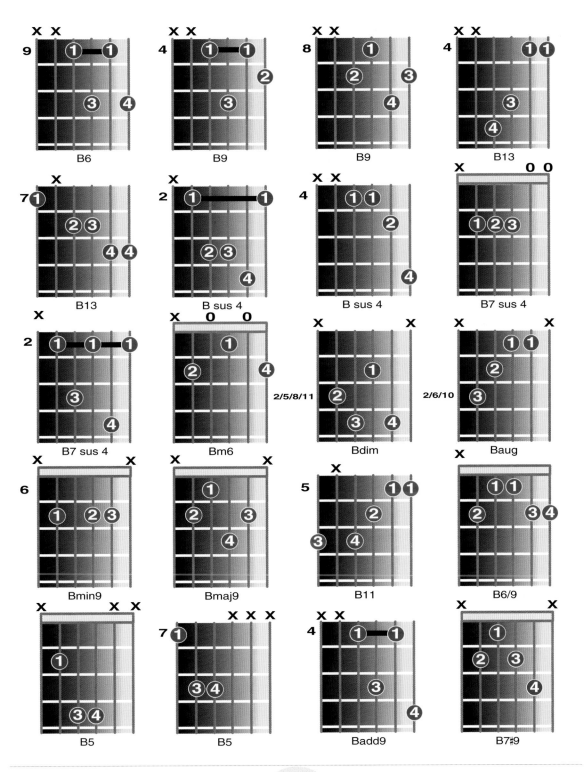

BIOGRAPHIES

Joe Bennett (Editorial Consutant)
Joe Bennett (*www.joebennett.co.uk*) is a musician, composer, tutor and writer. He is a former deputy editor of *Total Guitar* magazine where he was responsible for everything from writing equipment reviews, performing for cover CDs to transcribing music and interviewing famous names. Joe has worked for the City of Bath College as Head of Music, where he taught Creative Music Technology and Popular Music. He is now course director for the foundation degree in Commercial Music at Bath Spa University. As a freelance musician and composer, his clients have included Channel 4, the Theatre Royal, Newcastle, Bath Guitar Festival and Smallworld studios. Joe writes on a freelance basis for most of the leading music-related publishers, including Future Publishing, IMP, and Music Sales. He is the co-director of StudioDoctors, UK, an independent music studio consultancy company based in Bath, UK, specialising in small studios and music workstation setups.

Trevor Curwen (Effects, Recording)
Trevor Curwen started out his musical career as a guitarist and now works in the recording industry as an engineer and record producer, as well as hiring out his collection of vintage guitars, amps and effects pedals for recording projects. He has written on recording and guitar-related matters in magazines, such as *The Mix*, *Future Music*, *Guitarist*, *Total Guitar* and *Metal Hammer*, and is a part-time lecturer in music technology at Bath Spa University College.

Cliff Douse (Glossary, Singer-Songwriters)
Cliff Douse has written many articles and columns for some of the UK's foremost music and computer magazines including *Guitarist*, *Guitar Techniques*, *Computer Music*, *Rhythm*, *The Mix*, *MacFormat*, *PC Format* and *Internet Advisor*. He is a music technology expert and the author of several music tuition books for guitar. His first two books, *Scales & Modes for Guitar* and *Scales & Modes for Bass Guitar*, carry endorsements from Pete Townshend (The Who) and Mark King (Level 42) respectively. Cliff is currently working on a number of new guitar books and music software projects.

Douglas J Noble (Players)
Douglas J Noble (*www.djnoble.co.uk*) is a musician, guitar instructor and music journalist based in Edinburgh. He has a degree in Psychology and two Diplomas in Classical Guitar. Douglas is the Tablature Editor of *The Guitar Magazine* (UK) and the Music Director of *UniVibes*, the international Jimi Hendrix magazine. He has interviewed many of the world's top guitarists and has written books on Jimi Hendrix and Peter Green. He is also an examiner for Rock School/Trinity College of Music.

Richard Riley (Guitar Manufacturers, Recording, Repairs, Technical Details)
Richard Riley (*www.richardriley.co.uk*) is a guitar player and writer living in Bath, UK. He has recorded and performed with a wide range of artists from Natalie Imbruglia to Laurel Aitken in venues as diverse as The Old Grey Whistle Test, Abbey Road, London and The Royal Festival Hall, London. He is a long-time contributor to many of the UK's leading music technology publications including *Total Guitar*, *Future Music*, *MP3 Magazine* and *The Melody Maker*. He is the author of the highly successful *Electric Guitar Handbook* (PC Publishing, 1999). As an artist and musician his work is regularly seen in the mp3.com charts.

Tony Skinner (How to Play, Musical Styles, Theory)
Tony Skinner is the Director of the Registry of Guitar Tutors – the world's foremost organisation for guitar education. He is also the Principal Guitar Examiner for the London College of Music and has compiled examination syllabi in electric, bass and classical guitar playing and popular music theory. He has written and edited over 40 music-education books and is a regular contributor to *Total Guitar* magazine. Tony is widely respected as one of the UK's premier music educators.

Harry Wylie (Equipment, Tuning, Guitar Manufacturers)
Harry Wylie died on 15 March 2002 from a rare heart disease, aged only 33. His death marked the untimely end of his successful career in music journalism, most notably as editor of specialist magazine *Total Guitar*.

Harry attended Abingdon School in Oxford and used to jam regularly with a group of schoolmates, who later went on to form the band Radiohead. He then went to Manchester University, where he gained a double first in English Literature.

Harry joined the staff of *Total Guitar* in September 1994, and helped launch its first issue in December of that year. Two years later, he took on the role of editor and, under his influence, the magazine became hugely successful. During this period, Harry set a standard that the magazine still tries to achieve today. The apogee of Harry's career at *Total Guitar* was when, for its fiftieth issue (at the height of the Britpop years), he scooped other commercial magazines and featured exclusive interviews with Noel Gallagher and Paul Weller. After five extremely successful years at the helm of *Total Guitar*, Harry left to pursue a freelance career, continuing to write up until his death.

Harry had a dry wit, high standards and an impeccable taste in music. He will be sorely missed.

PICTURE CREDITS

All pictures courtesy of Foundry Arts except:
Aria 146 (b)
Arbiter Group plc 110 (©), 116 (br) Fender Musical Instruments inc. 50 (r), 105 (b), 106 (t)
Ampeg 146 (t)
C F Martin & Co. Inc., Nazareth, PA USA 151
Dorling Kindersley Ltd. 104 (l), 105 (t), 106 (b), 107, 108 (t), 110 (except c), 116 (l), 117 (r), 118 (l), 122 (tr, br), 140 (t), 147 (t), 149 (b), 152 (bl), 154 (r), 155, 163 (tl)
Hobgoblin Music 111
Live Photography 21, 49, 54, 60, 84, 89
London Features International 8 (b), 9 (r), 10, 14, 16, 17, 18, 19 (r), 20, 22, 23 (b), 25, 26 (l), 27, 29, 30 (r), 31 (r), 33 (r), 34 (l), 36 (r), 38, 39, 40, 42, 56 (r), 46 (t), 47, 48, 50, 52, 53, 56, 57, 59, 61, 63, 64, 65, 67, 68, 69, 70 (b), 71, 72, 73, 74, 75, 76, 77, 78, 79 (r), 80 (l), 81, 82, 83 (l), 85, 87 (t), 88, 91, 92, 94, 95, 96, 98, 99, 100, 101, 103, 104 (r), 109, 124 (r), 148 (r), 152 (t), 154 (l), 157 (b), 158, 159, 166, 167 (t), 169, 170, 183, 186, 195
Marshall Amplification 112 (tl), 139, 150, 153 (r), 161 (r)
Redferns Henrietta Butler 58, Michael Ochs Archive 86
Topham Picturepoint 12 (b), 44 (l), 62, 66, 90, 128, 129
William Worsley 137 (l), 141, 161 (l), 167 (b)

Special thanks to Lucy Bradbury and Tom Worsley for the photographic shoots. Gear provided by Nick Wells and Tom Worsley.

FURTHER READING

Anderton, Craig, *Home Recording for Musicians*, AMSCO, 1978
Bacon, Tony, *The Ultimate Guitar Book*, Dorling Kindersley, 1991
Bailey, Derek, *Improvisation*, Moorland, 1980
Bennett, Scotty, *Bob Marley*, Virgin, 1997
Bowman, David & Paul Terry, *Aural Matters*, Schott, 1993
Buckley, Jonathon (ed.), *The Rough Guide to Rock*, Rough Guides, 1996
Burrows, Terry, *The Kiss Guide to Playing Guitar*, Dorling Kindersley, 2000
Chapman, Richard, *The Complete Guitarist*, Dorling Kindersley, 1993
Clifford, Mike, *Play Rock Guitar*, Salamander, 1987
DeCurtis, Anthony (ed.), *The Rolling Stone Album Guide*, Virgin, 1992
Denyer, Ralph, *The New Guitar Handbook*, Pan, 1992
Douse, Cliff, *The Guitarists Book of Guitarists*, Music Maker Books, 1994
Hugh, Gregory, *1000 Great Guitarists*, IMP, 1992
Hanson, Mark, *The Alternate Tuning Guide for Guitar*, AMSCO, 1991
Larkin, Colin, *The Virgin Encyclopedia of the Blues*, Virgin, 1998
Larkin, Colin, *The Virgin Encyclopedia of Popular Music*, Virgin, 2002
Larkin, Colin, *The Virgin Illustrated Encyclopedia of Rock*, Virgin, 1998
Lewis, Dave, *The Complete Guide to the Music of Led Zeppelin*, Omnibus Press, 1994
Lowe, Leslie, *Directory of Popular Music*, Waterlow, 1975
Martín Juan, *El Arte de Flamenco de la Guitarra*, United Music, 1982
Oliver, Paul, *The Story of the Blues*, Pimlico, 1969
Pickow, Peter, *Guitar Case Chord Book*, AMSCO, 1983
Randall, Don, *The New Harvard Dictionary of Music*, Harvard University Press, 1986
Scott, Iain, *Electric Blues Guitar*, East River, 1998
Shearer, Aaron, *Classic Guitar Technique*, Franco Colombo, 1963
Traum, Happy, *Flat-Pick Country Guitar*, Oak, 1973
Turnbull, Harvey, *The Guitar*, Bold Strummer, 1991
Yudkin, Jeremy, *Understanding Music*, Prentice Hall, 1996

INDEX